Formula One MATHS

C3

Catherine Berry ● Margaret Bland

Anthony Eccles ● Dave Faulkner

Sophie Goldie ● Tim Holmes

Simon Jowett ● Habib Rashid

Leonie Turner ● Brandon Wilshaw

SERIES EDITOR: **Roger Porkess**

HODDER
EDUCATION
AN HACHETTE UK COMPANY

Acknowledgements

Every effort has been made to trace and acknowledge ownership of copyright. The publishers will be glad to make suitable arrangements with any copyright holder whom it has not been possible to contact.

Illustrations were drawn by Maggie Brand, Maureen Carter, Tom Cross, Jeff Edwards, Jackie Govier and Joe McEwan.

Photos supplied by Gianni Dagli Orti/CORBIS (page 50); Bruce Coleman (page 137); Bob Krist/CORBIS (page 139); Ruth Nossek (pages 148, 149); Harry Taylor/Dorling Kindersley (page 161, all); Barry Dowsett/Science Photo Library (page 171); Manchester Evening News (page 216).

Cover design and page design by Julie Martin.

Orders: please contact Bookpoint Ltd, 130 Milton Park, Abingdon, Oxon OX14 4SB. Telephone: (44) 01235 827720, Fax (44) 01235 400454. Lines are open from 9.00–5.00, Monday to Saturday, with a 24 hour message answering service.

British Library Cataloguing in Publication Data
A catalogue record for this title is available from The British Library

ISBN 978 0 340 77978 1

First published 2002
Impression number 10 9 8 7 6 5
Year 2009

Copyright © 2002 Catherine Berry, Margaret Bland, Anthony Eccles, Dave Faulkner, Sophie Goldie, Tim Holmes, Simon Jowett, Roger Porkess, Habib Rashid, Leonie Turner, Brandon Wilshaw

Cover photo from Jacey, Debut Art

Typeset by Tech-Set Ltd, Gateshead, Tyne & Wear.
Printed in Italy for Hodder Educational an Hachette UK Company,
338 Euston Road, London NW1 3BH by Printer Trento.

Introduction

This book is designed for Year 9 students and is part of a series covering Key Stage 3 Mathematics. Each textbook in the series is accompanied by an extensive Teacher's Resource including additional material. This allows the series to be used with the full ability range of students.

The series builds on the National Numeracy Strategy in primary schools and its extension into Key Stage 3. It is designed to support the style of teaching and the lesson framework to which students will be accustomed.

This book is presented as a series of double-page spreads, each of which is designed to be a teaching unit. The left-hand page covers the material to be taught and the right-hand page provides examples for the students to work through. Each chapter ends with a review exercise covering all its content. Further worksheets, tests and ICT materials are provided in the Teacher's Resource.

An important feature of the left-hand pages is the Tasks, which are printed in boxes. These are intended to be carried out by the student in mid-lesson. Their aim is twofold. In the first place they give the students practice on what they have just been taught, allowing them to consolidate their understanding. However, the tasks then extend the ideas and raise questions, setting the agenda for the later part of the lesson. Further guidance on the Tasks is available in the Teacher's Resource.

Another key feature of the left-hand pages is the Discussion Points. These are designed to help teachers engage their students in whole class discussion. Teachers should see the icon as an opportunity and an invitation.

Several other symbols and instructions are used in this book. These are explained on the 'How to use this book' page for students opposite. The symbol indicates to the teacher that there is additional ICT material directly linked to that unit of work. This is referenced in the teaching notes for that unit in the Teacher's Resource.

The order of the chapters in this book ensures that the subject is developed logically, at each stage building on previous knowledge. The Teacher's Resource includes a Scheme of Work based on this order. However, teachers are of course free to vary the order to meet their own circumstances and needs.

The first 22 chapters complete the new work needed for the Key Stage 3 National Test. Chapter 23 consists of questions on earlier work for students preparing for this National Test. The remaining two chapters are designed for use after the students have taken the National Test. Chapter 24 is about reasoning and proof; it covers ideas that will be really important to students as they continue their study of mathematics. Chapter 25 consists of Investigations in preparation for GCSE coursework.

The authors would like to thank all those who helped in preparing this book, particularly those involved with the writing of materials for the accompanying Teacher's Resource.

Roger Porkess   2002
Series Editor

How to use this book

 This symbol means that you will need to think carefully about a point. Your teacher may ask you to join in a discussion about it.

 This symbol next to a question means that you are allowed (and indeed expected) to use your calculator for this question.

 This symbol means exactly the opposite – you are not allowed to use your calculator for this question.

 This is a warning sign. It is used where a common mistake, or misunderstanding, is being described. It is also used to identify questions which are slightly more difficult or which require a little more thought. It should be read as 'caution'.

 This is the ICT symbol. It should alert your teacher to the fact that there is some additional material in the accompanying Teacher's Resource using ICT for this unit of work.

Each chapter of work in this book is divided into a series of double-page spreads – or units of work. The left-hand page is the teaching page, and the right-hand page involves an exercise and sometimes additional activities or investigations to do with that topic.

You will also come across the following features in the units of work:

 Task

The tasks give you the opportunity to work alone, in pairs or in small groups on an activity in the lesson. It gives you the chance to practise what you have just been taught, and to discuss ideas and raise questions about the topic.

 Do the right thing!

These boxes give you a set of step-by-step instructions on how to carry out a particular technique in maths, usually to do with shape work.

Do you remember?

These boxes give you the chance to review work that you have covered in the previous year.

This downline at the edge of the page indicates that this is a review (or revision) of material which you have already met.

Contents

Financial calculations

Sanjiv and Leila work out the price of this printer.

Sanjiv writes

Colour Printer
Usually £120
!SALE!
20% OFF
Marked Price

Leila writes

Sanjiv writes

20% of £120

$\frac{20}{100} \times £120 = £24$

Original price   £120

Reduction   £24

Sale price   £96

Leila writes

Original price   100%

Reduction   20%

Sale price   80%

Sale price $= \frac{80}{100} \times £120$

$= £96$

 Which method do you think is easier?

Task

1 Use Sanjiv's method to find the sale price of these items.
   (a) Board game £30   **(b)** Stationery pack £8.80
   (c) Calculator £40   **(d)** Computer mouse mat £6

SALE 15% OFF

2 Now use Leila's method to find the sale price of the items in question 1.

VAT (Value-added tax)

This tax is set by the Chancellor of the
Exchequer and is currently 17.5%.
Most things that you buy include VAT.

Tanya and Jo share a telephone.

Tanya's calls cost £48.

She works out how much she must
pay altogether, including VAT.

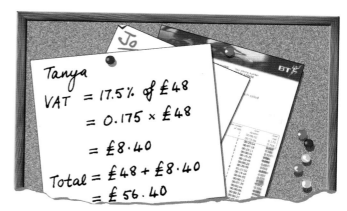

Jo

Tanya
VAT $= 17.5\%$ of £48
$= 0.175 \times £48$
$= £8·40$
Total $= £48 + £8·40$
$= £56·40$

 Calculate 1.175×48.
   Explain the connection between this calculation and the VAT calculation.

Exercise

1 In a sale in a sports shop prices are reduced by 20%.
Find the sale price of these items.
  (a) Football shirt £45   **(b)** Whistle   £3.20
  (c) Football boots £28   **(d)** Trainers   £35

2 Find the sale price of these items.
  (a) A T-shirt originally £18, reduced by 25%.
  (b) A computer desk: originally £170, reduced by 15%.
  (c) A bicycle: originally £159, reduced by 20%.
  (d) A camcorder originally £210, reduced by 12%.

3 VAT is 17.5% and is added to the original price (100%) of an item.
The prices below exclude VAT.
How much do these items cost including VAT?
  (a) Camera   £18   **(b)** Guitar   £180
  (c) Drum machine   £88   **(d)** Binoculars   £54

4 Ranulf pays tax at 23%.
How much tax must he pay if he earns
  (a) £16 000   **(b)** £23 000   **(c)** £19 000?

Investigation

Look at this diagram. It refers to the labour force in a particular country.

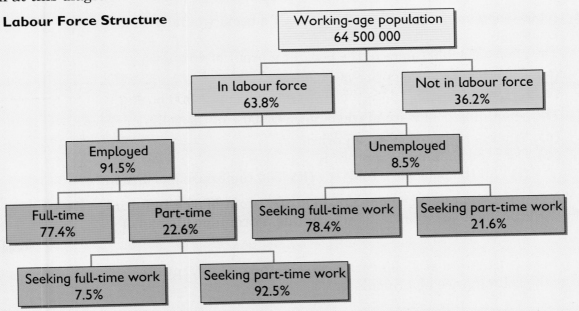

Labour Force Structure

1 Giving your answer to nearest hundred, how many people are
  (a) in full-time employment   **(b)** seeking full-time employment
  (c) seeking part-time employment   **(d)** not in the labour force?

2 Give your answers to question 1 as percentages of the working-age population.

Profit and loss

When shops sell articles they expect to make a profit.

A newsagent buys magazines for £1.80 each.
*This is called the **cost price** (C.P.).*

He sells each magazine for £2.25.
*This is called the **selling price** (S.P.).*

His profit is £2.25 − £1.80 = £0.45
Profit = S.P. − C.P.

Profit
Percentage profit = $\dfrac{0.45}{1.80} \times 100\% = 25\%$
C.P.

> **% profit** = $\dfrac{\textbf{profit}}{\textbf{C.P.}} \times 100\%$
>
> **% loss** = $\dfrac{\textbf{loss}}{\textbf{C.P.}} \times 100\%$

Task

1   A bookshop manager buys 2000 copies of a book by a famous footballer.
Each copy costs £16.00.
The shop sells 900 copies of the book at a profit of 40% each.
   (a) What is the selling price of the book?
   (b) How much money does the shop receive for the 900 books?
The remaining books are marked down by 50% of the selling price.
   (c) What is the marked-down price?
   (d) Does the shop make a profit if
       (i) all the books are sold   **(ii)** 200 copies are left unsold?

2   A new manager decides to make an initial profit of 80% in future.
Work through question 1 again with this percentage instead of 40%.

A shop buys calculators at £3.00 each and sells them at 55% profit.
What is the selling price of a calculator?

S.P. = 155% of £3.00
   = 1.55 × £3.00
   = £4.65

*Take the cost price as 100%.
The profit is 55%.
So the S.P. is 155% of the C.P.*

?   How does 155% turn into 1.55?

Exercise

1 **(a)** The cost price of a personal stereo is £40.
It is sold for £45.
What is the percentage profit?

(b) The cost price of a mobile phone is £49.
It is sold for £70.
What is the percentage profit?

(c) The cost price of a poster is £4.50.
It is sold for £3.60. What is the percentage loss?

(d) The cost price of a T-shirt is £15.
It is sold for £12. What is the percentage loss?

2 **(a)** The cost price of a guitar is £360.
A music shop sells it at a profit of 11%.
What is the selling price?

(b) A book of popular music costs £9.
More recent tunes have been written by the same composer, so the music shop sells the book at a loss of 23%.
What is the selling price?

(c) The cost price of a tracksuit is £45.
It is sold at a profit of 40%.
What is the selling price?

(d) The cost price of a pair of jeans is £30.
They are sold at a profit of 60%.
What is the selling price?

Investigation

You often make measurements in other subjects, for example in science experiments, and in real life. The percentage errors in these measurements are calculated in a manner that is similar to percentage profit calculations.

$$\text{Error} = \text{Measurement} - \text{Actual quantity}$$

$$\% \text{ Error} = \frac{\text{Error}}{\text{Actual quantity}} \times 100\%$$

Find **(a)** the error **(b)** the percentage error of these measurements.

1 Measurement = 3 m   Actual length = 3.05 m

2 Measurement = 600 ml   Actual volume = 612 ml

3 Measurement = 0.5 kg   Actual mass = 508 g

4 Measurement = 6 km   Actual length = 6200 m

Reverse percentage calculations

A shop sells boots at £56 a pair.
This includes a profit of 40%.
What price did the shop pay for the boots?

Arif writes

Cost Price	= 100%
Profit	= 40%
Selling price	= 140%
So 140% of C.P.	= £56
1% of C.P.	$= \dfrac{£56}{140}$
100% of C.P.	$= \dfrac{£56}{140} \times 100$
	= £40

? What is 140% as a decimal?
What is $\dfrac{£56}{1.4}$?

The shop has a sale.

SALE 10% OFF

What was the original price of the shoes?
Arif calculates:

Original Price	= 100%
Reduction	= 10%
Sale price	= (100 – 10)% = 90% of the original price
So 90% of the original price	= £45
1% of the original price	$= \dfrac{£45}{90}$
100% of the original price	$= \dfrac{£45}{90} \times 100$
	= £50

? What is 90% as a decimal? What is $\dfrac{£45}{0.9}$?

 Task

Juanita stays at three hotels. The costs of the rooms are
(a) first night £77.55   **(b)** second night £63.45   **(c)** third night £82.25.
All the bills include VAT at 17.5%.
Find the cost of each room before VAT is added.

Exercise

1 **(a)** Goalkeeper's gloves are sold at £34.50 per pair.
The shop makes a profit of 15%. What did the gloves cost the shop?

(b) A silver ring is sold at £11.70.
The retailer makes a loss of 35%. What was the cost price?

(c) A guitar is sold for £325.
The music shop makes a profit of 30%. Find the cost price.

(d) A bicycle is sold for £728.
The sports shop makes a profit 25%. What was the cost price?

2 These items are reduced in a sale. Find their original prices.
(a) A chess set selling at £19.80 after a 20% reduction in price.
(b) A quartz watch selling at £11.05 after a 15% reduction.
(c) A mobile phone selling at £52.50 after a 25% reduction.
(d) A CD selling at £11.90 after a 15% reduction.

3 The prices below include VAT at 17.5%.
Find the price of each of these items before VAT was added.

(a) Video recorder £329   **(b)** DVD £18.80
(c) Computer printer £258.50   **(d)** CD £13.63

4 Ranulf pays tax at 23%.
Find how much money he earns when the amount left after tax is:
(a) £18 480   **(b)** £13 475   **(c)** £21 868.

Investigation

A hotel's bill includes VAT at 17.5%.
Some customers want to know how much
VAT has been added.
The hotel works it out by using the formula

Multiply by 7 and divide by 47.

1 Use this method to find the VAT
on a bill of £82.25.
2 Check your answer with the answer
to part (c) of the Task on the
previous page.
3 Explain why this formula works.

A few years later the VAT rate changes.

The formula becomes

Multiply by 9 and divide by 49

4 What is the new VAT rate?

Interest

 Eddie invests the money at 8%. How much interest does he receive at the end of the first year?

 He receives this each year for the three years. How much is this altogether?

In this case the interest paid each year remains the same.
This is known as **simple interest**.
The interest is proportional to:

- the money invested, £P
- the interest rate, $R\%$ per year
- the time, T years.

*This is sometimes called the **principal**.*

The formula is $I = \dfrac{PRT}{100}$.

Check that substituting $P = 800$, $R = 8$ and $T = 3$ into the formula gives the same answer that you got before.

 How much money does Eddie have after three years?

This is called the **amount**.

Task

1 Find the simple interest payable on the following.
   (a) £600 invested at 12% per year for 4 years.
   (b) £480 invested at 3% per annum (per year) for $2\frac{1}{2}$ years.
   (c) £750 invested at 7.5% p.a. (per annum) for 5 years.
   (d) £250 invested at 6% p.a. for 18 months.

2 Rearrange the formula $I = \dfrac{PRT}{100}$ to make the subject **(a)** P **(b)** R **(c)** T.

3 Use the appropriate rearrangement from question 2 to answer these questions.
   (a) £5000 is invested for three years and earns £900 simple interest. What is the rate?
   (b) £680 is invested at 4% p.a. and earns £68 simple interest. What is the time?
   (c) An investment earns £720 in simple interest in 3 years at 8% p.a. What is the principal (the money invested)?

Exercise

① **Calculator revision:** find the value of the following.

(a) $\dfrac{540 \times 4 \times 6}{100}$

(b) $\dfrac{280 \times 8\frac{1}{4} \times 5\frac{1}{3}}{100}$

(c) $(1.07)^6$

(d) $\left(1 + \frac{13}{100}\right)^3$

(e) $550\left(1 + \frac{6}{100}\right)^5$

(f) $2000\left(1 - \frac{9}{100}\right)^2$

② Find the simple interest payable on the following.
  (a) £500 invested for 3 years at 7% p.a.
  (b) £640 invested for 4 years at 9% p.a.
  (c) £2500 invested for 6 years at 6.5% p.a.
  (d) £3700 invested for $5\frac{1}{2}$ years at 8.5% p.a.
  (e) £6480 invested for 18 months at 7.4% p.a.

③ **(a)** £1200 is invested for four years and earns £312 simple interest. Find the rate at which it is invested.
  (b) How much money must be invested at 6% p.a. to earn £360 simple interest after four years?
  (c) For how long would £2500 need to be invested at 3.5% p.a. to earn £437.50 simple interest?

Investigation

Some investments base the calculation for the second year's interest on the amount at the end of the first year.
This is called **compound interest**.
Leonie invests £800 at compound interest of 8% p.a.

1 **(a)** Copy and complete this table.

Year	Principal	Interest	Amount at end of year
1	£800	£64	£864 *Use this amount as the next principal.*
2	£864 *Amount from year before.*		
3			

(b) The amount, £A, can also be calculated by using the formula
$$A = P\left(1 + \frac{R}{100}\right)^T.$$
Use the formula with $P = 800$, $R = 8$ and $T = 1$, 2 and 3 to check your answers to part (a).

(c) Explain why the formula works.

2 Find **(i)** the amount **(ii)** the compound interest paid in these cases.
  (a) £900 invested for 5 years at 7.5% p.a. compound interest.
  (b) £650 invested for 4 years at 3.9% p.a. compound interest.
  (c) £110 invested for 18 months at 5.4% p.a. compound interest.

Finishing off

Review exercise

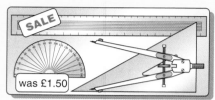

1 In a sale a stationery shop reduces its prices by 12%.
Find the sale price of these items.
(a) Geometry set £1.50
(b) Fountain pen £8.50

2 VAT must be added at 17.5% to these bills.
In each case find the total amount to be paid.
(a) A restaurant bill for £120.40
(b) A garage bill for £237.20   **(c)** A telephone bill for £98.80

3 Express
(a) 40p as a percentage of £2
(b) 300 g as a percentage of 5 kg
(c) 40 cm as a percentage of 3 m.

> ⚠ Start by converting both quantities into the same units.

4 A chemist buys hair gel at £2.40 per tube.
She makes a 30% profit.
(a) What is the selling price of the hair gel?
(b) In a special offer, she sells three tubes for the price of two.
Does she still make a profit?
What is her percentage profit or loss?

5 Find **(i)** the error   **(ii)** the percentage error
of these measurements.
(a) Measurement = 4.6 cm   Actual length = 4.5 cm
(b) Measurement = 4.5 cm   Actual length = 4.6 cm
(c) Measurement = 360 g   Actual mass = 350 g
(d) Measurement = 290 g   Actual mass = 280 g
(e) Measurement = 580 ml   Actual volume = 640 ml

6 Find the original price of these items.
(a) Designer label jeans selling at £51.20 after a 20% reduction.
(b) A designer label shirt selling at £31.50 after a 30% reduction.

7 These prices include VAT at 17.5%. Find the pre-VAT price.
  (a) Printer cartridge £22.09 **(b)** Telephone bill £101.05
  (c) Burger and chips £8.93 **(d)** Polo-neck sweater £42.30

8 A picture increases in value at 6% p.a.
It is initially worth £25 000. What is its value four years later?

9 A motorcycle decreases in value at a rate of 10% p.a.
Initially it was worth £8500. What is its value after 2 years?

10 One Monday, 100 people have a highly infectious disease.
The number of people with the disease increases by 20% every day.
How many people have the disease the following Monday?

11 A tank is 35 cm long and 20 cm wide.
It holds water which has a depth of 25 cm.
Water evaporates so that the volume decreases by 10%.
What is the percentage decrease in the depth?

12 **(a)** Simple interest of £120.60 is earned on £670 after 2 years.
    Find the rate at which the money was invested.
  (b) An investment of £850 at 7.2% p.a. earned £306 simple interest.
    For how long was the money invested?
  (c) An investment at 8.5% p.a. for 3 years earned £612 simple interest.
    How much money was invested initially?

13 For how many years must £1500 be invested at 8.5% p.a. compound interest
to amount to £2655?

14 At what rate of compound interest must £2800 be invested to amount to
£4308 in five years?

Investigation

1 Find the simple interest payable on the following.
  (a) £580 at 6.5% p.a. for 3 years.
  (b) £1650 at 8% p.a. for 4 years.
  (c) £24 000 at 12% p.a. for 10 years.

2 Look at this information on compound interest rates.
Find **(i)** the amount
      (ii) the compound interest
        paid on the following.
  (a) £580 invested for 3 years in a standard
    saver account.
  (b) £1650 invested for 4 years in a junior
    saver account.
  (c) £24 000 invested for 10 years in a super
    saver account.

3 Compare the three investments in **1** and **2**.

ALLIED AVON
Savings accounts
compound interest rates

Standard saver	6% p.a.
Junior saver	7.5% p.a.
Super saver	11% p.a.

2 Algebraic expressions

Review

Do you remember?

Vaya has been given some algebra questions. Here are the questions and her answers.

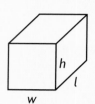

Find the value of $2(lw + wh + lh)$ when $l = 5$, $w = 4$ and $h = 2$.

$$2(lw + wh + lh) = 2(20 + 8 + 10)$$
$$= 2 \times 38$$
$$= 76$$

 What does this expression represent?

 What does *lw* mean?

 Why are *l*, *w* and *h* called variables?

Vaya

Simplify $3a + 2b + 4a - 5b$

Collect like terms

$$3a + 4a + 2b - 5b = 7a - 3b$$

 What are like and unlike terms?

Factorise $6a - 3b$

$$6a - 3b = 3(2a - b)$$

Expand $5(4x - 5y)$

$$5(4x - 5y) = 20x - 25y$$

Task

Write down the letters for the answers to questions 1 to 10 in order.
What do they spell?

1 What is the value of $2x + 5y$ when $x = 4$ and $y = 3$?

2 Factorise $12x - 18y$ fully.

3 Simplify $3x + 4y - 5x - 5y + 3x$.

4 Expand $3(x - 4y)$.

5 What is the value of $3(x + 4) + 2(x - 2)$ when $x = 5$?

6 Simplify $3(x + 2y) + 2(x - y)$.

7 What is the value of $3(x + 2y) - 2(x - 5)$ when $x = 5$ and $y = 3$?

8 Simplify $x + 4(x + y) - y$.

9 What is the value of $3(x + 2y) + x$ when $x = 4$ and $y = -1$?

10 Simplify $3(2x + y + 4) - 2(3x + 1) - 3y$.

A	$3x - 12y$
C	$3(x + 4y)$
E	$x - y$
F	10
G	23
L	$5x - 4y$
R	$6(2x - 3y)$
S	$5x + 4y$
T	33
U	$5x + 3y$

 You must be careful when expanding brackets if there is a minus sign outside. Look at this example.

EXAMPLE Simplify $2(5a - 3b + 4c) - 3(2a + b - 4c)$

Expand brackets $\quad = 10a - 6b + 8c - 6a - 3b + 12c$

Collect like terms $\quad = 10a - 6a - 6b - 3b + 8c + 12c$

$$= 4a - 9b + 20c$$

⚠ $-3 \times -4c$ gives $+12c$

Exercise

1 Simplify the following expressions.
  (a) $3x - 7 + 2x + 3x - 5$ (b) $3 - 2k - 7k - k + 6$
  (c) $3b - 2c + 3c - 4b + 2b$ (d) $5n + 3m - 2n - 4m + 3n$

2 (a) Group together the algebra cards with matching expressions.

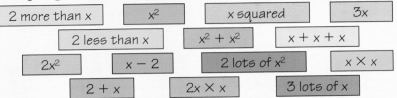

2 more than x	x^2	x squared	3x
2 less than x	$x^2 + x^2$	x + x + x
$2x^2$	x − 2	2 lots of x^2	x × x
2 + x	2x × x	3 lots of x

  (b) Find the value of each card when $x = 5$.
     Use your answers to check that you have grouped the cards correctly.

3 Emma works out 6×43 using brackets.
  Work out the following using brackets.

$$6 \times 43 = 6(40 + 3)$$
$$= 6 \times 40 + 6 \times 3$$
$$= 240 + 18$$
$$= 258$$

  (a) 7×42 (b) 8×963

4 Expand the following brackets.
  (a) $4(1 + 3g)$ (b) $11(5 - 6f)$ (c) $12(3b - 2c)$ (d) $-4(3f - 2)$

5 Factorise fully the following expressions.
  (a) $24 - 18p$ (b) $15b + 25$ (c) $48x - 30y$ (d) $12b - 4$

6 Expand and simplify these expressions.
  (a) $4(5a - 2) + 2(10a + 7)$ (b) $9(3b - 2) + 4(6b + 3)$
  (c) $2(5 - 3c) - (2c + 1)$ (d) $3(d + 2) - 2(5 + 3d)$
  (e) $4(2e - 3) - 3(e - 2)$ (f) $7(3f + 6) - 2(3 - f)$
  (g) $8(g - 1) - 7(g - 1)$ (h) $3(2h - 7) - (1 - h)$

Investigation

1 (a) What is: (i) $2 + 3 + 4$ (ii) $3 + 4 + 5$ (iii) $4 + 5 + 6$?
  (b) Show that each of your answers to part (a) is a multiple of 3.

2 These algebra cards represent three consecutive numbers.
  Write down the missing expressions.

| ? | n | ? |

3 Use all three of the expressions to prove that the sum of any
  three consecutive numbers is a multiple of 3.

Investigation

1 Look at this algebra wall.
  The expression in each brick is the sum of those in
  the two bricks beneath it.
  Copy the algebra wall and find the missing expressions.

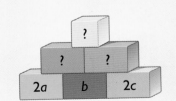

2 a, b and c are positive, whole numbers.
  Explain why the number in the top brick will always be even.

3 How could you change the expressions in the bottom three bricks so that the number
  in the top box is always odd?

4 What happens when $a = \frac{1}{2}$ and b and c are whole numbers?

Indices

Do you remember?

$n \times n \times n \times n \times n$ can be written as n^5.
n^5 is in **index form**.
n is the base. 5 is the power or index.

> Say this as
> 'n to the power 5'
> or just
> 'n to the 5'.

 What is the value of 5^1?

> Alan,
> simplify $a^6 \times a^2$
> and $a^6 \div a^2$.

Alan writes:

$$a^6 \times a^2$$
$$= \underset{1\ \ 2\ \ 3\ \ 4\ \ 5\ \ 6}{a \times a \times a \times a \times a \times a} \quad \times \quad \underset{7\ \ 8}{a \times a}$$
$$= a^8$$

 Simplify **(a)** $x^{106} \times x^{104}$ **(b)** $x^{106} \div x^{104}$
Explain why you don't need to write down
all the xs.
What rules do you use?

$$a^6 \div a^2$$
$$= \frac{a \times a \times a \times a \times \cancel{a} \times \cancel{a}}{\cancel{a} \times \cancel{a}}$$
$$= a^4$$

 Complete these statements.
'To multiply two numbers in index form,
you ... their powers.'

$$x^a \times x^b = x^?$$

> The numbers must all
> have the same base.

'To divide one number in index form by another, you ... their powers.'

$$x^a \div x^b = x^?$$

Task

Look at these algebra pyramids. The expression in each brick is found by multiplying
together those in the two bricks beneath it.
Copy each algebra pyramid and find the missing expressions.

1

2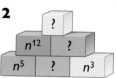

3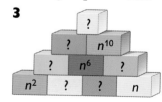

4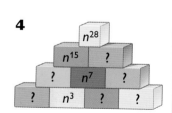

> Alan,
> simplify $(x^2)^3$.

Alan writes:
$$(x^2)^3 = x^2 \times x^2 \times x^2$$
$$= \underset{1\ \ 2}{x \times x} \quad \times \quad \underset{3\ \ 4}{x \times x} \quad \times \quad \underset{5\ \ 6}{x \times x}$$
$$= x^6$$

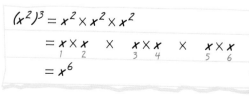

 Simplify $(x^3)^{100}$.
Explain why you don't need to write down all the xs.
Complete the following rule. $\quad (x^a)^b = x^?$

Exercise

1 Write each of the following as a single power.
   (a) $a^3 \times a^4$ **(b)** $b^2 \times b^2$ **(c)** $c^{15} \times c^{20}$ **(d)** $d^5 \times d$
   (e) $e^5 \div e^2$ **(f)** $f^5 \div f$ **(g)** $g^{50} \div g^{49}$ **(h)** $h^{100} \div h^{100}$

2 Jake simplifies $4x^3 \times 5x^2$ like this.

$$4x^3 \times 5x^2 = 4 \times 5 \times x^3 \times x^2$$
$$= 20x^5$$

Simplify the following.
   (a) $6a^3 \times 3a^5$ **(b)** $9b^7 \times 6b^5$ **(c)** $3c^5 \times 2c^9$ **(d)** $30d^{40} \times 20d^{60}$

3 Laila simplifies $\dfrac{12b^5}{4b^3}$ like this.

$$\frac{12b^5}{4b^3} = 3b^2$$

$12 \div 4 = 3$
$b^5 \div b^3 = b^2$

Simplify the following.

   (a) $\dfrac{15a^6}{3a^4}$ **(b)** $\dfrac{24b^8}{8b^3}$ **(c)** $\dfrac{150c^{27}}{15c^9}$ **(d)** $\dfrac{125d^{10}}{5d}$

4 **(a)** Write $2^5 \div 2^5$ as a single power of 2.
   (b) Evaluate $2^5 \div 2^5$.
   (c) Explain why your answers to parts (a) and (b) show that $2^0 = 1$.
   (d) Evaluate the following:
       (i) $3^2 \div 3^2$ **(ii)** $4^3 \div 4^3$ **(iii)** $10^4 \div 10^4$
   (e) Write each of your answers to part (d) as a single power.
   (f) What does n^0 equal? Give a reason for your answer.

5 Look at these algebra pyramids.
   The expression in each brick is found by multiplying together those in the two bricks beneath it.
   Copy each algebra pyramid and find the missing expressions.

   (a) 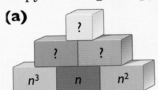   **(b)** 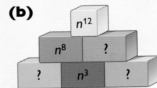   **(c)**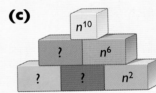

Investigation

Helen is investigating powers.
She works out $(2^3)^2$.
She writes: $(2^3)^2 = (8)^2 = 64$

Helen works out what is inside the brackets first.

1 Use Helen's method to work out the following. Use your calculator at the last stage.
   (a) $(3^4)^3$ **(b)** $(2^3)^5$ **(c)** $(4^3)^2$ **(d)** $(5^2)^4$

Richard uses another way to work out $(2^3)^2$.
He writes: $(2^3)^2 = (2 \times 2 \times 2)^2 = (2 \times 2 \times 2) \times (2 \times 2 \times 2) = 2^6 = 64$

This is the rule $(x^a)^b = x^{ab}$.

2 Use Richard's method to write the expressions in question 1 as single powers.
   Use a calculator to check your answers.

3 Write each of the following as a single power.
   (a) $(a^5)^2$ **(b)** $(b^2)^3$ **(c)** $(c^3)^4$ **(d)** $(d^{40})^{20}$

Expanding two brackets

Alan asks Sophie to multiply 73 by 34 in her head.

Sophie

That's easy. I split it into rectangles.

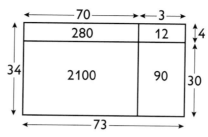

This is how Sophie thinks of 73 × 34.

$73 \times 34 = (70 + 3) \times (30 + 4)$
$= 70 \times 30 + 70 \times 4 + 3 \times 30 + 3 \times 4$
$= 2100 + 280 + 90 + 12$
$= 2482$

 Use this method to multiply 87 × 56.

You can use the same method for expanding brackets in algebra.

	p	q	
$(r + s)$	pr	qr	r
	ps	qs	s

$p + q$

$(p + q)(r + s) = pr + ps + qr + qs$

	x	4	
$(x + 3)$	x^2	$4x$	x
	$3x$	12	3

$x + 4$

$(x + 4)(x + 3) = x^2 + 3x + 4x + 12$
$= x^2 + 7x + 12$

Task

Expand the following.

1 $(a + b)(c + d)$ **2** $(a + b)(a + d)$ **3** $(x + 9)(x + 11)$ **4** $(x + 2)(x + 2)$

Another way to expand two brackets is to use long multiplication.
This is how you do it for $(x + 4)(x + 3)$.

Step 1

Multiply by x. Keep the x^2, x and numbers in separate columns.

$$\begin{array}{r} x + 4 \\ x + 3 \\ \hline x^2 + 4x \end{array}$$

Step 2

Now multiply by 3.

$$\begin{array}{r} x + 4 \\ x + 3 \\ \hline x^2 + 4x \\ +3x + 12 \\ \hline \end{array}$$

Step 3

Add up.

$$\begin{array}{r} x + 4 \\ x + 3 \\ \hline x^2 + 4x \\ +3x + 12 \\ \hline x^2 + 7x + 12 \end{array}$$

 Use this method to expand $(x + 5)(x + 2)$. Explain where each term comes from.

Now use this method with negative numbers.
Expand $(x - 4)(x + 3)$ and $(x - 4)(x - 5)$.
Why is it hard to use the rectangle method when negative numbers are involved?

Exercise

1 Expand the following brackets.
   (a) $a(2a - 5)$ **(b)** $b(2 - b)$ **(c)** $6c(3 - 2c)$
   (d) $5d(2d + 3)$ **(e)** $3e(2e^2 + 7)$ **(f)** $4f(3 - 2f^2)$
   (g) $g(3g^2 - 2g + 2)$ **(h)** $2h(1 - h + h^2)$ **(i)** $7i(3i^2 - 4i + 5)$

2 Look at how this expression is factorised. $6y^2 + 4y = 2y(3y + 2)$
   Factorise the following expressions fully.

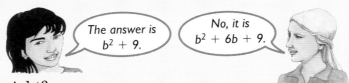

   (a) $4a^2 + 5a$ **(b)** $3b^2 - 6b$
   (c) $8c^2 - 4c$ **(d)** $d^3 + d^2 + d$ **(e)** $12e^3 - 8e^2 + 4e$ **(f)** $15f^3 - 6f^2 - 9$

3 Expand the following brackets. Simplify your answers.
   (a) $(a + 1)(a + 2)$ **(b)** $(b + 1)(b + 3)$ **(c)** $(c + 3)(c - 2)$
   (d) $(d - 2)(d - 5)$ **(e)** $(e - 2)(e + 7)$ **(f)** $(f - 9)(f - 4)$

4 **(a)** Find and simplify an expression for the area
        of this square. $(a + 3)$ cm

   (b) **(i)** What does 37^2 mean?   **(ii)** What does x^2 mean?
       (iii) What does $(x + 7)^2$ mean?   **(iv)** Expand $(x + 7)^2$.
       (v) Use your answer to part (iv) to work out 37^2.
           What value of x should you use?

5 Vaya and Sarah have both expanded the expression $(b + 3)^2$.

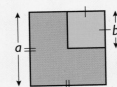

         The answer is   No, it is
         $b^2 + 9$. $b^2 + 6b + 9$.

   (a) Who is right?
   (b) How would you show the other person that she is wrong?
   (c) Expand and simplify the following.
      (i) $(n + 3)^2$ **(ii)** $(x - 3)^2$ **(iii)** $(y - 30)^2$

Investigation

1 **(a)** Expand the brackets $(a + b)(a - b)$. Simplify your answer.
   (b) Expand and simplify the following.
      (i) $(a + 3)(a - 3)$ **(ii)** $(a + 5)(a - 5)$ **(iii)** $(a + 2)(a - 2)$

2 **(a)** Expressions in the form $a^2 - b^2$ are often called the 'difference of two squares'.
     Why do you think this is?
   (b) Factorise the following.
      (i) $a^2 - 16$ **(ii)** $a^2 - 36$ **(iii)** $a^2 - 64$ **(iv)** $a^2 - 1$

3 Show how you would use the 'difference of two squares' to work out the following
   without using a calculator.
   (a) $26^2 - 16^2$ **(b)** $378^2 - 376^2$ **(c)** $1025^2 - 1024^2$

4 Find as many different expressions as you can for the
   blue-shaded area.
   Show algebraically that your expressions are equivalent.

Further expressions

Look at this shape.
It consists of four cuboids.
Its volume is given by the expression:

$$a^3 + a^2b + a^2c + bc^2.$$

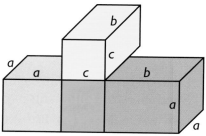

 This expression has four terms, one for each colour in the shape.
Which term goes with which colour?

Notice two things about $a^3 + a^2b + a^2c + bc^2$.

• It cannot be simplified. All four terms are unlike.
• You know what it stands for. It is the volume of the shape.

You often meet expressions in algebra where you do not know what they stand for.
You treat them just the same.

Sandy, what is
$2a^2b^3 \times 5ab^4$?

Sandy writes:

$$2a^2b^3 \times 5ab^4$$
$$= 2 \times 5 \times a^2 \times a^1 \times b^3 \times b^4$$
$$= 10a^3b^7 \checkmark$$

 Explain what Sandy has done.

Task

1 (a) Find expressions for the volume
and surface area of this shape.
(b) Find the value of each of your
expressions when $a = 2$ cm
and $b = 4$ cm.

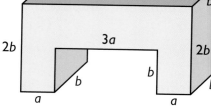

All the
angles
are 90°.

2 Simplify the following.
(a) $p^3 + p - p^3 + 2$ **(b)** $2a^2b + 3aab - c^2$ **(c)** $3x^2y^3 \times 5x^2y^4$ **(d)** $12x^5y^7 \div 3x^2y^5$

Look at this question and the answer.

Simplify $2a(a^2 + 3b^2 + c^2) - 3b(2ab - c^2)$

$$2a(a^2 + 3b^2 + c^2) - 3b(2ab - c^2) = 2a^3 + 6ab^2 + 2ac^2 - 6ab^2 + 3bc^2$$
$$= 2a^3 + 6ab^2 - 6ab^2 + 2ac^2 + 3bc^2$$
$$= 2a^3 + 2ac^2 + 3bc^2$$

 Explain each step of the working.

Exercise

1 Simplify the following.
(a) $5a^2 + 3a + 2a + 7a^2$
(b) $7b^2 - 4ab + 3b^2 + 2ab$
(c) $5c^3 + 2c^2 - 4c^3 - c^2$
(d) $3d^2 - 5c^2d + 4d^2 - 7d^2 + 6c^2d$
(e) $5e^2 + 3e - 2e^2 - e^2 + 2e$
(f) $7fg - 3fg + 6f^2g - 4fg - 5f^2g$

2 Simplify the following.
(a) $5a^2b \times 3ab$
(b) $7bc^2 \times 6b^5c^3$
(c) $4c^3d^2 \times 3cd$
(d) $3de \times 2d^2e^6$
(e) $9ef^6 \times 4e^2f^3$
(f) $10f^{100}g^{50} \times 7f^{75}g^{25}$

3 Alice and Ben are simplifying the expression $\dfrac{15x^2y^5}{5xy^3}$.

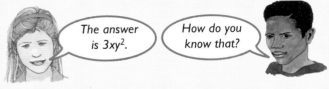

The answer is $3xy^2$.

How do you know that?

Here is Alice's working:

$\dfrac{15x^2y^5}{5xy^3} = 3xy^2$

$15 \div 5 = 3$
$x^2 \div x = x$
$y^5 \div y^3 = y^2$

(a) Explain how Alice can check that her answer is right.

(b) Simplify the following.

(i) $\dfrac{12a^2b^3}{4ab}$

(ii) $\dfrac{18b^7c^4}{6b^4c^3}$

(iii) $\dfrac{20c^6d^4e^2}{4c^4d^2e}$

(iv) $\dfrac{5ef^4}{ef}$

(v) $\dfrac{10f^3g^2}{5fgg}$

(vi) $\dfrac{100f^{20}g^{100}h^{50}}{25f^{20}g^{99}h^{48}}$

4 Thena is designing a garden pond for her Design and Technology project. It consists of metal rods joined together. They are then covered in a strong waterproof fabric.

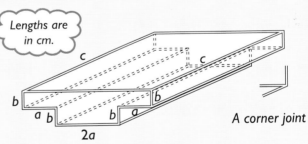

Lengths are in cm.

A corner joint

(a) Find expressions for
(i) the total length of metal rod
(ii) the area of fabric
(iii) the volume of the pond
(iv) the number of corner joints.
Factorise your answers fully where possible.

(b) Find the values for the four quantities when $a = 40$, $b = 30$ and $c = 300$. State the units for each answer.

Thena decides to make a and b the same value.

(c) Rewrite your four expressions, using the variables a and c. Factorise your answers fully.

(d) Find the value of each quantity when $a = 40$ and $c = 150$.

5 Look at how Sam factorises this expression.

$24x^2y - 18xy = 6xy(4x - 3)$

$6xy \times 4x = 24x^2y$

$6xy \times 3 = 18xy$

Factorise these expressions fully.

(a) $12ab + 8b$
(b) $15bc - 9c$
(c) $12c - 24cd$
(d) $18d^2 + 3d$
(e) $6e^2 - 2e$
(f) $9f^2g - 6fg$
(g) $24g^2h + 6g$
(h) $15h^3j - 5h^2$

Finishing off

Now that you have finished this chapter you should be able to:

- simplify expressions
- understand the terms: *simplify*, *expand*, *factorise*, *base*, *index* and *power*
- factorise expressions
- expand two sets of brackets
- multiply and divide simple powers.

Review exercise

1 Simplify the following expressions.

(a) $2e - 3 + 5e + 5 - e$

(b) $4f + 3g - 2f + 4g + f$

(c) $4h - h + j - 2h + 3j$

(d) $3k - 2m - k - 3m - k + 4m$

(e) $n^2 + m^2 + n^2 + m^2 - 3n^2$

(f) $4p^2 + 3p + 2p^2 - 2p - 3p^2 - 5p$

(g) $5gh + 3g^2h - 3gh - 2g^2h - 7gh$

(h) $7rs - 3r^2 - 2rs + r^2 - 2r^2$

2 How should you write the following expressions?

(a) $5 \times 3 \times d$

(b) $2 \times e \times 5$

(c) $3 \times f \times f$

(d) $5 \times g \times g$

(e) $3 \times h \times j$

(f) $3 \times g \times 6 \times h$

(g) $p \times 3 \times r \times r$

(h) $m \times 4 \times n \times m$

3 Expand the following brackets. Simplify your answers where possible.

(a) $5(a - 2)$

(b) $2(7b - 3)$

(c) $2c(3c + 4)$

(d) $(d + 4)(d - 3)$

(e) $(e + 7)(e - 7)$

(f) $(f - 4)^2$

4 Factorise the following expressions fully.

(a) $12 - 6a$

(b) $3 + 6b$

(c) $c^2 - 2c$

(d) $4d^3 + 3d^2 + d$

(e) $18e + 24e^2 + 6e^3$

(f) $10f^3 - 12f^2$

(g) $5gh + 10g$

(h) $33cd - 22c$

(i) $36j^2k - 60jk$

5 (a) Expand the following. Simplify your answers.

(i) $(a + 1)^2$

(ii) $(a - 1)^2$

(b) Use your answers to part (a) to work out the following.

(i) 201^2

(ii) 99^2

(iii) 199^2

6 Write the following as single powers.

(a) $a^6 \times a^3$

(b) $b^7 \times b^2$

(c) $c^5 \times c^4$

(d) $d^{50} \times d$

(e) $e^6 \div e^4$

(f) $f^6 \div f^2$

(g) $g^{10} \div g^{10}$

(h) $h^{50} \div h^{49}$

(i) $(i^3)^2$

(j) $(j^2)^3$

(k) $(k^5)^8$

(l) $(l^{100})^2$

7 Simplify the following.

(a) $2a^5 \times 5a^7$

(b) $3b^4 \times 2b$

(c) $6c^3 \times 2c^{10}$

(d) $5d^4 \times 2d^0$

(e) $\dfrac{3ef^3}{ef^2}$

(f) $\dfrac{12fg^2}{3fg}$

(g) $\dfrac{8g^{10}}{4g^{10}}$

(h) $\dfrac{4gh^6}{2gh^0}$

Activity Use all of these algebra dominoes to make a rectangle.
Touching tiles must have equivalent expressions on them.

| $2a^2 \times 3a^4$ | $\dfrac{2a^4}{a^3}$ | | 3 | $\dfrac{a^3 \times a^2}{a^5}$ | | $(2a^3)^2$ | $\dfrac{3a^2}{a^2}$ | | $6(a^3)^2$ | $4a^6$ |

| 2a | $\dfrac{a^3}{a^3}$ | | $8a^6$ | 1 | | a^0 | $(2a^2)^3$ |

Investigation

Meena, what is $(3\frac{1}{2})^2$?

Dad

That is easy, I have a special trick for squaring halves. One more than 3 is 4 so you do 3 times 4 and then add $\frac{1}{4}$. Answer $12\frac{1}{4}$.

Meena

(a) Is it true that $(3\frac{1}{2})^2 = 12\frac{1}{4}$?

(b) Check Meena's method for **(i)** $(1\frac{1}{2})^2$ **(ii)** $(2\frac{1}{2})^2$ **(iii)** $(5\frac{1}{2})^2$ **(iv)** $(10\frac{1}{2})^2$.

(c) Use algebra to describe the method. You will need to write two expressions, one for the question and another for the answer.

(d) Use your answer to part **(b)** to prove that the method works for squaring any positive (+) number of this type.

Investigation

The expression in the top brick of each of these algebra pyramids has been found by multiplying together the expressions in the two bricks beneath it. Copy each algebra wall.

1 Expand and simplify the expressions in each of the top bricks.

(a)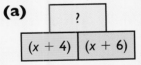

(b)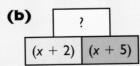

(c)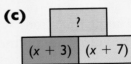

2 Complete the expressions in the bottom bricks.

(a)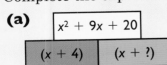

(b)

| $x^2 + 5x + 6$ |
| $(x + 2)$ | $(x + ?)$ |

(c)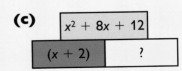

(d)

| $x^2 + 13x + 40$ |
| $(x + ?)$ | $(x + ?)$ |

(e)

| $x^2 + 11x + 10$ |
| $(x + ?)$ | $(x + ?)$ |

(f)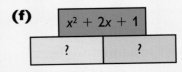

What rules should you use to find the expressions in the bottom bricks?

Collecting information

Jack wants to show his mother that she is wrong. He decides to do his own survey. He makes this questionnaire.

When you write a question for a survey, ask these three things.

- Are people allowed to tick more than one box?
- Do the boxes cover all possible answers?
- Is the question biased?

1. Do you watch a lot of TV?
   Yes ☐   No ☐

2. What sort of programmes do you watch?
   Comedy ☐   Films ☐   Soaps ☐

? What is wrong with Jack's questions?

Jack tells his friends Molly and Karl about his questionnaire.

Molly

Karl

Task

Write a questionnaire that Jack could use.
Include some questions which will help Jack to find out whether Molly or Karl is right.
Compare your questionnaire with the rest of the class.

? What advice would you give Jack?

When you carry out a survey, make sure you have a **representative sample**. Depending on the purpose of the survey, you might need to

- ask the same number of males and females
- ask the same numbers in a variety of age groups.

? Jack finally decides to ask a lot more people to answer his questionnaire. How might he choose who to ask?

Exercise

1 Sally is doing a survey on pocket money.
Here is her questionnaire.

> **1** How often do you get pocket money?
> weekly ☐   monthly ☐
>
> **2** What do you spend it on?
> clothes ☐   sweets ☐   CDs ☐   magazines ☐   going out ☐
>
> **3** How much do you get?
> £0–£2 ☐   £2–£5 ☐   £10 ☐   more ☐
>
> **4** Do you save any of your pocket money?
> yes ☐   no ☐   some of it ☐   all of it ☐   sometimes ☐
>
> **5** Everyone should save some of their pocket money, shouldn't they?
> yes ☐   no ☐   *These questions need improving, Sally.*
> *Please try again.*

Sally's teacher says her questions need improving.

(a) Explain what is wrong with each question.

(b) Write a better questionnaire for Sally.

2 Sally wants to ask 50 people to answer her questionnaire.
Suggest how she could decide who to ask.

3 Write *one* survey question which you could use to find out about each
of the following issues.
Make sure you write down a sensible set of responses for each question.

(a) How people travel to school.

(b) What people think about wearing fur clothes.

(c) How much exercise people do.

(d) How often people visit the cinema.

4 **(a)** Write a questionnaire to find out what people think about
school uniform.
Your questionnaire should cover
  ● whether people agree with having a school uniform
  ● what sort of uniform people would prefer
  ● whether there should be rules about jewellery, make-up, etc.

(b) Explain how you would choose a sample of people to complete the
questionnaire.

5 Choose a topic that you are interested in.
Write a questionnaire to find out about your chosen topic.

Displaying data

Here is part of Jack's questionnaire.

> How many TV sets are there in your household?
> 0 ☐   1 ☐   2 ☐   3 ☐
> 4 ☐   5 ☐   more than 5 ☐
>
> Which of the following do you like best?
> comedy ☐   films ☐   soaps ☐   game shows ☐
> drama ☐   sport ☐   science fiction ☐   factual ☐

*The answer to this question is always a number. This kind of data is called **numerical** data*

*The answer to this question is not a number. This kind of data is called **categorical** data.*

 Think of some examples of data which you might collect for a survey. Are the data categorical or numerical?

Jack displays his data from the second question like this.

Category	Tally	Frequency
Comedy	⊪	5
Films	‖‖	3
Soaps	⊪ ‖‖	8
Game shows	‖	1
Drama	‖‖	3
Sport	⊪	5
Science fiction	‖‖	3
Factual	‖	2

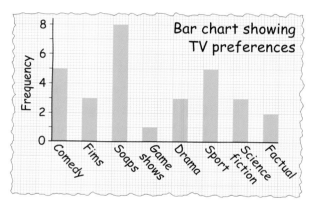

Bar chart showing TV preferences

 What are the advantages of the bar chart over the tally chart?

Task

Jack makes this two-way table to show the TV preferences of the boys and girls in his class separately.

Category	Comedy	Films	Soaps	Game shows	Drama	Sport	Science fiction	Factual
Boys	2	2	1	0	1	5	2	1
Girls	3	1	7	1	2	0	1	1

Make a display to show these data.
Your display should make it easy to compare boys with girls.

 What do these data tell you about the TV preferences of boys and girls in Jack's class?

Exercise

1 Mr Berry is a teacher.
He wants to know how well his students have done in their GCSE maths exams.
Here is a list of his students' grades.

C E B B D E E A F C C C
C D G B E C B E F B C B
A D D E C C D

(a) Make a tally chart to show these results.
(b) How many students are there in Mr Berry's class?
(c) What percentage of the students obtained a grade A, B or C?
(d) Draw a bar chart to show these results.

2 Sarah is doing research for a travel agent. She uses this questionnaire.

1 Which of these holiday destinations would you prefer?
Ibiza ☐   Kenya ☐   Florida ☐   Sydney ☐

2 What is your age group?
Under 30 ☐   30–50 ☐   Over 50 ☐

Sarah draws this compound bar chart to show her results.

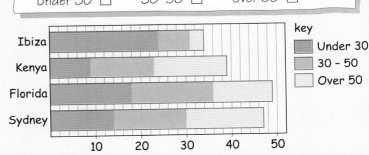

key
■ Under 30
▨ 30 – 50
☐ Over 50

(a) Copy and complete this two-way table.

	Ibiza	Kenya	Florida	Sydney
Under 30	24			
30–50				
Over 50				
Total				

(b) What is the most popular resort for people aged
(i) under 30   (ii) 30–50   (iii) over 50?

3 This two-way table shows the ages of boys and girls on an adventure holiday for teenagers.

Age	13	14	15	16	17	18
Boys	8	12	13	17	11	9
Girls	15	16	12	8	7	4

(a) Draw a compound bar chart to illustrate these data.
(b) What does the chart show you about the data?

4 (a) Throw two dice 50 times, adding the scores together each time. Record your scores in a tally chart.
(b) Draw a bar chart to illustrate your results.
(c) Describe the shape of the bar chart. Why is it this shape?

Pie charts

Here is another of the questions Jack asks.

> Which of these TV channels do you watch most often?
> BBC1 ☐   BBC2 ☐   ITV1 ☐   C4 ☐

Here are the results from this question.

Channel	BBC1	BBC2	ITV1	C4
Frequency	11	6	5	8

Jack wants to draw a pie chart to illustrate these data.
This is how he works out the size of the sector for BBC1.

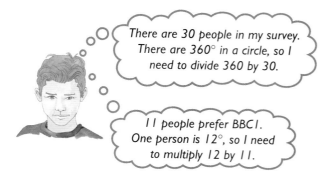

> There are 30 people in my survey.
> There are 360° in a circle, so I need to divide 360 by 30.

> 11 people prefer BBC1.
> One person is 12°, so I need to multiply 12 by 11.

> Number of degrees per person
> = 360 ÷ 30
> = 12
>
> Size of slice for BBC1
> = 12 × 11
> = 132°

? What are the sizes of the other three sectors of the pie chart?

Here is Jack's pie chart.

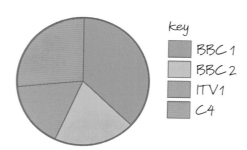

key
- BBC 1
- BBC 2
- ITV1
- C4

? Which do you think is better for categorical data, a bar chart or a pie chart?
Which do you think is better for numerical data?

Task

Ask 20 people which TV channel they watch most often.
Draw a pie chart to illustrate your results.

? Compare your pie chart with Jack's.
What are the differences between them?

Exercise

1 These two pie charts show the results of two football teams last season.

Avonford Town   Brentbridge United

key

- Win
- Draw
- Lose

(a) What percentage of their matches did Avonford Town win?
(b) What percentage did they lose?
(c) What percentage of their matches did Brentbridge United draw?
(d) Which team had the better season?

2 Philip wants to draw a pie chart to show how he spends his time one day. He writes down how many hours he spends on each activity.

Sleeping	Eating	Lessons	Watching TV	Doing homework	Other
10	1	5	2	2	4

(a) How many degrees should Philip use to represent 1 hour?
(b) Draw Philip's pie chart.

3 Melanie is doing a survey about sport.

Boy ☐   Girl ☐

Which is your favourite sport from the following list?

athletics ☐   football ☐   hockey ☐

swimming ☐   tennis ☐

Here are her results.

	Athletics	Football	Hockey	Swimming	Tennis
Boys	4	19	2	10	5
Girls	5	3	11	9	8

Melanie draws two pie charts to show her results.

(a) How many boys did Melanie ask?
(b) How many degrees does she use to represent each boy?
(c) How many girls did she ask?
(d) How many degrees does she use to represent each girl?
(e) Draw Melanie's two pie charts.

Working with grouped data

Here is some more of Jack's questionnaire.
Both these questions deal with numerical data.

> How many TV sets are there in your household?
> 0 ☐   1 ☐   2 ☐   3 ☐   4 ☐
> 5 ☐   More than 5 ☐
> How much TV did you watch last week? (t = no. of hours)
> $0 < t \leqslant 5$ ☐ $5 \leqslant t < 10$ ☐ $10 \leqslant t < 15$ ☐
> $15 \leqslant t < 20$ ☐ $20 \leqslant t < 25$ ☐ $t \geqslant 25$ ☐

The answer to this question can only take certain values. You cannot have $2\frac{1}{2}$ TV sets! Data like these are called **discrete** *data.*

The answer to this question could take any value. You could have any fraction of an hour. Data like these are called **continuous** *data.*

 What does $0 < t \leqslant 5$ mean?
Janice watched TV for exactly 10 hours. Which box should she tick?

Jack draws a bar chart to illustrate the results to the second question.
This kind of bar chart is called a **frequency chart**.
He also draws a **frequency polygon** by joining the mid-points of the top of each bar.

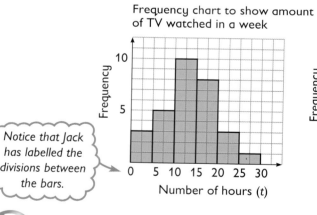

Frequency chart to show amount of TV watched in a week

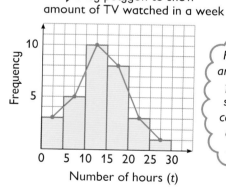

Frequency polygon to show amount of TV watched in a week

Notice that Jack has labelled the divisions between the bars.

Frequency polygons are particularly useful for comparing two sets of data as you can draw more than one graph on the same set of axes.

 Look back to Jack's conversation with his mother on page 22.
Look at the frequency chart. Who is right, Jack or his mother?

Task

1 Measure the height of everybody in the class.
   Record the data for each person individually.
2 Choose suitable class intervals and make two tally charts, one for boys and one for girls.
3 Draw two frequency polygons on the same axes to illustrate your results.

 What do your frequency polygons tell you about the heights of boys and girls in your class?

Exercise

1 State whether each of the following sets of data is categorical, discrete numerical or continuous numerical.
  (a) The political parties voted for by people in a village.
  (b) The heights of a class of school children.
  (c) The shoe sizes of a class of school children.
  (d) The flavours of crisps preferred by a group of people.

2 Paul and Sophie each do a survey to find out the ages of people using a swimming pool over a 1-hour period. The charts below show their results.

Paul's chart

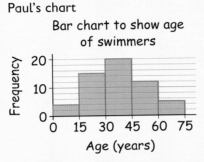

Sophie's chart

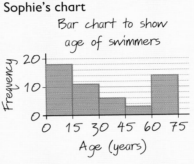

  (a) How many people aged 60 or over used the pool during each survey?
  (b) How many people aged under 30 used the pool during each survey?
  (c) One survey was carried out between 7 p.m. and 8 p.m. on a Monday. The other was carried out between 10 a.m. and 11 a.m. on a Tuesday. Which do you think was which? Why?

3 Every time Julie uses the internet, she records the length of time, t minutes, she is on-line. This frequency table shows her results.

$0 < t \leqslant 30$	$30 < t \leqslant 60$	$60 < t \leqslant 90$	$90 < t \leqslant 120$	$120 < t \leqslant 150$
15	35	22	9	2

Draw a frequency chart to illustrate these data. What does it show you? Comment on the results.

4 Liz is a midwife at Avonford Hospital.
One week, she records the birth weights, w kg, of all the babies born.

Boys	3.21	3.64	3.52	2.93	4.13	3.10	3.34	3.81
	3.27	2.75	3.04	3.18	4.09	3.61	3.70	3.15
	2.48	4.46	3.56	3.75	3.22	3.67	2.81	3.94
	3.43	3.87	4.01	2.52				

Girls	2.83	3.42	3.69	3.15	3.04	3.17	2.56	3.21
	3.81	3.60	3.58	2.80	2.95	3.73	3.15	3.31
	2.69	4.12	3.49	3.64	3.52	3.71	3.42	3.83

  (a) Draw separate grouped tally charts to show the data for boys and girls. Use the groups $1.80 < w \leqslant 2.20$, $2.20 < w \leqslant 2.60$, ..., $4.60 < w \leqslant 5.00$.
  (b) Draw two frequency polygons on the same axes to show the boys' weights and the girls' weights.
  (c) What differences are there between the two sets of data?

Scatter diagrams

Vicki is in the same class as Jack. She is interested in Jack's survey.
Vicki thinks that her older sister watches a lot more TV than she does.

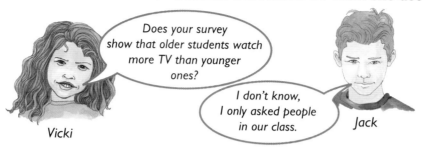

Does your survey show that older students watch more TV than younger ones?

I don't know, I only asked people in our class.

Vicki

Jack

Vicki decides to carry out her own survey. She chooses 20 people in a variety of year groups. They keep a record of how much TV they watch one week.

Name	Age	Hours of TV	Name	Age	Hours of TV
Amy	11	8	Emily	12	7
Euan	13	9	Matthew	13	16
Hassan	14	23	Vicki	14	19

Vicki rounds the times to the nearest hour.

Vicki draws this **scatter diagram** to show her results for her survey report.
She also draws a **line of best fit** through the points.

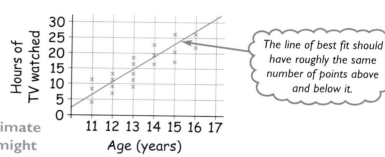

The line of best fit should have roughly the same number of points above and below it.

 Use the line of best fit to estimate how much TV a 17-year-old might watch and how much a 10-year-old might watch.
Do you think that your estimates are accurate?

 **Task**

1 For the Task on page 28 you measured the height of everybody in your class.
   Look again at these data.
2 Now ask everybody their shoe size.
3 Draw a scatter diagram to illustrate these data.

    What does you scatter diagram tell you about these data?

Vicki's scatter diagram shows **positive correlation**. As one variable increases, the other increases too.

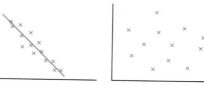

*This scatter diagram shows **negative correlation**. As one variable increases the other decreases.*

*This scatter diagram shows **no correlation**. There is no connection between the two variables.*

 What do you think these scatter diagrams might represent?

Exercise

1 Anita thinks that people who are
good at maths are also good at science.
She uses the results from Class 9B's
maths and science tests to draw this
scatter diagram.

(a) What is
  (i) the lowest mark in the maths test?
  (ii) the highest mark in the maths test?
  (iii) the lowest mark in the science test?
  (iv) the highest mark in the science test?

(b) Katie got 40% in the science test.
What did she get in the maths test?

(c) James got 61% in the maths test.
What did he get in the science test?

(d) Look at the scatter diagram. Do the data support Anita's idea?
Explain your answer.

2 The table below shows the maximum temperature and the number of hours
of sunshine in 12 British cities on one day in August.

City	Max. temp (°C)	Hours of sunshine	City	Max. temp (°C)	Hours of sunshine
London	24	10	Southampton	25	9
Birmingham	22	9	Norwich	23	11
Manchester	20	8	Liverpool	22	8
Edinburgh	17	9	Exeter	25	10
Glasgow	18	6	Newcastle	20	9
Bristol	23	7	Nottingham	21	8

(a) Draw a scatter diagram to illustrate these data.
(b) Draw a line of best fit on your diagram.
(c) The maximum temperature in York that day was 19°C.
Estimate the number of hours of sunshine that York had.
(d) Brighton had 12 hours of sunshine.
Estimate the maximum temperature in Brighton.

3 What do each of the scatter diagrams below tell you?

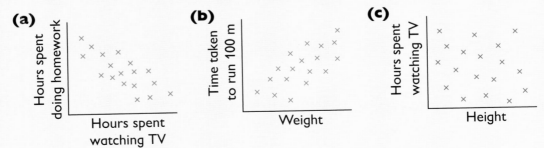

Finishing off

Now that you have finished this chapter you should be able to:

- design a questionnaire and use it to collect data
- draw and interpret tally charts, bar charts, pie charts and two-way tables
- tell the difference between categorical data, discrete numerical data and continuous numerical data

- group data when appropriate
- draw and interpret frequency charts for continuous data
- draw and interpret frequency polygons
- draw and interpret scatter diagrams
- draw and use the line of best fit on scatter diagrams.

Review exercise

1 A council has a budget of £900 million to spend on services. It is divided up as shown in the table.

Education services	£580 million
Social services	£200 million
Environmental services	£110 million
Other services	£10 million
Total	£900 million

Jo works for the council.
She wants to draw a pie chart to show these data.

(a) How many degrees should Jo use to represent £1 million?

(b) Draw Jo's pie chart.

2 This is a special kind of bar chart called a population pyramid.
This population pyramid shows the population of the U.K. in 1991.

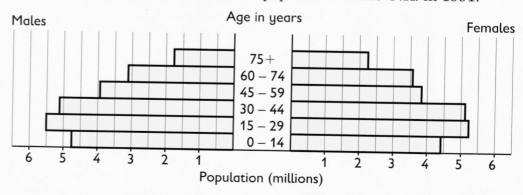

(a) What is the most numerous age group for both males and females?

(b) In which age groups are there more females than males?
Why do you think this is?

3 Stephen and his sister Anna
share a computer.

Stephen and Anna both keep a record
of the length of time, in minutes, that
they use the computer each day for one month.

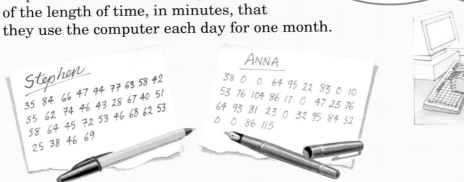

*It's not fair.
You use the computer
more than I do.*

Stephen
35 84 66 47 94 77 63 58 42
55 62 74 46 43 28 67 40 51
58 64 45 72 53 46 68 62 53
25 38 46 69

ANNA
38 0 0 64 95 22 83 0 10
53 76 104 86 17 0 47 23 76
64 93 81 23 0 32 95 84 52
0 0 86 115

(a) Make a grouped tally chart to show Stephen's data and another
to show Anna's data.
Use the groups $0 \leqslant t < 15$, $15 \leqslant t < 30$, etc.

(b) Draw a frequency chart to show Stephen's data and another
to show Anna's data.

(c) Draw two frequency polygons on the same axes to illustrate the
two sets of data.

(d) Do you think that Anna is right?

4 Sarah says 'I think that people who are good at sprinting are also good
at the long jump.'
Sarah collects some data to find out if she is right.

Time to run 100 m (seconds)	Distance jumped (m)	Time to run 100 m (seconds)	Distance jumped (m)
14.3	1.81	17.3	1.52
15.1	1.76	12.8	2.03
14.4	1.78	16.0	1.68
18.6	1.57	15.3	1.75
13.5	1.95	13.4	1.88
16.1	1.68	13.6	1.92
12.7	1.94	14.7	1.78
13.9	1.84	12.5	2.08
15.4	1.72	16.4	1.58
14.0	1.88	13.7	1.87

(a) Draw a scatter diagram to show Sarah's data.

(b) Describe the relationship between the time taken to run 100 m and
the distance jumped.

(c) Draw a line of best fit on your diagram.

(d) Sarah's friend Richard runs 100 m in 14.8 seconds.
Use your line of best fit to estimate how far Richard can jump.

4 Equations

Solving equations

Do you remember how to solve equations?

> ### Task
>
> Work with a friend. Each of you takes one of these equations (1 (a) or (b)).
>
> **1 (a)** $5x - 3 = 2x - 12$ **(b)** $7x + 8 = 3x + 28$
>
> Solve your equation, step-by-step, then pass your work to your partner.
> Your friend describes your steps in words, like 'Divide both sides by 2'.
> You do the same for your friend's equation.
> Check your answers.
> Now do the same for the next two pairs of equations.
>
> **2 (a)** $3(x + 1) = x + 7$ **(b)** $2(5x - 2) = 7x + 20$
>
> **3 (a)** $3(x + 5) + 2(2x - 3) = 5(x + 3)$ **(b)** $8(x + 2) + 3(2x - 11) = 9(x + 2)$

Steffi is given this equation. $\frac{2}{3}(x + 1) = \frac{x}{5} + 3$

Help!
It has fractions in it.

Steffi

It's easy, you
do it like this.

Suleman

Suleman writes

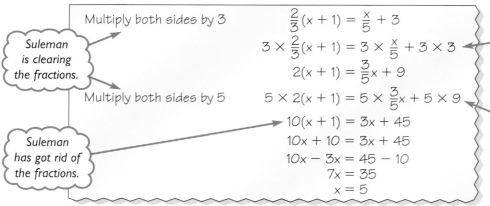

Suleman
is clearing
the fractions.

Multiply both sides by 3

$\frac{2}{3}(x + 1) = \frac{x}{5} + 3$

$3 \times \frac{2}{3}(x + 1) = 3 \times \frac{x}{5} + 3 \times 3$

$2(x + 1) = \frac{3}{5}x + 9$

Multiply both sides by 5

$5 \times 2(x + 1) = 5 \times \frac{3}{5}x + 5 \times 9$

Suleman
has got rid of
the fractions.

$10(x + 1) = 3x + 45$

$10x + 10 = 3x + 45$

$10x - 3x = 45 - 10$

$7x = 35$

$x = 5$

 Remember
to multiply
everything
by 3.

 Remember
to multiply
everything
by 5.

 Why does Suleman multiply by 3 and 5?   **Suleman did not explain all the steps. Do so for him.**

> ### Task
>
> Work with your friend again, just like you did for the first Task.
> These equations all have fractions in them.
>
> **1 (a)** $\frac{x}{5} = 2$ **(b)** $\frac{x}{3} - 6 = 0$
>
> **2 (a)** $\frac{1}{3}(x - 8) = \frac{1}{4}(x - 7)$ **(b)** $\frac{(x - 3)}{2} = \frac{(x - 2)}{3}$
>
> **3 (a)** $\frac{1}{4}(x + 5) = \frac{1}{5}(x + 3) - 1$ **(b)** $\frac{1}{2}(x + 1) = \frac{1}{5}x - 2$

Exercise

In this exercise set out your working step-by-step.

1 Solve these equations and check your answers.

(a) $7x + 3 = 2x + 13$

(b) $4x - 2 = 5x - 5$

(c) $2x + 3 = 8x - 27$

(d) $6x - 4 = 5x + 1$

(e) $6x - 7 = 3x$

(f) $2(x + 4) = 4$

(g) $3(x + 2) + x = 22$

(h) $5(x + 1) - 4(x - 1) = 0$

(i) $5(x + 1) - 1 = 9$

(j) $2(x + 1) + 3(x + 2) = 2(x + 6) - 1$

2 Solve each of these equations and check your answers.

(a) $\frac{x}{5} = 4$

(b) $\frac{(x + 2)}{20} = \frac{1}{4}$

(c) $\frac{x}{12} = -\frac{1}{48}$

(d) $\frac{3}{x} = \frac{1}{5}$

(e) $\frac{x}{3} - 3 = 2$

(f) $\frac{1}{4}(x + 6) = \frac{1}{3}(x + 4)$

(g) $\frac{(x + 10)}{3} = \frac{(x + 5)}{2}$

(h) $\frac{1}{5}(2x + 8) = x + 1$

(i) $\frac{1}{3}(x + 4) + \frac{1}{5}(x + 3) = 3$

(j) $\frac{1}{2}(x + 3) = \frac{1}{5}(x + 8) + 2$

3 Alan and Ruth are making up number puzzles for each other.

*I think of a number.
I multiply it by 3, then add 3.
My answer is 4 times my
first number.*

Alan

*I think of a number.
I double it and then subtract 5.
My answer is the same as
my first number.*

Ruth

(a) (i) Write down an equation for Alan's number.
(ii) What number was Alan thinking of?
(b) (i) Write down an equation for Ruth's number.
(ii) What number was Ruth thinking of?

4 Solve these equations. Some of the solutions are negative and they are not all whole numbers.

(a) $3x + 1\frac{1}{4} = 6x - 2\frac{1}{2}$

(b) $\frac{(x + 5)}{2} = \frac{(x + 6)}{3}$

(c) $2.1x + 0.4 = 1.6x + 2.4$

(d) $\frac{(4x + 7)}{10} = \frac{(6x + 6)}{6}$

(e) $\frac{1}{2}(4x + 0.2) = 3x - 0.1$

(f) $\frac{(5x + 5)}{5} = \frac{1}{4}(x + 4)$

(g) $\frac{1}{2}(2x - 2) + 3 = \frac{(x + 7)}{2}$

(h) $(x + 0.6) - 0.1 = \frac{1}{3}(3x + 1.5)$

Solving more equations

Ahmed has this equation to solve. $12 - 2x = 10$

I know the answer is x = 1 but Mrs Wilson wants it written down step-by-step. Help!

It's easy. Look I'll show you.

The 'subtract 2x' is the problem. I'll deal with that first.

Ahmed

Sophie

Sophie writes

$$12 - 2x = 10$$

Add 2x to both sides $12 - 2x + 2x = 10 + 2x$

Tidy up $12 = 10 + 2x$

Subtract 10 from both sides $12 - 10 = 10 + 2x - 10$

Tidy up $2 = 2x$

Divide both sides by 2 $1 = x$

$$x = 1$$

She now has an equation without the −2x.

This is the same as 1 = x.

Check:

Substitute x = 1 in $12 - 2x = 10$

$12 - 2 \times 1$

$10 = 10$ ✓

This is called the root of the equation.

⚠ Always deal with the 'subtract x' bit of the equation first.

Task

Make up an equation with a 'take away x' bit in it.
Write down the answer without showing anybody.
Ask your partner to solve the equation step-by-step.
Do you both get the same answer?

I can solve that equation a different way.

Subtract 12 from both sides
Divide both sides by −2

$12 - 2x = 10$
$-2x = -2$
$x = 1$

Remember that −2 ÷ −2 = 1.

Zeynah

  Which method do you think is better, Sophie's or Zeynah's? Why?

Exercise

You have met two ways of solving these equations. Do some of this exercise like Sophie does and the rest like Zeynah does.

1 Solve these equations showing all your working.

(a) $27 - 4x = 15$ (b) $19 - 9y = 1$ (c) $13 - 3t = 7$

(d) $11 - 3x = 2$ (e) $20 - 2r = 17$ (f) $29 - 5w = 16.5$

(g) $7.5 - 6x = 5.1$ (h) $12 - \frac{y}{2} = 8$ (i) $55 - 5t = 0$

2 Natalie was going shopping with £250.
When she checked her wallet she found that three notes, all of the same value of £x, were missing. She had £190 left. Write this as an equation. Solve it to find the value of the missing notes.

3 Solve these equations.
Be careful, some answers are negative and some are not integers.

(a) $10 - 3x = 4$ (b) $12 - 2x = 18$

(c) $17 - 4x = 21$ (d) $10 - \frac{x}{2} = 7$

(e) $\frac{2x}{3} = 5$ (f) $32 - 5x = 42$

(g) $3x - 7 = -13$ (h) $4(x - 1) - 5(x + 1) = 0$

(i) $2.4x + 5.9 = 14.3$ (j) $4(x - 1) + 5(x + 1) = 100$

> An integer is a whole number.

Check by substitution that all your answers are correct.

Investigation

Look at the equation $x^2 = 9$. It has two roots, $+3$ and -3. ($+3 \times +3 = +9$ and $-3 \times -3 = +9$)
Solve the following equations. All the roots are given in the list.

(a) $x^2 + 5 = 30$ (b) $30 - x^2 = 14$ (c) $2x^2 - 8 = 10$

(d) $\frac{4x^2}{2} = 2$ (e) $12x^2 = 3$ (f) $\frac{1}{2}(2x^2 - 12) = 30$

> Remember the opposite of square is square root.

Roots

$x = +1$ $x = -3$ $x = +5$ $x = -\frac{1}{2}$

$x = -1$ $x = +6$ $x = -6$ $x = +4$

$x = +\frac{1}{2}$ $x = -4$ $x = +3$ $x = -5$

Investigation

Find the values of $2(x + 2) + 1$ and $3x + 5 - x$ when

(a) $x = 2$ (b) $x = 5$ (c) $x = 100$. What do you notice?

Try to solve $2(x + 2) + 1 = 3x + 5 - x$. What happens?

 How many more values of x can you find that make the two expressions equal?

A statement that is true for **all** values is called an **identity**. The symbol $\equiv$ is used. For example, $3(a - 2) \equiv 3a - 6$. Write three identities of your own.

Forming equations

Len is a Park Keeper at Avonford Park.
He needs to fence a rectangular plot to make a playground.
He has 140 metres of fencing.
He makes the playground 25 metres wide.

I'll let x stand for the length.

Len

25 m

x

Len writes:

> *x* + 25 + *x* + 25 = 140
> 2*x* + 50 = 140
> 2*x* = 90
> *x* = 45
> The playground will be 45 metres long.

? **Explain Len's equation.**

? **Look at Len's solution and say what he has done at each line. How can you check Len's answer?**

Task

1 Len tries out some different widths. Form an equation and find the value of *x* when the width is

(a) 20 m   **(b)** 10 m   **(c)** 40 m   **(d)** 15 m.
Show all your working.

2 Investigate the cases when
 (a) the playground is a square
 (b) the length of the playground is four times the width.

Look at what Julian says.

How old is he now?

Start by letting *j* stand for Julian's age.

In seven years' time I will be twice as old as I was three years ago.

Julian

? **Does it have to be *j*?**

? **Find an expression for Julian's age in seven years' time.**
Find another expression in terms of *j* for Julian's age three years ago.

? **What does 'in terms of' mean?**

? **Explain the equation**
$j + 7 = 2(j - 3)$.

? **Solve the equation to find Julian's present age.**

Exercise

1 Bethany makes a run for her rabbit.
She builds it against her garden wall.
She has 60 m of wire netting.

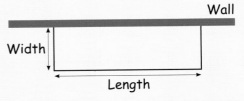

(a) She make the run 10 m wide.
Let x stand for the length.
Form an equation to work out the
length of the run.
Set out your working clearly.

(b) Bethany wants to make the area
of the run as large as possible.
She tries some different widths.
Copy and complete Bethany's table
of values to find the width that will give the maximum area.

Width	Length	Area
10		
8		
6		
4		
12		

2 (a) Copy this arithmagon. The number in the
square is the sum of those in the two circles on either side.
Fill in the bottom circles in terms of a.

(b) Use your answers to part (a) to write an
equation in terms of a and the number 28.

(c) Solve your equation to find a.
Check your answer in the arithmagon.

3 Tim and his mother have the same birthday.
When Tim is 12, his mother is 48.
They want to know the answer to his
mother's question.
Let this happen in n years.

Mum you are four times as old as me.

How old will we be when my age is three times yours?

(a) Write down an expression for
Tim's mother's age in n years.

(b) Write down an expression for
Tim's age in n years.

(c) Write down an equation connecting
the first two expressions.

(d) Solve your equation to find n.

(e) How old will they each be when
Tim's mother is three times as old as Tim?

(f) How old will they be when Tim's mother is twice as old as Tim?

 Activity   (a) Think of two numbers that add up to 1.
(b) Square the larger and add this to the smaller number.
(c) Square the smaller and add this to the larger number.
(d) Repeat for other pairs of values that add up to 1.
(e) Use algebra to explain your results.

Trial and improvement

Miriam is designing a container to hold 200 cm³ of bubble bath.
She tries a cube.

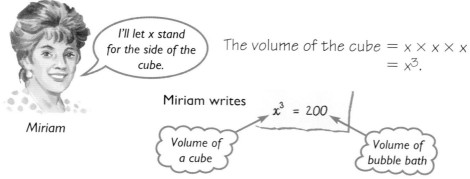

I'll let x stand for the side of the cube.

Miriam

The volume of the cube = x × x × x
= x^3.

Miriam writes

$x^3 = 200$

Volume of a cube

Volume of bubble bath

Then she makes this table.

x cm	x³	small / large
4	4×4×4 = 64	too small
6	6×6×6 = 216	too large

It must be between 4 and 6, I'll try 5.

Miriam

5	5×5×5 = 125	too small
5.5	5.5×5.5×5.5 = 166.375	too small
5.8		

Task

Copy and continue Miriam's table.
Keep going until your answer is correct to the nearest mm.

Miriam uses this spreadsheet to help her find the answer.

? Explain what the spreadsheet is set up to do.

? How could you adjust it to give a more accurate answer?

Task

Set up your own spreadsheet to work out an answer to Miriam's problem, correct to 3 decimal places.

	A	B
1	x	x³
2	5	A2^3
3	=A2+0.1	A3^3
4	=A3+0.1	A4^3
5	=A4+0.1	A5^3
6	=A5+0.1	A6^3

Exercise

1 Copy and complete this table to solve the equation $x^3 + x = 100$
Give your answer correct to 2 decimal places.

x	x^3	$x^3 + x$	small/large

2 Make your own table to solve the equation $x^3 - x^2 = 50$
Give your answer to 2 decimal places.

3 Jane is making a tray out of a 20 cm square
piece of card.
She cuts a square out of each corner
and then folds the card into a tray.

I want the tray to hold as much as possible.

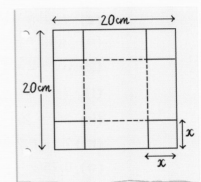

(a) Copy and complete
Jane's table of values.
Find the value of x that
gives the largest volume.
Give your answer to
2 decimal places.

x cm	volume
2	$16 \times 16 \times 2 = 512$
3	$14 \times 14 \times 3 = 588$

(b) Why must the value of x always be less than 10 cm?

(c) Use a spreadsheet to find the value of x that gives the largest volume,
to 3 decimal places.

4 Make tables or use a spreadsheet to solve the following equations.
Give your answers to 2 decimal places.

(a) $x^2 + x^3 = 150$ **(b)** $2x^2 + x = 75$

(c) $x(x + x^2) = 150$ **(d)** Explain your answers to parts (a) and (c).

Investigation

Miriam changes the shape of the economy
size box.
Its ends are squares but the length of the
new box is twice the width.

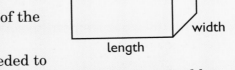

width
length

NEW ECONOMY SIZE
BUBBLE BATH
500 CM³
OF YOUR FAVOURITE BUBBLES

1 Compare the amount of card needed to
make this box with the amount needed to make the original box.

2 What happens if the length of the box is three times the width?

Finishing off

Now that you have finished this chapter you should be able to:

- solve equations with fractions
- use trial and improvement to solve equations.
- form your own equations

Review exercise

1 Solve these equations.
Use your answer to check that you have solved each equation correctly.

(a) $9x - 7 = 29$ **(b)** $2x + 9 = 3x - 5$

(c) $7x - 8 = 4x + 4$ **(d)** $6x + 7 = 37$

(e) $2(4x + 3) = 10$ **(f)** $3(3x + 10) = 12$

(g) $3x - 2 = 4x - 5$ **(h)** $\frac{1}{2}(4x + 12) = 3$

(i) $7x + 3 = 3x + 7$ **(j)** $\frac{1}{4}(5x + 1) = 4$

(k) $3(x + 2) + 2x = 4x + 6$ **(l)** $\frac{1}{2}(x - 3) = \frac{1}{3}(x - 2)$

(m) $7x - 0.2 = 2.4 - 6x$ **(n)** $2(x + 2.5) + \frac{1}{2}(4x - 6) = 0$

(o) $0.75(x - 1) = 0.5(5x - 3)$ **(p)** $\frac{1}{3}(x - 2) + \frac{1}{4}(x + 2) = 1$

(q) $\frac{1}{5}(x - 6) = \frac{1}{6}(x + 7) - 2$ **(r)** $\frac{3}{4}(x + 3) = \frac{2}{3}(x - 1) + 3$

2 Tom and Pat are playing a number game.

I think of a number and multiply it by 2. I take it away from 10 and the answer is 4.

I think of a number and treble it. I then take it away from 13 and the answer is 1.

(a) Write down an equation for Tom's number.
(b) Solve your equation.
(c) Write down an equation for Pat's number.
(d) What number was Pat thinking of?

3 **(a)** Copy and complete this table of values for $x^2 + \frac{1}{x}$.

x	1	2	3	4	5
x^2	1	4			
$\frac{1}{x}$	1				0.2
$x^2 + \frac{1}{x}$	2				

(b) Use trial and improvement to solve the equation

$$x^2 + \frac{1}{x} = 11$$

Give your answer correct to 1 decimal place.

4 This tent frame is made from aluminium tubing.
The measurements are in metres.
The length x is called the 'size' of the tent.

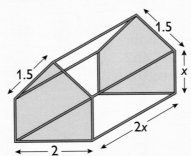

(a) Write down the formula for the total length of tubing needed.
(b) (i) The size of a tent is 1.8 m. How much tubing is needed?
    (ii) A tent uses 25 m of tubing. What is its size?
    (iii) A tent uses 30 m of tubing. What is its size?

Investigation

Solve each of these equations and write down the corresponding letter from the table.
What word do you spell?

(a) $\dfrac{3x}{14} = \dfrac{3}{7}$

(b) $\dfrac{(x - 5)}{4} = \dfrac{(3x - 1)}{10}$

(c) $\dfrac{(x - 1)}{5} = \dfrac{(x + 1)}{7}$

(d) $\dfrac{2}{(x - 5)} = \dfrac{9}{(x + 2)}$

(e) $\dfrac{1}{(4x - 1)} = \dfrac{2}{4x}$

6	7	$\frac{1}{2}$	8	10	-6	-23	-4	2
P	E	R	D	G	T	U	A	S

Investigation

$x - 3$	$x + 2$	$x + 1$
$x + 4$	x	$x - 4$
$x - 1$	$x - 2$	$x + 3$

(a) Copy this square substituting the value $x = 5$.
(b) What do you notice about the sum of all the rows, columns and diagonals?
(c) Copy it again but this time substituting $x = 8$.
(d) What do you notice this time?
(e) What is the connection between parts (b) and (d) and the value of x each time?
(f) Prove that this will always be the case.
(g) Copy and complete this magic square.

$x - 4$	$x + 1$	
	$x - 1$	

Angles

This diagram shows you the convention for describing angles. Two angles together on a straight line are called **adjacent angles**.

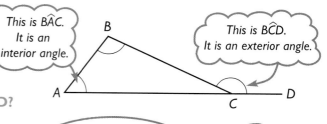

This is BÂC. It is an interior angle.

This is BĈD. It is an exterior angle.

 Which interior angle is adjacent to BĈD?
What do adjacent angles add up to?
How do you form an exterior angle?

Jenny and Alison know that the angles in a triangle always add up to 180°.
They each use a different method to explain why.

Jenny and Alison, convince me that the angles of a triangle always add up to 180°.

Jenny

1. Jenny draws a large triangle on a piece of paper.
   She marks each angle and shades them in different colours.

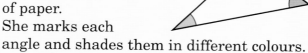

2. She tears each angle out from the triangle and glues them next to each other on another piece of paper. The 'points' are at the same place.

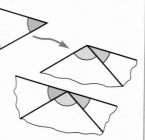

 How does Jenny know that her angles add up to 180°?

Alison

Alison uses angle facts.
She sketches a triangle between two parallel lines.

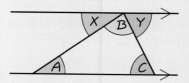

Then she writes

$X + B + Y = 180°$ [Angles on a straight line]

$A = X$ [Alternate angles]

$C = Y$ [Alternate angles]

$\therefore A + B + C = 180°$ [$A = X$ $C = Y$]

 Jenny has cut up just one triangle. Is this enough to convince you?

 Has Alison convinced you? Whose method is better?

 Jenny's method is a **demonstration**. Alison has used a **proof**. What is the difference?

Task

Quadrilateral PQRS has been split into two triangles by the diagonal QS.

 How does this show that the sum of the interior angles of a quadrilateral is 360°?

Copy the diagram and write a proof of this fact.
Your proof should start with:

Sum of interior angles = SP̂Q + PQ̂R + QR̂S + RŜP.

Hint: PQ̂R = PQ̂S + SQ̂R.

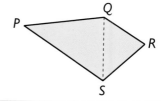

Exercise

1 Calculate the size of each lettered angle in these shapes.

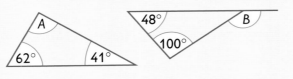

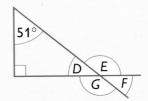

2 Find the lettered angles in these isosceles shapes.

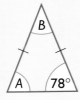
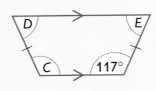
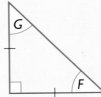

3 ABCDE is a regular pentagon. Angle BAE is 108°.

(a) Make a sketch copy of the diagram.

(b) Calculate the size of the following angles.

    (i) AB̂E   **(ii)** AÊB   **(iii)** BÊD

    (iv) BD̂E   **(v)** EB̂D   **(vi)** DB̂C.

(c) What sort of triangle is   **(i)** triangle EBD

                              (ii) triangle ABE?

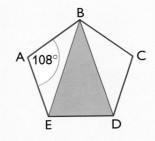

Karl cuts the pentagon into three
separate triangles.
He fits triangles EBD and BCD together.

(d) Prove they make another triangle.

(e) What sort of triangle has Karl made?

(f) Prove that Karl can fit all three triangles together to make a trapezium.

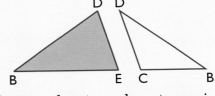

4 The angles on a straight line add up to 180°.
The interior angles of a triangle add up to 180°.

Use these two facts to prove that the exterior
angle of a triangle equals the sum of the two
interior opposite angles.

Prove BĈD = BÂC + AB̂C

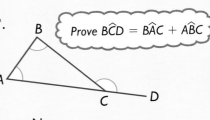

5 An aircraft flies from A to B then from B to C.
AB and BC are equal distances.
The flight paths are shown on this diagram.

(a) Make a sketch copy of the diagram.

(b) Calculate the bearing of A from B.

(c) Calculate AB̂C.

(d) What sort of triangle is ABC?

(e) What can you say about BĈA and BÂC?

(f) Calculate BĈA and BÂC.

(g) Find the bearing the aircraft must follow to
fly from C back to A.

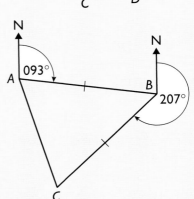

Angles of polygons

A polygon is a two-dimensional closed shape with straight sides.

 What is **(a)** the smallest **(b)** the largest number of sides a polygon can have?
What is a *regular* polygon?

Task

1 Look at this heptagon.
Four diagonals have been drawn from one **vertex**.
The diagonals split the heptagon into five triangles.

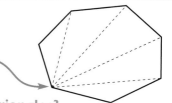

 What is the sum of all the interior angles of the five triangles?
What is the sum of the interior angles of the heptagon?

2 Copy and complete this table.

Diagram	Sides of polygon	Diagonals	Triangles	Sum of interior angles
	3	0	1	$1 \times 180° = 180°$
	4	1	2	$2 \times 180° = 360°$
	5	2		
	6			
	7	4	5	
	19			
	n			

 Let *S* be the sum of the interior angles of a polygon with *n* sides.
Write down a formula for *S* in terms of *n*.

This diagram shows part of a polygon.
There is an interior angle and an exterior angle at
each vertex.

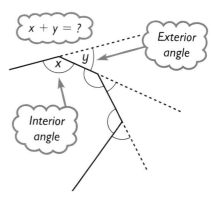

 A polygon has *n* sides.
What is the sum of all its interior and exterior angles?
What is the sum of its interior angles?
What is the sum of the exterior angles of a polygon?

Exercise

1 Calculate the sum of the interior angles of
    (a) a hexagon   **(b)** an octagon
    (c) a polygon with 23 sides   **(d)** a square
    (e) a triangle   **(f)** a polygon with 501 sides.

2 Calculate the size of the interior angle of
    (a) a regular hexagon   **(b)** a regular octagon
    (c) a regular triangle   **(d)** a regular quadrilateral.
    (e) a regular decagon (10 sides)   **(f)** a regular heptagon.

3 The tessellation of a regular polygon is called a **regular** tessellation.

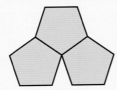

    (a) Explain why regular   **(b)** Explain why equilateral
         pentagons *cannot* form   triangles do form a regular
         a regular tessellation.   tessellation.
    (c) Find the two other regular polygons which form regular tessellations.
         Draw sketches to show how they tessellate.
    (d) Explain why there are only three regular tessellations.

4 This diagram shows a pentagon split into five triangles.
    (a) What is the sum of all the angles in all the triangles?
    (b) What is the sum of the angles at the centre?
    (c) What is the sum of the interior angles
         of the pentagon?
    (d) Use the diagram to explain why the sum of the
         interior angles of a polygon with n sides is $n \times 180° - 360°$.
    (e) Show that the formula in part (d) is the same as $(n - 2) \times 180°$.

5 Explain why the sum of the interior angles of a polygon cannot add up to 1320°.

Investigation

Erika runs a cross country race.
The course starts and finishes at A.
1 In what direction does she run at the beginning of the race?
2 In what direction does she run at the end of the race?

When she gets to B she turns through 63° and runs along BC.
During the race she turns through five angles in all.
3 What must the angles add up to? Explain your answer.
4 Explain why the interior angles of the pentagon
     must add up to 540°. (Use your answer to part 3.)

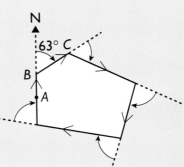

Regular polygons

 Which of these polygons are regular?

Also called a nonagon.

 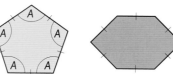 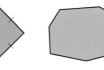 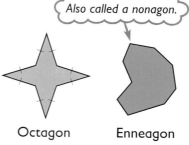 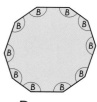

| Pentagon | Hexagon | Heptagon | Octagon | Enneagon | Decagon |

Task

I Follow these steps to make an accurate construction of a regular octagon.

Each angle is $\frac{360°}{8} = 45°$.

Sector

Chord

(a) Mark a centre and draw a circle.

(b) Divide the circle into 8 equal sectors.

(c) Join the ends of the radii with chords.

 How do you know that your regular octagon is made of eight congruent isosceles triangles?

2 (a) Look at these diagrams.

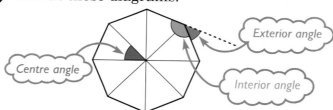

Exterior angle

Centre angle

Interior angle

Regular octagon

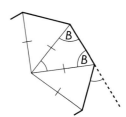

Part of a regular n-sided polygon

(b) Copy and complete this table.

	Regular octagon	Regular n-sided polygon
Sum of exterior angles	360°	360°
Exterior angle	$\frac{360°}{8} = 45°$	$\frac{360°}{n}$
Interior angle	$180° - 45° = 135°$	
Sum of interior angles	$8 \times 135° = 1080°$	
Centre angle	45°	
Sum of two base angles, $B + B$	$180° - 45° = 135°$	

 On page 46 you found that: The sum of the interior angles of a polygon $= (n - 2) \times 180°$.

Does this agree with your result in the Task above?

 Notice that the centre angle of a regular polygon is the same as its exterior angle? Explain why.

Exercise

1 A regular polygon has exterior angles of 18°.
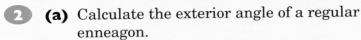
   (a) What is the sum of the exterior angles?
   (b) How many sides does the polygon have?
   (c) What is the size of each interior angle?
   (d) What is the sum of the interior angles of the polygon?

2 **(a)** Calculate the exterior angle of a regular
      enneagon.
   (b) Make an accurate construction of an enneagon.
      You will need a protractor.
   (c) Extend the sides of the enneagon to
      create exterior angles.
   (d) Measure all the exterior angles and check the
      accuracy of your construction.

3 Make accurate constructions of the following regular polygons without
using a protractor.
   (a) hexagon   **(b)** triangle   **(c)** quadrilateral   **(d)** octagon
   (e) Explain why you cannot construct a regular heptagon without a protractor.

4 A regular polygon has 360 sides.
   (a) What is the size of the exterior angle?
   (b) What is the size of the interior angle?
   (c) What is the sum of the interior angles?
   Imagine you constructed a regular polygon with 360 sides.
   (d) What other shape would it nearly be?

Investigation

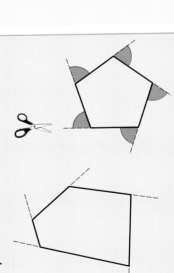

1 Make an accurate construction of a regular pentagon.

2 Extend the sides to form exterior angles.

3 Cut out each exterior angle.

4 Glue the exterior angles next to each other on
another piece of paper with the points at the same place.

? Do the exterior angles fit together as you expected?

5 Now draw an irregular pentagon and extend the sides to
form exterior angles.

6 Cut out the exterior angles and glue them together as before.

? What can you say about the exterior angles of your
irregular pentagon?

7 Repeat parts 5 and 6 for two more irregular polygons which have
different numbers of sides.

? What does this investigation show you about the exterior angles of polygons?
Is it a demonstration or a proof?

Pythagoras' rule

Look at these special triangles. They are all *right-angled*.
The side opposite the right angle is called
the **hypotenuse**.

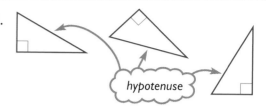

hypotenuse

 Why is the hypotenuse always the longest side?

Task

You will need centimetre squared paper, scissors
and glue.

1 Draw and label triangle ABC as shown.
AĈB is a right angle. AC = 3 cm and CB = 4 cm.

2 Draw squares ACDE and CBFG.

3 Measure length AB.
Draw square ABHI *on a separate piece of
squared paper*.

4 Glue square ABHI onto hypotenuse AB.

5 Shade the two smaller squares in one colour.
Shade the largest square in a different colour.

6 Repeat steps 1 to 5 for right-angled triangles with sides AC and CB as shown
in the table. Copy and complete the table.

| Shorter sides | | Hypotenuse | Sum of areas of smaller squares | Area of largest square |
AC	CB	AB		
3 cm	4 cm		9 cm² + 16 cm² = 25 cm²	
5 cm	12 cm			
2.5 cm	6 cm			

 What do you notice about the areas of the squares for each triangle?

 **A right-angled triangle has shorter sides AC = 9 cm and CB = 40 cm.
What is the length of the hypotenuse?**

Pythagoras' rule: The square of the hypotenuse of a right-angled
triangle is equal to the sum of the squares of
the other two sides.

This famous rule was known in Babylonia over 2500 years ago.
It was first proved to be true for *all* right-angled triangles by Pythagoras.
Pythagoras was a Greek philosopher who lived from 560 to 480 BC.

Pythagoras

 **Write down the equation connecting
a, *b* and *c*.**

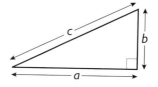

Exercise *You will need to use a calculator to find square roots in this exercise.*

1 Copy and complete this calculation to find h.

$$h^2 = 24^2 + 5^2$$
$$h^2 = 576 + 25$$
$$h^2 = \ldots$$
$$h = \ldots$$

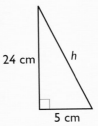

24 cm h

5 cm

2 Find the length of the hypotenuse of each of these triangles.

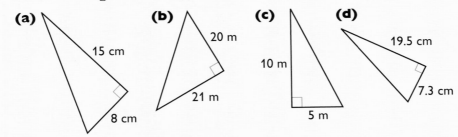

(a) 15 cm 8 cm

(b) 20 m 21 m

(c) 10 m 5 m

(d) 19.5 cm 7.3 cm

3 A ship leaves harbour and sails North for 17 miles, then West for 11 miles.
It then sails straight back to the harbour.
How far does it sail in total?

4 A small room has a cupboard
in one corner.
Is the room wide enough to
move the cupboard to the
new position?
Give a mathematical
explanation for your answer.

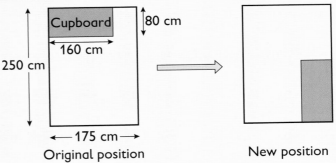

Cupboard   80 cm
160 cm
250 cm
175 cm
Original position   New position

Investigation

Look at this triangle.
The longest side is l cm and the largest angle is $X°$.
The two shorter sides are a cm and b cm.
Draw a triangle with $a = 6$, $b = 8$ and $l = 10$. Measure X.
Copy and complete the table below.

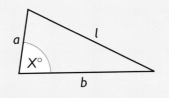

a l $X°$ b

a	b	l	X	Compare l^2 to $a^2 + b^2$	Compare X to $90°$
				Answer $<$, $=$ or $>$	Answer $<$ (acute), $=$ (right) or $>$ (obtuse)
6	8	10	90°	=	=
6	8	12			
6	8	9			

Now draw some triangles of your own. Enter your results in the table.
What do you notice?

Using Pythagoras' rule

Finding a shorter side

Gill is a decorator.
She uses a ladder 6 m long.
The safety instructions on the ladder say that the foot of
the ladder must be at least 1.75 m from the wall on
horizontal ground.
Gill calculates the maximum height her ladder will reach
up a vertical wall.

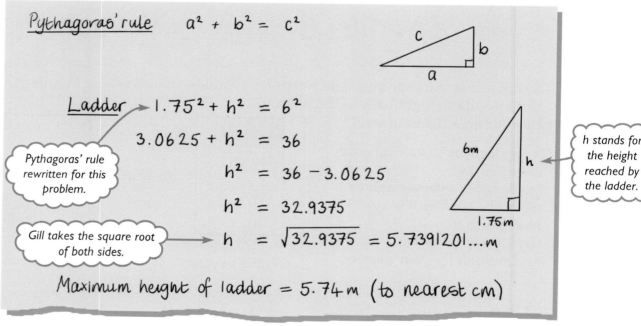

Pythagoras' rule $a^2 + b^2 = c^2$

Ladder ⟶ $1.75^2 + h^2 = 6^2$

$3.0625 + h^2 = 36$

Pythagoras' rule rewritten for this problem.

$h^2 = 36 - 3.0625$

$h^2 = 32.9375$

Gill takes the square root of both sides. ⟶ $h = \sqrt{32.9375} = 5.7391201...\,m$

h stands for the height reached by the ladder.

Maximum height of ladder = 5.74 m (to nearest cm)

 Why has Gill rounded her answer?

 How does Gill know that the triangle is right-angled?

Task

Here are the safety instructions
for Gill's ladder.

 ATTENTION!
Foot of ladder must be between 1.75 m
and 2.35 m from vertical surface.
Ground must be horizontal.

Calculate the *minimum* height the
ladder can reach up the wall.

 What could happen if the safety instructions are not obeyed?

Exercise

1 Find the lengths of the sides marked with a letter in each of these triangles.
Give your answers correct to one decimal place.

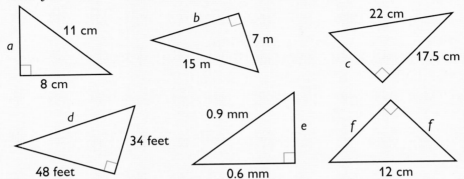

2 Sarah makes earrings.
Here is one of her designs, called 'Isosceles'.

(a) Explain why the perpendicular bisector of the
base passes through the top of the triangle.

(b) Calculate the perpendicular height of the triangle.
Give your answer in mm correct to 1 decimal place.

(c) Use your answer to part (b) to calculate the area
of the earring.

Sarah makes the earrings from sheet aluminium which weighs 0.27 g per cm^2.

(d) Calculate the weight of ten pairs of earrings.
Ignore the hole in your calculations.

3 An aircraft leaves an airport and flies south-east for 200 km.

(a) Calculate how far east the aircraft has flown.
Draw a diagram to help you.

(b) How far south has the aircraft flown?

4 The diagram shows a ball touching a floor and a wall.
Using Pythagoras' rule, calculate distance SR.

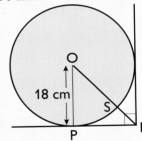

Investigation

Builders use Pythagoras' rule to make sure that corners
are 'square'.
They measure around the corner and 'three-four-five' it.

 How does this ensure the corner is a right angle?
How are the measurements shown in the picture
an example of 'three-four-five'?

The number set 3, 4, 5 is called a **Pythagorean triple**.

Find as many different Pythagorean triples as you can.
Do not include any which are simply a multiple of one
you have already found.

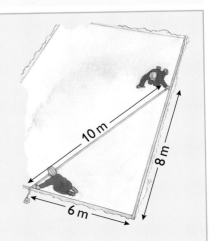

Finishing off

Now that you have finished this chapter you should know:

- how to prove that the angles in a triangle add up to $180°$
- how to prove that the angles in a quadrilateral add up to $360°$
- that the sum of the interior angles of a polygon with n sides is $(n-2) \times 180°$
- that the sum of the exterior angles of a polygon is $360°$
- how to construct a regular polygon
- how to use Pythagoras' rule.

Review exercise

1 Calculate the size of each lettered angle in these shapes.

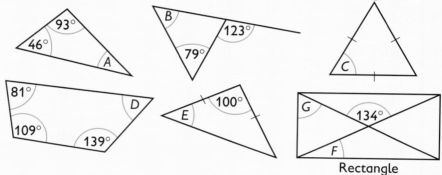

Rectangle

2 A regular polygon has 60 sides.
    (a) What is the size of **(i)** an exterior angle **(ii)** an interior angle?
    (b) What is the sum of the interior angles?

3 A regular polygon has n sides.
    The sum of the interior angles is $1980°$. Find the value of n.

4 The three shapes in this pattern are identical rhombi.
    What can you say about the hexagon they form?
    Explain your answer.

5 Look at this diagram of a heptagon.
    (a) Write down the size of angle A.
    (b) Explain why angle A = angle B.
    (c) Find the sum of its interior angles.
    The heptagon is symmetrical.
    (d) Calculate the size of angle C.

Notice the parallel sides.

6 Calculate the lengths of the unknown sides in each of these triangles.

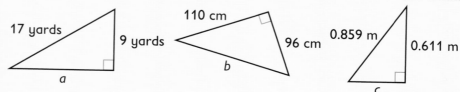

7 The diagram shows a quadrilateral inside a regular dodecagon.

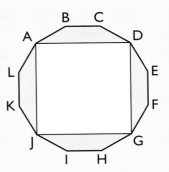

(a) Calculate the size of AB̂C.

(b) Calculate the size of BÂD.

(c) Write down the size of LÂJ.

(d) Explain why quadrilateral ADGJ must be a square.

8 Find whole number lengths that will fit these right-angled triangles. There may be more than one answer.

(a)
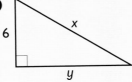

(b)

(c)
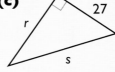

Investigation

The tiled floor below is a tessellation made from octagons and squares. Any tessellation made from two or more *regular* polygons is called a **semi-regular** tessellation.

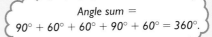

Angle sum =
$135° + 135° + 90° = 360°$.

There are two semi-regular tessellations which can be made from triangles and squares.
Here is one of them.

Angle sum =
$90° + 60° + 60° + 90° + 60° = 360°$.

 How does the angle sum show you that the triangles and squares may tessellate?

? Another way to write the angle sum is
$90° + 90° + 60° + 60° + 60° = 360°$.
How does this make a *different* tessellation?

1 Sketch the other semi-regular tessellation of equilateral triangles and squares.

2 There are two semi-regular tessellations which can be made from hexagons and triangles. Use isometric paper to draw them.

6 Sequences and functions

Generating sequences

A party of 18 people is going to the Space Centre.
How much will it cost?

Manchester Space Centre	
Special group rates for 10 or more	
No. of people	**Price (£)**
10	55
11	58
12	61
15	70 and so on

Joe writes   *15 people cost £70.*
For each extra person, add £3.

$$70 \xrightarrow{+3} 73 \xrightarrow{+3} 76 \xrightarrow{+3} 79 \;\; (\pounds79)$$

Joe is using a **term-to-term rule**.
You have to use the previous term to
work out the next term.

Kate is using a **position-to-term** rule.
You find the 18th term by substituting
$n = 18$ into the formula.

There is an easier way.
The formula is £(25 + 3n).
So £(25 + 3 × 18)
= £79.

Kate

Task

1. Write down the first five terms of each of the following sequences.
   - **(a)** all the even numbers
   - **(b)** all the odd numbers
   - **(c)** multiples of 7
   - **(d)** the numbers 12, 9, 6, …
2. You can write term-to-term rules for each of these sequences:
   First term a. To find the next term add d to the previous term.
   Find the values of a and d for each sequence in part 1.
3. Find a position-to-term rule for each sequence.

Kate uses this **function** to make a sequence: $T(n) = 2n^2 + 1$

*This can also be
written as $n \rightarrow 2n^2 + 1$.*

1st term is when $n = 1$: $T(1) = 2 \times 1^2 + 1 = 3$
2nd term is when $n = 2$: $T(2) = 2 \times 2^2 + 1 = 9$

? **What are the next three terms of Kate's sequence?**

*For a function you put a
number in, such as 1 or 2,
and get an answer out.*

Task

*a_n is another way of saying
the nth term of the sequence
$a_1, a_2, a_3, \ldots$.*

1. Match these sequences with their functions.
   - **(a)** 0, 2, 6, 12, …
   - **(b)** 1, 4, 9, 16, …
   - **(c)** −2, 1, 6, 13, …
   - **(d)** $\frac{1}{2}$, 0, $-\frac{1}{2}$, −1, …
   - **(i)** $n \rightarrow n^2$
   - **(ii)** $T(n) = 1 - \frac{1}{2}n$
   - **(iii)** $a_n = n^2 - n$
   - **(iv)** $n \rightarrow n^2 - 3$
2. Find the 20th term of each of the sequences in part 1.

Exercise

1 Find the first five terms of each of the following sequences.

(a) The first term of the sequence is $-\frac{3}{4}$.
To find the next term add $\frac{1}{2}$ to the previous term.

(b) $T(n) = n^2 + 2n$ (c) $n \rightarrow 4 - 2n$

2 The first seven terms of a sequence are: $6, ?, ?, 18, ?, ?, 30$.

The term-to-term rule is: The first term is 6.
To find the next term add d to the previous term.

(a) Find the value of d.
(b) Find the missing terms of the sequence.
(c) Find a position-to-term rule for this sequence.
(d) What is the 50th term?

3 Joanne is organising a tombola for her Youth Club.
To win a prize the number on the ticket must be a term in one of the
following sequences.

> 1 $n \rightarrow n^2 + 1$ Chocolates CHOCO
>
> 2 The first term is 1.   Cuddly toy
>   The next term is double the previous term.
>
> 3 The first two terms are both 1.   CD Music
>   The next term is the sum of the previous two terms.
>
> 4 $T(n) = 2n^2 - 1$ Video

(a) Which prizes will these tickets win?

$$\boxed{17}\ \boxed{20}\ \boxed{1}\ \boxed{9}\ \boxed{13}\ \boxed{45}\ \boxed{50}\ \boxed{7}\ \boxed{64}\ \boxed{36}\ \boxed{91}\ \boxed{56}$$

(b) Which tickets will win more than one prize?

Investigation

The first term of a sequence is $a_n = 1$.
The term-to-term rule is 'Divide the previous term by 3 and then add 4'.

You can write this in algebra as $a_{n+1} \rightarrow \dfrac{a_n}{3} + 4$.

> Keep pressing **EXE** to get the
> next term. The 1st term is $a_1 = 1$.
> The 2nd term is $a_2 = 4.333333333$.

1 What are the values of a_2, a_3, and a_4?

2 What happens eventually?

3 Does the value you use for a_1 matter?

4 What is the solution to the equation $a = \dfrac{a}{3} + 4$?

5 Why are the answers to question 2 and question 4 the same?

6 What happens when you use numbers different from 3 and 4?

```
1
                    1
ANS/3+4
       4.333333333
       5.44444444
       5.814814815
       5.938271605
```

Linear patterns

John has some money in a savings account.
He makes a New Year resolution to add
£5 to it every week.

He records his savings on a graph.

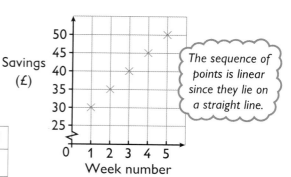

The sequence of
points is linear
since they lie on
a straight line.

 Copy and complete this table.

Week	1	2	3	4	5	6
Savings	30					

**What is the difference between one
term and the next?**

 **Is the difference always the
same for a linear sequence?**

Task

Which of the following sequences are linear?

1 5 8 11 14 17 ...

2 13 17 21 25 29 ...

3 1 4 9 16 25 ...

4 50 48 46 44 42 ...

5 1 1 2 3 5 ...

6 7.5 9 10.5 12 13.5 ...

For John's sequence, nth term $= 25 + 5n$.
Check: For $n = 1$, 1st term $= 25 + 5 \times 1 = 30$
               For $n = 2$, 2nd term $= 25 + 5 \times 2 = 35$
               For $n = 3$, 3rd term $= 25 + 5 \times 3 = 40$

This can also be sometimes
written as $n \rightarrow 25 + 5n$
or $T(n) = 25 + 5n$.

 **John's sequence starts at term 1. What would term 0 be?
What does the '5n' do? Where does the '25' come from?
What is the 50th term in John's sequence?
How long will it take him to save £100?**

Emily starts a savings account.
The table shows how much she has
in her account at the end of each week.

End of week	1	2	3	4	5	6
Savings (£s)	10	14	18	22	26	30

At the end of the nth week Emily's savings in pounds $= 6 + 4n$.

This can be written
as $n \rightarrow 6 + 4n$.

 **Where does the '6' come from in Emily's formula? What about the '4n'?
If this savings pattern continues, how much will Emily have saved after 52 weeks?**

Exercise

1 Peter's family help him to collect CDs.
By the end of a month he has nine CDs.
After that he buys two more every month.

I am starting a CD collection. All contributions welcome.

The table shows how his collection grows.

Number of months	1	2	3	4	5	6
Number of CDs	9	11	13	15	17	19

  (a) Write down a formula to show how many CDs Peter has after n months.
  (b) Explain where the '7' comes from in your formula.
  (c) How many CDs will he have after one year?
  (d) How long will it take for Peter's collection to exceed 100 CDs?
  (e) Is this sequence linear?

2 For each of these linear sequences find
  (i) the formula for the nth term   **(ii)** the 80th term.
  (a) 8, 12, 16, 20, ...   **(b)** 19, 21, 23, 25, ...   **(c)** 2, 5, 8, 11, ...
  (d) 300, 306, 312, 318, ... **(e)** 10, 15, 20, 25, ...   **(f)** 4, 6.25, 8.5, 10.75, ...

3 **(a)** Write down the next two terms of the sequence 50, 45, 40, 35, ...
  (b) The nth term of this sequence is $55 - 5n$.
    (i) Explain where the '$-5n$' comes from.
    (ii) Explain where the '55' comes from.
  (c) Which term in this sequence has the value 0?
  (d) Is this sequence linear?

4 For each of these sequences find
  (i) a formula for the nth term   **(ii)** the 40th term.
  (a) 200, 198, 196, 194, ... **(b)** 60, 53, 46, 39, ...   **(c)** 71, 70, 69, 68, ...
  (d) 82, 85, 88, 91, ...   **(e)** 12, 11.5, 11, 10.5, ... **(f)** 9, 8.8, 8.6, 8.4, ...

5 Which of the following sequences are linear?
  (a) 20, 23, 26, 29, ...   **(b)** 25, 36, 47, 58, ...   **(c)** 1, 4, 9, 16, ...
  (d) 31, 27, 23, 19, ...   **(e)** 1, 8, 27, 64, ...   **(f)** 1, 1, 2, 3, 5, 8, ...

6 Nadia is driving at a steady speed on the motorway. She notes mileage readings at ten-minute intervals. The first four readings are:

23402   23411   23420   23429

  (a) What are the next two readings?
  (b) Work out a formula for the nth term of this sequence.
  (c) What is the speed of the car in miles per hour?
  (d) What is the 50th term of the sequence?
  (e) Why is the answer to part (d) likely to be meaningless?

Using spreadsheets

How does Marsha use a spreadsheet to print the first 20 terms of $5n + 4$?

n	$5n + 4$
1	9
2	14
3	19

Computers don't make silly mistakes like I sometimes do!

Task

1 Copy this spreadsheet on your computer.
2 Complete all the entries.

n	$7n + 3$	1st difference	2nd difference
1	10		
2	17	7	
3	24	7	0
4	31	7	0
10			

? Where do the numbers in the 1st difference column come from?

? What about those in the 2nd difference column?

? What do you notice about the 1st and 2nd difference columns?

? Marsha says that for any linear sequence the 1st differences are always the same and the 2nd differences are always zero. Is she right?

Ellie visited a car showroom with her father.

LATEST MODEL!
THE GALILEO

0 to 108 km per hour in just 6 seconds

TIME IN SECONDS	0	1	2	3	4	5	6
SPEED OF CAR (km per hour)	0	3	12	27	48	75	108

Look Dad there's a pattern to these speeds!

? What pattern can Ellie see?

Task

You can find Ellie's pattern using a spreadsheet.
1 Set it up to print the first 10 terms.
2 Make columns for the 1st, 2nd and 3rd differences.

t	Speed	1st diff.	2nd diff.	3rd diff.
0	0			
1	3	3		
2	12	9	6	
3	27	15	6	0

? In this sequence the speed after t seconds is at^2. What is the value of a?

3 Complete the spreadsheet.

? Will the *Galileo's* speed obey this formula for large values of t? Explain.

Exercise

1 Four sequences are given by these formulae.

(A) nth term $= 3n + 1$ **(B)** nth term $= 4n + 9$

(C) nth term $= 302 - 7n$ **(D)** nth term $= \dfrac{n}{n + 5}$

(a) For each sequence
    (i) use a spreadsheet to print the first 20 terms
    (ii) make an extra column to calculate the first differences.

(b) Which of the sequences are linear and which are not?

2 **(a)** Use your spreadsheet to print the first 12 terms and 1st, 2nd and 3rd differences of each of these sequences.

(A) nth term $= n^2 + 7$ **(B)** nth term $= 6n^2$ **(C)** nth term $= n^2 + 5n$
(D) nth term $= 800 - 3n^2$ **(E)** nth term $= n^2 + 13n - 9$

The first has been started for you.

Term	Value	1st difference	2nd difference	3rd difference
1	8			
2	11	3		
3	16	5	2	
4	23	7	2	0
5	32	9	2	0
6				

(b) Ellie says that a **quadratic sequence** always has a 2nd difference which is constant and a 3rd difference of 0.
    (i) Do these sequences fit in with Ellie's statement?
    (ii) How can you prove Ellie's statement?

> The formula for the nth term of a quadratic sequence is of the form $an^2 + bn + c$, where a, b, and c are numbers.

3 **(a)** Write down the first four terms of the cubic sequence given by $n \rightarrow n^3 + 7$.
(b) Put the sequence on a spreadsheet and print the first 16 terms.
(c) Add columns for the 1st, 2nd and 3rd differences and complete the spreadsheet.
(d) What do you notice about the 3rd difference column?

Investigation

Fibonacci's famous sequence is 1, 1, 2, 3, 5, 8, 13, 21, ...

1 How does the sequence work?
2 What are the next two terms?
3 Put the sequence on a spreadsheet and make columns for the 1st and 2nd differences.
Complete the spreadsheet.
4 Look carefully at the 1st and 2nd difference columns. What has happened?
5 Is the Fibonacci sequence linear, quadratic or neither?

Spatial patterns

Scott is designing a new park for Avonford.
He has several different plans.
Here are two.

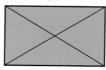

There is an entrance to the park at each vertex.

Scott has made the plans so that there is a path from each entrance to every other entrance.

There are two diagonal paths crossing the park in the rectangular plan.
How many diagonals are there in the pentagon?
How would you find the number of diagonals for a 50-sided shape?

Scott makes a table to help him solve the problem.

Number of sides	Number of diagonals
4	2
5	
6	
7	

1 (a) Copy and complete the table.
(b) What pattern do you notice?
(c) Predict how many diagonals are needed for an enneagon.

Sometimes called a nonagon; it has nine sides.

2 Follow these steps to help you find a formula for the number of diagonals for any polygon.

(a) Think about a decagon (10 sides).
(i) How many vertices does the shape have?
(ii) How many diagonals does each vertex have leading from it?
(iii) How can you use your answer to part (ii) to find out the number of diagonals in a decagon?

(b) Check your method works for the polygons in part 1.

3 Copy and complete these statements.

An *n*-sided polygon has ... vertices.
Each vertex has ... diagonals from it.
There are ... diagonals altogether.

You need to find expressions in terms of *n*.

4 Check your formula works for polygons with six, seven and eight sides.

Look through the Task.
Describe the stages involved in solving Scott's problem.

Exercise

1 Look at these patterns.

Pattern 1   Pattern 2   Pattern 3

(a) Draw the next two patterns.

(b) (i) How many new discs have been added each time?

(ii) What type of numbers are these?

(c) How many discs are added to the ninth pattern to make the tenth pattern?

(d) How many discs are there in each of the first five patterns?

(e) How many discs are in these patterns?

(i) 8th   (ii) 10th   (iii) 50th

(f) (i) What is the sum of the first eight odd numbers?

(ii) What pattern has this number of discs?

(g) What is the sum of the first

(i) 10   (ii) 50   (iii) 100   odd numbers?

(h) What is the sum of the first n odd numbers?

2 Look at these patterns.

(a) Draw the next two patterns.

(b) How many discs are there in each triangle?

(c) What patterns do you notice? These numbers are called **triangular numbers**. You can put two triangles together to make a rectangle.

Triangle 1   Triangle 2   Triangle 3

(d) Copy and complete this table.

Rectangle 1   Rectangle 2   Rectangle 3

Triangle	Rectangle	Length of rectangle	Width of rectangle	Number of discs in rectangle	Number of discs in triangle
1	1	2	1	2	1
2	2	3	2	6	
3	3				
4	4				
5	5				
10	10				
100	100				
n	n				

(e) t_{n-1} represents the $(n-1)$th triangular number. t_n represents the nth triangular number. Find an expression for $t_{n-1} + t_n$. Use a table like the one in part (d) to help you.

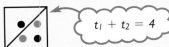

$t_1 + t_2 = 4$

Finishing off

Review exercise

1 Write down the first four terms of these sequences:
(a) $n \to 2n + 1$
(b) nth term $= 3n - 1$
(c) $n \to n^2$
(d) nth term $= 3n^2 - 4$
Which of these sequences are linear?

2 The rule for a sequence is given by:

> The first term of the sequence is a.
> To find the next term add d to the previous term.

Find the values of a and d so that the rule generates these sequences.
(a) The numbers 4, 8, 12, 16, …
(b) Positive multiples of 3
(c) The numbers 100, 95, 90, 85, …
(d) The numbers $-20, -18, -16, -14$

3 The first five terms of a linear sequence are: $60, ?, ?, 51, 48, …$
(a) Find values for the missing terms.
(b) Find the rule for the nth term.
(c) Show that the 100th term is -237.
(d) Find the 101st term.

4 Find the rule for the nth term of these linear sequences.
(a) 3, 5, 7, 9, …
(b) 4, 7, 10, 13, …
(c) 1, 3, 5, 7, …
(d) 3, 8, 13, 18, …
(e) 60, 56, 52, 48, …
(f) 20, 19.8, 19.6, 19.4, …

5 Use a spreadsheet to help you complete this table for each of the following sequences.
(a) nth term $= 4n^2 - 3$
(b) nth term $= 2n^2 - n + 3$
(c) nth term $= 10 - 4n$
(d) nth term $= \dfrac{n}{n - 5}$

Term	Value	1st difference	2nd difference	3rd difference
1				
2				
⋮				
9				
10				

Which of the sequences are linear, which quadratic and which neither?

Investigation

Look at this pattern.
It is called a **mystic rose**.
It has five vertices.
Each vertex is joined to every other vertex.

(a) Copy and complete this table.

Number of vertices	Number of lines
1	0
2	1
3	
4	
5	
6	
10	

(b) Copy and complete the following statements.

In a mystic rose with n vertices there are . . . lines from each vertex.
So there are . . . lines altogether.

(c) Test your formula for mystic roses with
(i) 7 vertices
(ii) 8 vertices
(iii) 10 vertices.

Investigation

Look at this jigsaw puzzle.
It is a 4 by 4 jigsaw.

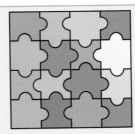

I (a) Copy and complete this table.

Jigsaw size n by n	Number of corner pieces, c	Number of edge pieces, e	Number of middle pieces, m	Total number of pieces, t
2 by 2				
3 by 3				
4 by 4	4	8	4	16
5 by 5				
10 by 10				

(b) Find formulae for c, e, m and t for an n by n jigsaw.
(c) Use your formulae to show that $c + e + m = t$ for an n by n jigsaw.

2 Investigate rectangular jigsaw puzzles.
    (a) Start by finding a rule for
        (i) 2 by n jigsaws   **(ii)** 3 by n jigsaws   **(iii)** 4 by n jigsaws.
    (b) Find formulae for the number of corner, edge and middle pieces in an l by n jigsaw.
    (c) Show that $c + e + m = t$ for an l by n jigsaw.

7 Circles

Circumference and diameter

? How is the radius of a circle related to its diameter?
Is the circumference related to the diameter?

Task

For this task you will need: string, ruler, pencil,
graph paper, a selection of circular objects.

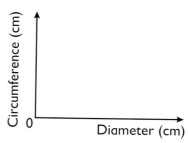

1 Use a piece of string to find the circumference of
   a circular object.

2 Measure the diameter of the circular face.

3 Repeat parts 1 and 2 using different circular objects.
   Make a table of results, like this.

Object	Circumference (cm)	Diameter (cm)	Circumference ÷ Diameter
Can			
10p piece			

4 For each object plot circumference against diameter.
   Arrange the axes as shown.

? What do you notice about the points on your graph?
What can you say about the circumference and
diameter of *any* circle?

5 Draw a line of best fit through the points on
   your graph.

6 A circular object has a diameter of 5.3 cm.
   Use your graph to estimate the circumference of the object.

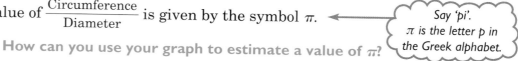

The ratio Circumference:Diameter is the same for *all* circles.

The value of $\dfrac{\text{Circumference}}{\text{Diameter}}$ is given by the symbol π.

> Say 'pi'.
> π is the letter p in
> the Greek alphabet.

? How can you use your graph to estimate a value of π?

? $\pi = 3.141\,592\ldots$ .The decimal goes on for ever.
You will often use 3.14 for π. How many decimal places is this correct to?

? What is the formula for the circumference, C, of a circle in terms of
(a) the diameter, d (b) the radius, r?

? *Part* of a circumference is called an arc.
Explain why the length of the red arc in this diagram is $\dfrac{60}{360} \times \pi \times 10$.

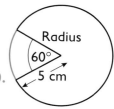

Exercise   *Use π = 3.14 in questions 1, 2, 3, 6 and 7.*

1 Calculate the circumference of circles with these dimensions.

(a) diameter = 10 cm   **(b)** diameter = 8 cm   **(c)** diameter = 2 m

(d) diameter = 23.6 cm   **(e)** radius = 5 cm   **(f)** radius = 3.8 m

2 The large wheel on Andy's wheelchair has a diameter of 60 cm.
Andy pushes the wheel round exactly once.

(a) How far has Andy moved?

Andy crosses a busy road, 20 m wide.

(b) How many times does he have to rotate
the large wheel to do this?

3 A circle has a circumference of 6.28 m.
Calculate **(a)** the diameter and **(b)** the radius of the circle.

4 You cannot write π exactly as a fraction, a terminating
decimal or even a recurring decimal.
A rough approximation for π is 3.

Some calculators have a button for π.
A ten digit display calculator gives π
as 3.141 592 654.

(a) Phil says 'π is 3.142'. Is Phil right?

Other approximations are $\frac{22}{7}$ and $\sqrt{10}$.

(b) Use a calculator to change **(i)** $\frac{22}{7}$ **(ii)** $\sqrt{10}$ to a decimal.
Compare your answers with the value given by the π button.

5 Use $\pi = \frac{22}{7}$ to calculate the circumference of circles with these dimensions:

(a) diameter = $3\frac{1}{2}$ cm   **(b)** diameter = $1\frac{3}{4}$ m   **(c)** radius = $4\frac{3}{8}$ km

6 **(a)** Calculate the lengths of these arcs.

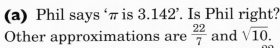

(i) 120° 8 cm   **(ii)** 180° 3.7 m   **(iii)** 161° 5.5 cm   **(iv)** 290° $10\frac{1}{2}$ inches

(b) Find a formula for the length of
the arc in this diagram.
θ is the angle between the two radii.

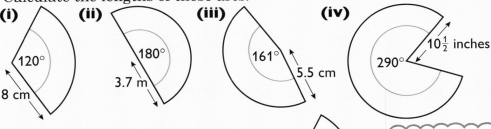

*This is the Greek
letter 'theta'.*

θ° r

7 A circular table has a diameter of 10 feet.
20 children are invited to a party tea.
Each child needs one foot six inches around the table's circumference.
Can all the children sit around the table together?

Area of a circle

 How do you deduce the formula for the area of (a) a triangle (b) a parallelogram? How can you find the area of a circle?

Task

You will need: centimetre squared paper, a pair of compasses, scissors, glue.

1 **(a)** Draw a circle of radius 8 cm on squared paper.
Make sure the centre is at the corner of a square.

(b) Count the squares to estimate the area of the circle.

2 **(a)** Cut out the circle.

(b) Fold it in half four times.

(c) Open it out and cut along the folds.
You should have sixteen **sectors** of the circle.

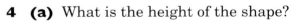

3 Glue the sectors onto another piece of paper.
Arrange them centre to arc, as shown.

 What shape have you almost made?

4 **(a)** What is the height of the shape?

(b) Measure the length of the shape.

(c) Use the length and height to estimate the area of the shape.

 How does your answer compare with your estimate from part 1?

In this diagram a circle of radius r is cut into lots of sectors and arranged to form a shape like a parallelogram.

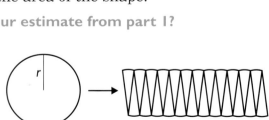

 Why is the length of the parallelogram approximately πr?
Use this length to calculate the area of the circle.

 What is the formula for the area of a circle?

 What is the area of the red sector in this diagram?

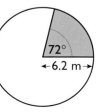

Exercise *Use π = 3.14 to calculate the answers in this exercise.*

1 Calculate the areas of circles with these dimensions:
   (a) radius = 10 cm   **(b)** radius = 5 cm   **(c)** radius = 42.7 cm
   (d) radius = 2.6 m   **(e)** diameter = 30 feet **(f)** diameter = 2 km
   (g) radius = 7.5 inches **(h)** diameter = 3.4 km   **(i)** diameter = 5 mm

2 The radius of a pizza is 15 cm. Calculate the area of
   (a) the pizza   **(b)** half the pizza
   (c) each of these sectors

   (i) 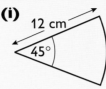   **(ii)** 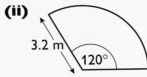   **(iii)**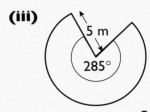

3 Find a formula for the area of the sector in this diagram.
   θ is the angle between the two radii.

4 **(a)** Calculate the area of the
       concrete surround of this
       circular swimming pool.
   Rehana covers the concrete
   with non-slip paint.
   Each tin of paint covers 8.5 m².
   (b) How many tins does she have to buy?

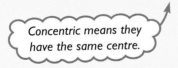

5 Calculate the area of the shaded region.
   These two circles are **concentric**.

   Concentric means they have the same centre.

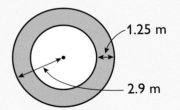

6 The inside lane of a running track is 400 m long.
   Each straight stretch of track is 100 m long.
   (a) Explain why the distance round each
       semicircular end is 100 m.
   (b) Find the inside radius of the
       semicircular ends.
   Field sports take place on the area inside the track.
   (c) Find the area used for field sports.

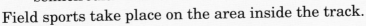

7 These diagrams consist of circles and squares.
   Each circle has a diameter of 20 cm.
   (a) Find the shaded area in each diagram.
   (b) Find the length of the chords in the
       right-hand diagram.

Circle constructions

 P is a fixed point.
What is the locus of all points 5 cm from P
(a) in two dimensions (b) in three dimensions?

P •

Do the right thing!

Follow these steps to construct a **tangent**.
You will need a pencil, a pair of compasses and a ruler.

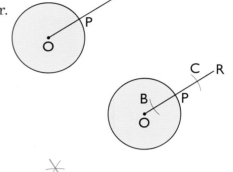

Step 1 Draw a circle of radius 5 cm with centre O.

Step 2 Draw a line OR cutting the circle at P.

Step 3 Use compasses to mark two points, B
and C, on OR.
B and C are equidistant from P.

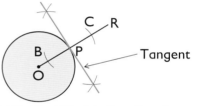

Step 4 Construct the perpendicular bisector of BC.
This is the tangent at P.

 A tangent touches a circle at just one point.
What can you say about the angle between a
tangent and the radius to this point?

In this diagram a line intersects a circle at two points, A and B.
Chord AB of the circle divides the circle into two **segments**.

 What do you call a chord which passes through the centre?

 What is the difference between a segment and a sector?

Task

1 Draw a circle and a chord which is not a diameter.

2 Construct the perpendicular bisector of the chord.

3 Draw two more chords in the circle.
Construct their perpendicular bisectors.

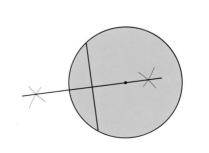

 What do you notice about your three
perpendicular bisectors?

 Think about the locus of a perpendicular bisector.
Think about the locus of a circle.
Explain why the centre of a circle must lie on the perpendicular bisector of a chord.

Exercise

1 (a) Draw a triangle ABC with sides of any lengths.

(b) Construct the perpendicular bisectors of each side. One is shown in the diagram.

(c) The three bisectors should all intersect at the same point. Call it Q.

   (i) Draw a circle with centre Q, through A.

   (ii) What do you notice about your circle? Why does this happen?

The circle you have drawn is called the **circumcircle** of the triangle. The centre of this circle is called the **circumcentre**.

2 (a) Draw a circle and mark the centre O.

(b) Draw two radii, OA and OB.

(c) Construct tangents at A and B. Label their intersection T.

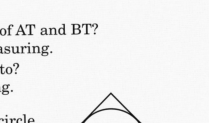

(d) What can you say about

   (i) lengths OA and OB

   (ii) angles OAT and OBT?

(e) Construct the bisector of angle ATB.

   (i) What shape is OATB?

   (ii) What can you say about the lengths of AT and BT? Explain your answers. Check by measuring.

(f) What must angles AOB and ATB add up to? Explain your answer. Check by measuring.

3 The sides of this triangle are tangents to the circle. The circle is the **inscribed circle** of the triangle.

(a) Draw a triangle with sides of any lengths.

(b) Think about your construction in question 2.

   (i) Find the position of the centre of the inscribed circle.

The inscribed circle is also called the incircle.

   (ii) Draw the inscribed circle.

Activity

1 Mark a point C.
Draw a circle with centre C and mark a point P on its circumference.

2 Use a ruler to draw a tangent at P *by eye*.
Your tangent should touch the circle at P only.
There is only one line which is the tangent at P.

3 Check the accuracy of your tangent by constructing a perpendicular to your line from P.

 How does constructing the perpendicular check the accuracy of your tangent?

Finishing off

Now that you have finished this chapter you should know:

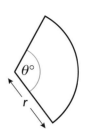

- that $\frac{\text{circumference}}{\text{diameter}}$ is the same for all circles, and is called π
- that two approximate values of π are 3.14 and $\frac{22}{7}$
- the circumference of a circle $= 2\pi r = \pi \times$ diameter
- the area of a circle $= \pi r^2$
- arc length $= \frac{\theta}{360} \times 2\pi r$
- sector area $= \frac{\theta}{360} \times \pi r^2$
- how to construct a tangent to a circle, the circumcircle of a triangle and the incircle of a triangle.

Review exercise

Use $\pi = \frac{22}{7}$ for questions 1 and 2.

1 For each circle calculate **(i)** the circumference **(ii)** the area.

(a)
14 cm

(b)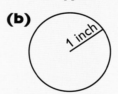
1 inch

(c)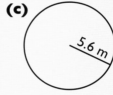
5.6 m

(d)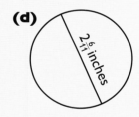
$2\frac{6}{11}$ inches

2 A bicycle has wheels of diameter 70 cm.

(a) How far does the bicycle go when a wheel makes:
(i) one rotation   **(ii)** five rotations?

(b) How many rotations does the wheel make when the bicycle travels
(i) 10 m   **(ii)** 100 m   **(iii)** 10 km?

Use $\pi = 3.14$ for the rest of this exercise.

3 Here are three timpani.

(a)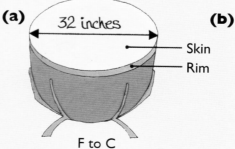
32 inches
— Skin
— Rim
F to C

(b)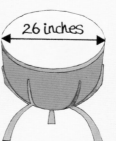
26 inches
B♭ to F

(c)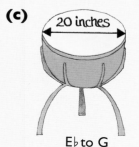
20 inches
E♭ to G

For each timpani find:
(i) the circumference of the rim   **(ii)** the area of the skin.

4 All these curves are semicircles, quarter circles or three-quarter circles.
Calculate the perimeter of each shape.

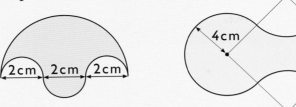

5 Here is a church door.
The arch at the top is a semicircle.
Calculate the area of the door.

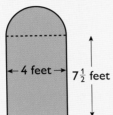

6 Look at this wrought iron gate.
The curve at the top is a semicircle.
Calculate the total length of iron
rod used to make the gate.

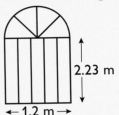

7 Here is a circular pond, surrounded by a path.
Calculate the area of **(a)** the pond **(b)** the path.
Give your answers to the nearest 0.01 m².

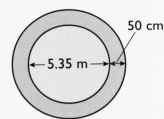

Investigation

1 (a) Find out the markings of a football pitch.
These are given at the Football Association's web site *www.the-fa.org/index.htm*
(b) Calculate the total length of lines on an international pitch of maximum size.
(c) The lines are 12 cm wide marked in chalk. What area of grass is covered by chalk?

2 A donkey and a goat graze in a 60 m by 60 m square
field with a diagonal path.
Each animal can just reach the path but cannot cross it.

The donkey is tethered to a post at A in the corner
making the largest possible quarter circle for the
donkey to graze.

The goat is tethered to a post at B somewhere on the
field boundary, making the largest possible semicircle.

Which animal has the larger grazing area?
Use scale drawing and measurement to help calculate the answer.
Use loci and construction techniques to find the position of B.
Repeat this question for a rectangular field, say 60 m by 80 m.

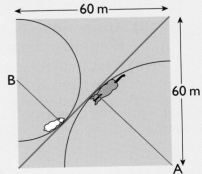

8 Ratio

Do you remember?

Zak does these questions about ratio.

> **1** Simplify 1 kg : 12.5 g
>
> 1000 g : 12.5 g
> 10 000 : 125
> Answer 80 : 1

 Explain each line of Zak's work.

 Where do the fractions $\frac{7}{9}$ and $\frac{2}{9}$ come from?

 Explain Zak's check.

> **2** Share £270 between A and B in the ratio 7:2
>
> $7 + 2 = 9$ parts
> $\frac{7}{9} \times £270 = £210$ A's share
> $\frac{2}{9} \times £270 = £60$ B's share
> Check £210 + £60 = £270 ✓

Task

Carly and Simon are making candles.
They decide to colour them with wax dye.

(a) Carly wants to make *pink* candles.
She uses six parts white dye and one part red dye.
The ratio is, white : red = 6 : 1.
Which of these ratios would make the same shade of pink?

(i) 30 : 5   **(ii)** 42 : 6   **(iii)** 3 : 0.5

(iv) $1 : \frac{1}{6}$ **(v)** $1.5 : \frac{1}{4}$ **(vi)** 600 : 10

(b) Simon decides to colour his candles *moss green*.
To make moss green needs blue, yellow and red in the ratio 3 : 3 : 2.

(i) He uses 24 drops of wax dye altogether.
How many drops of each colour does he use?

(ii) Another time he uses 56 drops of dye.
How many drops of blue, yellow and red does Simon use this time?

(iii) Next time Simon uses 16 drops of red dye to make moss green candles.
How many drops of blue and of yellow does Simon need?

To find a missing quantity it is sometimes useful to use algebra.
Jo writes

$$x : 7 = 1 : 4$$
$$\frac{x}{7} = \frac{1}{4}$$
$$x = \frac{1}{4} \times 7$$
$$x = 1.75$$

 How would you find x in 2 : x = 3 : 5?

Exercise

1 Simplify these ratios.

    (a) $180:324$ **(b)** $216:192:240$ **(c)** $392:441:294$

    (d) $14\frac{1}{2}:15\frac{1}{2}$ **(e)** $13\frac{1}{3}:7\frac{1}{2}$ **(f)** $2\frac{1}{5}:7.7$

    (g) $5.1:8.5$ **(h)** $0.04:0.2$ **(i)** $0.4:2.4$

    (j) $2.1\,\text{kg}:700\,\text{g}$ **(k)** $42\ \text{minutes}:1\ \text{hour}$ **(l)** $4.2\,\text{m}:56\,\text{cm}$

2 Find the missing quantities.

    (a) $5:8=\ldots:72$ **(b)** $6:7=54:\ldots$ **(c)** $2\frac{1}{2}:4\frac{1}{2}=\ldots:18$

    (d) $1.5:7.5=\ldots:22.5$ **(e)** $1.7:3.2=15.3:\ldots$ **(f)** $5\frac{1}{3}:\ldots=48:17$

3 A map is drawn to a scale of $2\,\text{cm}:1\,\text{km}$.

    (a) What distance is represented by **(i)** 12 cm   **(ii)** 3.2 cm   **(iii)** 5.3 cm?

    (b) What distance on the map represents **(i)** 8 km   **(ii)** 3.6 km?

    (c) Write the scale in the form $1:n$, where n is a number.

4 In a hockey season the ratio of penalty goals scored to penalties saved is $15:2$.
51 penalties are awarded.
How many penalty goals are scored and how many penalties are saved?

5 In biscuits the ratio of butter, caster sugar and flour is $2:1:4$.
The total mass of the ingredients is 350 g.
How much of each ingredient is used?

6 The table shows the ratio of how goals were scored by two teams in a football league.
How many goals of each type were scored by each team?

	Left-footed : Right-footed : Headed			Total
Shellbury	5 :	7 :	3	60
Plystar	3 :	5 :	1	72

Investigation

1 (a) Construct accurately this right-angled triangle ABC.
    Measure BC.
    Work out the ratio BC : AB in the form $1:n$.

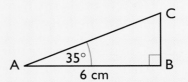

    (b) Repeat part (a) with **(i)** AB = 8 cm   **(ii)** AB = 10 cm.
    Find the ratio BC : AB each time.

2 Choose a different value for angle A and repeat the investigation.
What do you notice?

Ratios and similar figures

Look at these two rectangles.

12 cm

4 cm

3 cm

B

1 cm | A

? They are similar. What does this mean?
What is the ratio of the lengths in **A** to the lengths in **B**?
What about the areas?

? Two cuboids are similar.
The ratio of their
lengths is 1 : 3.
What is the ratio of
their volumes?

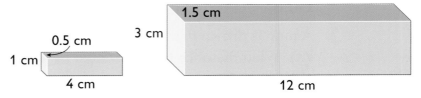

1.5 cm

3 cm

0.5 cm

1 cm

4 cm

12 cm

Task

Tom is a film star. He sends out souvenir models of his Oscar.
The souvenirs are packed in boxes. There are two sizes, large and small.
The boxes are similar.
On the front of each box is a photograph of Tom.
Photograph C is an enlargement
of photograph D.

16 cm

8 cm

height

24 cm

Photograph D

I (a) What is the ratio, width : height,
for photograph C?
(b) What is the height of photograph D?

Photograph C

The small box is 10 cm by 8 cm, and 12 cm high.
The ratio of the heights of the two boxes is 2 : 1.

2 What are the dimensions of the larger box?

3 What is the surface area of **(a)** the larger box
(b) the smaller box?

12 cm

4 (a) What is the ratio of the surface areas (large : small)
in its simplest form?
(b) What is the connection between this and the 2 : 1 ratio
of the heights?

8 cm

10 cm

5 Calculate the volume of each box and write down the ratio of
their volumes in its simplest form.

6 Find a connection between this ratio and that of the heights.

? Two cuboids are similar. The ratio of their lengths is 1 : *n*.
What is the ratio of their surface areas?
What is the ratio of their volumes?
Do these rules apply to any similar shapes?

Exercise

1 **(a)** Draw these triangles accurately.

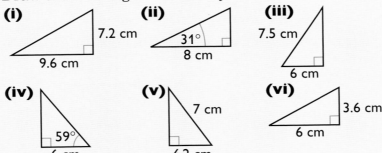

(i) 7.2 cm, 9.6 cm

(ii) 31°, 8 cm

(iii) 7.5 cm, 6 cm

(iv) 59°, 6 cm

(v) 7 cm, 4.2 cm

(vi) 3.6 cm, 6 cm

(b) Measure the lengths of the unknown sides to the nearest 0.1 cm.
Sort the triangles into two groups of similar triangles.

(c) Are any of these triangles congruent?

2 A photograph is 10 cm by 15 cm.

15 cm, 10 cm

(a) The diagrams show some possible enlargements.
Find the missing measurements.

E 30 cm, ?

F 60 cm, ?

G ?, 15 cm

(b) Calculate the areas of the photographs E, F and G.

(c) **(i)** What is the ratio, the width of E : the width of F?
(ii) What is the ratio, the area of E : the area of F?

3 These rectangles are similar.
(a) Find the lengths marked x and y.

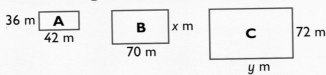

36 m, A, 42 m

B, x m, 70 m

C, 72 m, y m

(b) The rectangles represent gardens.
Fauzia does scale drawings with a scale of 1 : 2000.
What are the measurements of her scale drawings?

4 Cuboid A is 3 cm by 9 cm by 7.5 cm. Cuboid B is 2 cm by 6 cm by 5 cm.
(a) Write down and simplify the ratio of
(i) the widths **(ii)** the lengths **(iii)** the heights.
Are the cuboids similar?
(b) Find the volumes of the two cuboids.
(c) Work out the ratio, volume of cuboid A : volume of cuboid B.
What do you notice?
(d) Joe works out the surface area of each cuboid.
From this he finds the ratio, surface area A : surface area B.
Without doing any further calculations, write down his answer.

Proportionality

The circumference of a circle **is proportional to** the radius.

You can also say the circumference of a circle **varies as** the radius.
This can be written as $C \propto r$ or as $C = kr$.
In this case $k = 2\pi$ so $C = 2\pi r$.

> k is the **constant of proportionality**.

> This is called the **law of variation**.

 When do you use the symbol $\propto$
and when do you use an equals sign?

 The area of a circle is $A = \pi r^2$. Describe the relationship between A and r.

66 Do the right thing!

Look at this example. It shows you how to set out your work.

1   y varies as $\sqrt{x}$.
(a) Write this in symbols.
(b) When $x = 4$, $y = 10$.
Find the constant of proportionality
and hence the law of variation.
(c) Find y when $x = 9$.
(d) Find x when $y = 500$.

ERASER

> 1 (a) $y = k\sqrt{x}$
> (b) $10 = k\sqrt{4}$
> $10 = k \times 2$
> so $k = \frac{10}{2}$
> $k = 5$
> So the law of variation
> is $y = 5\sqrt{x}$
> (c) When $x = 9$,
> $y = 5 \times \sqrt{9}$
> $y = 5 \times 3$
> $y = 15$
>
> (d) When $y = 500$,
> $500 = 5\sqrt{x}$
> $\frac{500}{5} = \sqrt{x}$
> $\sqrt{x} = 100$
> $x = 100^2$
> $x = 10\,000$

Task

1 **(a)** $y \propto x$. Write this as an equation.
(b) When $x = 16$, $y = 40$.
Find the constant of proportionality and hence the law of variation.
(c) **(i)** Find y when $x = 30$. **(ii)** Find x when $y = 15$.

2 **(a)** s varies as t. Write this in symbols.
(b) When $t = 2$, $s = 50$.
Find the constant of proportionality and hence the law of variation.
(c) **(i)** Find s when $t = 4$. **(ii)** Find t when $s = 150$.

3 **(a)** V is proportional to L^3. Write this in symbols.
(b) When $L = 4$, $V = 192$.
Find the constant of proportionality and hence the law of variation.
(c) **(i)** Find V when $L = 5$. **(ii)** Find L when $V = 3000$.

4 Which of the graphs, A or B, could represent
the situations in questions 1, 2 and 3?

Exercise

1 **(a)** p is proportional to q. Write this in symbols.
   (b) When $q = 7$, $p = 28$.
   Find the constant of proportionality and hence the law of variation.
   (c) **(i)** Find p when $q = 7.5$.   **(ii)** Find q when $p = 444$.

2 **(a)** d is proportional to h. Write this in symbols.
   (b) When $h = 16$, $d = 272$.
   Find the constant of proportionality and hence the law of variation.
   (c) **(i)** Find d when $h = 4.2$.   **(ii)** Find h when $d = 102$.

3 **(a)** A varies as x^2. Write this in symbols.
   (b) When $x = 6$, $A = 72$.
   Find the constant of proportionality and hence the law of variation.
   (c) **(i)** Find A when $x = 5$.   **(ii)** Find x when $A = 98$.

4 **(a)** $v \propto \dfrac{1}{t}$. Write this as an equation.
   (b) When $v = 80$, $t = 6$.
   Find the constant of proportionality and hence the law of variation.
   (c) **(i)** Find v when $t = 4$.   **(ii)** Find t when $v = 60$.

5 $T \propto \sqrt{l}$ and when $l = 25$, $T = 10$. Find
   (a) the law of variation   **(b)** T when $l = 36$ **(c)** l when $T = 8$.

6 E varies directly as v^2 and when $v = 15$, $E = 1800$. Find
   (a) the law of variation   **(b)** E when $v = 8$ **(c)** v when $E = 288$.

Investigation

Amanda presents the following data in a piece of Science coursework on photosynthesis.

Distance from light source (d cm)	Rate of photosynthesis, r (bubbles per minute)
4	62
8	15
16	5
32	1
64	0

Amanda thinks that r varies as $\dfrac{1}{d^2}$ and that the constant of proportionality is 1000.

1 Draw the graph of the curve $r = \dfrac{1000}{d^2}$. Plot the five data points on your graph.

2 How closely do the data fit this theory?

Finishing off

Review exercise

1 **(a)** Simplify these ratios giving your answers in the form $m : n$ where both m and n are whole numbers.

  (i) $51 : 85$ **(ii)** $45 : 36$ **(iii)** $57 : 38 : 152$
  (iv) $0.04 : 0.12$ **(v)** $2.5 \, \text{kg} : 100 \, \text{g}$ **(vi)** $300 \, \text{kg} : 1 \, \text{tonne}$

  (b) Write these ratios in the form $1 : n$.

  (i) $4 : 500$ **(ii)** $13 : 91$ **(iii)** $3.5 : 8.4$
  (iv) $8 : 100$ **(v)** $0.06 : 0.12$ **(vi)** $1\frac{1}{2} : 4\frac{1}{2}$

2 **(a)** A skirt is made of viscose and polyester in the ratio $9 : 11$.
  What is the percentage of viscose in the shirt?

  (b) A jacket is made of viscose, wool, polyamide and cotton in the ratio $11 : 18 : 33 : 38$.
  What is the percentage of viscose in the jacket?

  (c) Which garment has the greater proportion of viscose?

3 The alloy constantin is 60% copper and the rest is nickel.
Cupro–nickel is also an alloy of copper and nickel in the ratio $0.25 : 0.75$.
Nickel–silver is an alloy of copper, zinc and nickel in the proportions $5 : 2 : 3$.
Which of these has the greatest proportion of nickel?

4 Brown paint is made with five parts orange and one part black.
Orange paint is made with one part red and one part yellow.
What is the ratio of red : yellow : black needed to make brown paint?

5 Find the missing quantity in these ratios.

  (a) $5 : 8 = \boxed{} : 48$ **(b)** $2 : 7 = 18 : \boxed{}$ **(c)** $3.2 : \boxed{} = 16 : 9$

6 Share 48 sweets between Simon and Mandy in the ratio $5 : 11$.

7 **(a)** Share £96 000 profits between Ms Craig, Mr Fulford and
  Mrs McIntosh in the ratio $7 : 4 : 5$.

  (b) On another occasion Ms Craig's share of the profits is £105 000.
  What is the total that is shared out on this occasion?

8 **(a)** Use Pythagoras' theorem to find the lengths x and y.

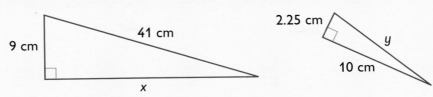

(b) Write down the ratio of
    (i) the shortest side of triangle A : the shortest side of triangle B
    (ii) the middle-sized sides   **(iii)** the longest sides.
(c) Are the triangles similar?
(d) Without any further working, write down the ratio of the area of triangle A to the area of triangle B.

9 **(a)** For these two cuboids, write down the ratio of
    (i) the heights   **(ii)** the lengths   **(iii)** the widths.

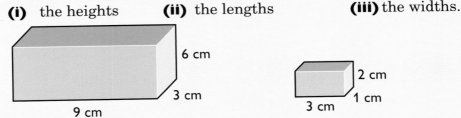

(b) Are the cuboids similar?
(c) Without doing any further working, write down the ratio of
    (i) the surface areas **(ii)** the volumes.

10 You are given that $V \propto h^3$ and that $V = 1000$ when $h = 5$. Find
  (a) the law of variation   **(b)** V when $h = 3.5$ **(c)** h when $V = 512$.

11 You are given that $y \propto x^3$ and $z \propto \sqrt{y}$.
You are also given that $x = 4$, $y = 576$ and $z = 48$.
  (a) Find z when $x = 16$.   **(b)** Find x when $z = 96$.

12 A cylinder has a radius of 4 cm and a volume of 512 ml.
A similar cylinder has a volume of 64 ml.
  (a) Write down the ratio of
    (i) their volumes   **(ii)** their radii.
  (b) What is the radius of the smaller cylinder?

13 An experiment involves two quantities E and h.
E is proportional to h.
At the start of the experiment $E = 5$ and $h = 50$.
  (a) h increases by 10%.
    (i) What is the new value of h? **(ii)** What is the new value of E?
  (b) Later the value of h is 40.
    (i) What is the percentage decrease of h from its original value of 50?
    (ii) What is the percentage change in the value of E?

Solving pairs of equations

Amy is trying to find out where the lines $x + y = 5$ and $y = x + 1$ **intersect**.
She draws their graphs.

cross

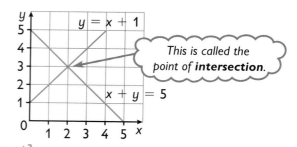

This is called the point of **intersection**.

 Which point lies on both lines?
How can you check that your answer is correct?

The equations $x + y = 5$ and $y = x + 1$ are called a pair of **simultaneous equations**.

There are two equations and two unknowns, x and y.

The solution of these equations is a value of a x *and* a value of y.

In this example $x = 2$ and $y = 3$

You can solve simultaneous equations graphically like Amy did.
The point of intersection of the lines gives the solution.
You can also solve simultaneous equations using algebra. Look at Laura's working out:

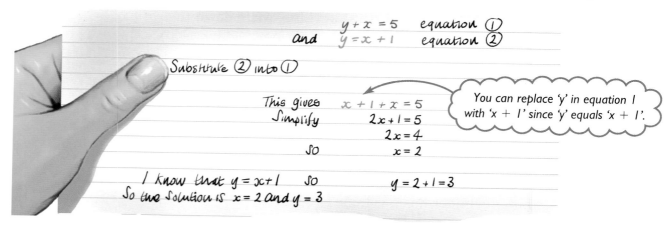

and $y + x = 5$ equation ①
$y = x + 1$ equation ②

Substitute ② into ①

This gives $x + 1 + x = 5$
Simplify $2x + 1 = 5$
$2x = 4$
So $x = 2$

You can replace 'y' in equation 1 with 'x + 1' since 'y' equals 'x + 1'.

I know that $y = x + 1$ So $y = 2 + 1 = 3$
So the solution is $x = 2$ and $y = 3$

This is an example of solving simultaneous equations by **substitution**.

Task

Make a square by plotting these lines.

A $y = x + 4$ B $x + y = 14$

C $y = x - 4$ D $x + y = 6$

1 Write down the coordinates of the vertices of the square.

2 Show how to find the co-ordinates of the vertices algebraically.

3 Explain why the simultaneous equations $x + y = 14$ and $x + y = 6$ have no solution.

 How would you solve the following pair of equations? $b = 3a$ and $7a - 2b = 1$

Exercise

1 **(a)** Copy and complete this table.

x	0	1	2	3	4
$y = 4x - 2$	-2			10	

(b) Make a table for the line $y = 2x + 1$.

(c) Draw the lines $y = 2x + 1$ and $y = 4x - 2$ on the same axes.

(d) Use your graph to solve these simultaneous equations.

$$y = 2x + 1$$
$$y = 4x - 2$$

2 Use algebra to solve the following pairs of equations.

(a) $y = x$
$x + 3y = 12$

(b) $a = b$
$6b + a = 28$

(c) $g = 2h$
$g + 3h = 15$

(d) $m = 2n$
$2m + 2n = 12$

(e) $c = d + 3$
$c + 2d = 21$

(f) $f = 5 - e$
$3e + f = 9$

(g) $s = t$
$3s + 2t = 25$

(h) $p = 2r$
$4p - 3r = 20$

(i) $y = 2x + 3$
$2y + x = 11$

(j) $c = 5d$
$c + 2 = 3d + 8$

(k) $2j = 3k - 1$
$4j + k = 5$

(l) $3r = 2s$
$4s - 12 = 12 - 6r$

3 Jane wants to buy some books with her birthday money.

I am buying three paperbacks and one hardback for £30.

Jane

(a) Write down an equation for what Jane buys using £p for the price of a paperback book and £h for the price of a hardback.

(b) Jane writes down the equation

$$h = 2p$$

AVONFORD BOOKS

Hardbacks only twice the price of paperbacks!!

What does this equation mean?

(c) Solve the two equations to find the price of each type of book.

4 **(a)** At the local shop birthday cards cost five times as much as postcards.
Write down an equation for this information using b pence for the cost of one birthday card and p pence for the cost of one postcard.

Happy Birthday

Greetings from SCOTLAND

(b) Michael buys three birthday cards and six postcards for £4.20.
Write down an equation for this information in terms of b and p.

(c) Solve your equations to find the cost of one birthday card and one postcard.

Simultaneous equations

Felicity and John bought some CDs and DVDs from SPIN-A-DISC.

I bought four CDs and two DVDs for £80.

I bought two CDs and two DVDs for £56.

SALE!! 🎵🎵🎵 **SALE!!**
SPIN-A-DISC
Lowest ever prices
on all CDs and DVDs!!

Amir wants to know how much one CD would cost from Spin-a-disc.
Look at what Amir writes.

? **What do c and d stand for?**

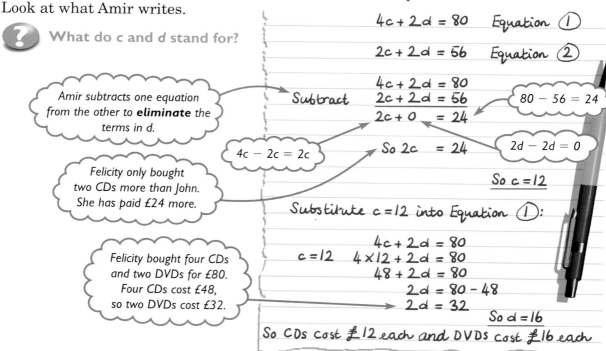

$4c + 2d = 80$ Equation ①

$2c + 2d = 56$ Equation ②

Subtract
$4c + 2d = 80$
$2c + 2d = 56$
$2c + 0 = 24$ $80 - 56 = 24$

Amir subtracts one equation from the other to **eliminate** the terms in d.

$4c - 2c = 2c$

So $2c = 24$ $2d - 2d = 0$

Felicity only bought two CDs more than John. She has paid £24 more.

So $c = 12$

Substitute $c = 12$ into Equation ①:

Felicity bought four CDs and two DVDs for £80. Four CDs cost £48, so two DVDs cost £32.

$c = 12$ $\begin{aligned} 4c + 2d &= 80 \\ 4 \times 12 + 2d &= 80 \\ 48 + 2d &= 80 \\ 2d &= 80 - 48 \\ 2d &= 32 \end{aligned}$

So $d = 16$

So CDs cost £12 each and DVDs cost £16 each

This is an example of solving simultaneous equations by **elimination**.

? **How can Amir check his answer is correct?**

Task

(a) Charlotte spends £60 on 2 skirts and 3 T-shirts.
Copy and complete this table. It shows possible whole number values of the prices.

Cost of one skirt	£3	£6					£24	
Cost of one T-shirt			£14	£12		£8		

(b) Sam buys 2 skirts and 6 T-shirts for £84. Their prices are the same as Charlotte paid.
Write down two possible whole number solutions to the equation $2s + 6t = 84$.
(c) How many more skirts and T-shirts did Sam buy than Charlotte?
How much more did Sam pay?
(d) What is the price of **(i)** one T-shirt   **(ii)** one skirt?
(e) Show how you would use algebra, as Amir did, to answer part (d).

Exercise

1 Look at this pair of simultaneous equations:

$$5p + 4q = 23$$
$$2p + 4q = 14$$

    (a) What does $3p$ equal?

    (b) What are the values of p and q?

2 Solve the following simultaneous equations.
Remember to find values for both unknowns.

    (a) $4a + 3b = 13$ **(b)** $3x + 5y = 29$ **(c)** $5p + 4r = 23$
            $2a + 3b = 11$ $3x + 3y = 21$ $3p + 4r = 17$

    (d) $8c + 4d = 28$ **(e)** $5s + 3t = 41$ **(f)** $12f + 4g = 36$
            $6c + 4d = 26$ $5s + 6t = 47$ $12f + 6g = 42$

    (g) $3m + 2n = 40$ **(h)** $3j + 2k = 29$ **(i)** $8e + 3f = 43$
            $5m + 2n = 60$ $3j + 7k = 64$ $12e + 3f = 51$

3 Dan buys four candles and two rockets.
He spends £26.

Fireworks
Special offer on all
candles and rockets !

    (a) Write an equation for what Dan buys
using c for the cost of a candle and r for
the cost of a rocket.

Nesrene buys one candle and two rockets.
She spends £11.

    (b) Write down a second equation in terms of c and r.

    (c) Solve your two equations to find the cost of one candle and the cost of
one rocket.

4 Cynthia buys two ballpoint pens and four pencils for £1.

    (a) Write down an equation for what
Cynthia buys using b pence for the
cost of a ballpoint pen and p pence for
the cost of a pencil.
        (*Hint*: Write 100 pence rather than £1.)

Darrell buys five ballpoint pens and four pencils for £1.90.

    (b) Write down a second equation in terms of b and p.

    (c) Solve the two equations to find the cost of one ballpoint pen and the cost
of one pencil.

5 A rail company works out the new
summer train timetable.

*How much time does each
stop add to the journey?*

	Number of stops	**Journey time (in mins)**
Slow train	23	143
Fast train	5	89

    (a) Write down two equations using the information in the table.
Use j minutes for the journey time without any stops and s minutes for
the time taken for each stop.

    (b) Solve your two equations to find out:

        (i) how long each stop takes

        (ii) how long the journey would be without any stops.

Solving simultaneous equations

John

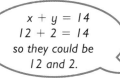

I will give a prize to whoever works out the ages of my two children. The sum of their ages is 14.

x + y = 14
12 + 2 = 14
so they could be 12 and 2.

Sarah

 What does Sarah mean by $x + y = 14$?
How many other possible answers are there to this equation?

The difference between the ages of John's children is 2.

 How do you write 'difference' in maths?

Sarah now writes

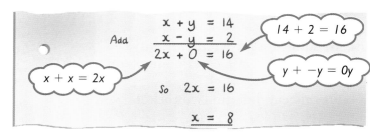

Add

$$x + y = 14$$
$$x - y = 2$$
$$2x + 0 = 16$$

14 + 2 = 16

x + x = 2x

y + −y = 0y

So $2x = 16$

$$\underline{x = 8}$$

*Sarah notices that when the two equations are added together the terms in y are **eliminated.***

 How can you work out the value of y? How old are John's children?

 Sarah solved the problem by adding the two equations together.
Could she have solved it by subtracting one equation from the other?

 Task

Hannah and Graeme are playing a game of mystery numbers.

The sum of my two numbers is 24. The difference between them is 6.

Hannah

One of my numbers is double the other. The sum of my two numbers is 15.

Graeme

1 Write down two equations for Hannah's mystery numbers.
Use a and b for her two numbers.
2 Solve your equations to find Hannah's mystery numbers.
3 Repeat parts 1 and 2 to find Graeme's mystery numbers.
4 Play your own game of mystery numbers with a partner.

 How do you solve these simultaneous equations?
(a) $2a - 3b = 4$ **(b)** $6f - 3g = 15$
       $4a + 3b = 26$ $4f - 3g = 7$
How can you decide whether to add or subtract the equations?

Exercise

1 Solve these simultaneous equations by adding the two equations together.

(a) $x - 2y = 4$
  $2x + 2y = 14$

(b) $4e + 2f = 16$
  $3e - 2f = 5$

(c) $5g + 2h = 12$
  $8g - 2h = 14$

(d) $4d - 2c = 10$
  $3d + 2c = 11$

(e) $3a - 2b = 13$
  $4a + 2b = 36$

(f) $5s - 6t = 22$
  $3s + 6t = 42$

2 Simplify

(a) $3x - 5x$

(b) $2x + (-2x)$

(c) $2x - (-2x)$

(d) $(-5x) - (-5x)$

3 Solve the following simultaneous equations by subtracting one from the other. *Be very careful with your signs.* Remember that $-3g - -3g = 0$.

(a) $6x - 3y = 12$
  $4x - 3y = 6$

(b) $3e + 2f = 10$
  $3e - f = 4$

(c) $6s - 2t = 0$
  $4s - 2t = 0$

(d) $7j - 3k = 19$
  $7j + k = 31$

(e) $12a - 4b = 4$
  $10a - 4b = 2$

(f) $4m + 2n = 14$
  $4m + 7n = 19$

4 Solve the following simultaneous equations. In each case you will need to decide whether to add or subtract.

(a) $3a + 6b = 24$
  $3a + 4b = 18$

(b) $4m + 2n = 34$
  $6m - 2n = 16$

(c) $5x - 2y = 8$
  $7x + 2y = 16$

(d) $4s - 2t = 22$
  $2s - 2t = 8$

(e) $6f - 4g = 32$
  $6f + 2g = 38$

(f) $2a + 3b = 7$
  $2a - b = 3$

(g) $4c - 2d = 16$
  $2c - 2d = 6$

(h) $2p + 3r = 18$
  $p + 3r = 15$

(i) $15g + 3h = 42$
  $15g - h = 6$

5 Joanne is thinking of two mystery numbers. Call them m and n.

(a) Write down two equations for m and n.

(b) Solve your equations to find the two numbers.

(c) How can you check that your answer is correct?

(d) Are there other possible answers for m and n?

When my two numbers are added together the answer is 21.

The difference between my two numbers is 3.

6 The perimeter of the rectangle is 10 cm. The perimeter of the triangle is 7 cm.

(a) Write down an equation for the perimeter of the rectangle.

(b) Write down an equation for the perimeter of the triangle.

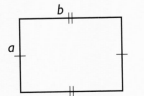

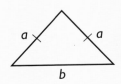

(c) Solve your two equations to find the dimensions of the rectangle.

(d) How can you check that your solution is correct?

More simultaneous equations

I bought three goldfish and two tench for £13.

David

I bought six goldfish and six tench for £30.

Serina

Serina writes

$$3g + 2t = 13 \quad \text{Equation ①}$$
$$6g + 6t = 30 \quad \text{Equation ②}$$

? Can Serina solve these simultaneous equations by adding or subtracting the two equations?

Serina bought twice as many goldfish as David.

? How much would David have spent if he had bought six goldfish and four tench?

Serina writes

Serina has multiplied each term by 2.

× by 2

$$3g + 2t = 13 \longrightarrow 6g + 4t = 26$$

$$6g + 6t = 30 \; ②$$
$$\underline{6g + 4t = 26} \; ① × 2$$
subtract
$$0 \; + 2t = 4$$

$$2t = 4$$
$$\text{so } t = 2$$

? How much does one goldfish cost?

? Serina eliminated g. How could she have eliminated t?

Task

I You are to solve the equations

$$3a + 2b = 21 \; ①$$
$$2a - 3b = 1 \; ②$$

(a) Multiply equation 1 by 3. **(b)** Multiply equation 2 by 2. **(c)** Now solve the equations.

2 Solve these equations.

(a) $3x + 2y = 21$
  $7x - 6y = 17$

(b) $3x + y = 10$
  $x + 2y = 5$

(c) $5x - 2y = 10$
  $3x - 4y = 6$

Exercise

1 Solve the following simultaneous equations.

(a) $3a + 2b = 13$
$5a + 4b = 23$

(b) $2c + 3d = 17$
$6c + 4d = 26$

(c) $4m - 6n = 4$
$3m + 2n = 29$

(d) $4p - 2r = 12$
$8p - 5r = 22$

(e) $2f + 3g = 21$
$6f - 4g = 24$

(f) $2s - t = 5$
$5s - 4t = 11$

(g) $6x - 3y = 3$
$2x + 5y = 7$

(h) $5j + 2k = 45$
$3j + 6k = 75$

(i) $2e - 3f = 10$
$6e + f = 130$

(j) $2m - 5n = 1$
$5m + 3n = 49$

(k) $3s - 2t = 4$
$5s + 3t = 13$

(l) $2a - 3b = 2$
$3a - 2b = 8$

2 Natalie buys three toffees and four chocolates for 38p.
Scott buys nine toffees and two chocolates for 64p.

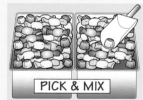

PICK & MIX

(a) Write down two equations for this information
using t pence for the cost of a toffee and c pence
for the cost of a chocolate.

(b) Find the cost of one toffee and the cost of one chocolate.

3 Mary works at Avonford Pet Rescue Centre.
One Saturday she feeds each large dog six
biscuits and each small dog four biscuits.
There are 15 dogs altogether and between
them they eat 80 biscuits.
How many large dogs are in the rescue centre?

Investigation

1 **(a)** Solve these simultaneous equations.

(i) $x - 2y = 3$
$2x - 4y = 8$

(ii) $3x - 2y = 6$
$9x = 6y + 18$

(b) What do you notice? Why does this happen?

(c) Use a graphic calculator to plot the graphs of each pair of equations.
You will need to make y the subject of each equation. What do you notice?

(d) Find some other pairs of equations where the same thing happens.

Activity

With a friend design a poster showing how to solve simultaneous equations.
Choose three of the pairs of equations below to illustrate your poster.
Your poster should include an explanation of the following.

1 How to solve simultaneous equations
(a) graphically **(b)** by substitution **(c)** by elimination.

2 How to decide what to multiply an equation by prior to solving.

3 How to decide whether to add or subtract the two equations.

$3a + 2b = 16$
$2a - b = 6$

$d = 2c$
$d = 3c - 4$

$e + f = 7$
$3e - 2f = 6$

$3g + 2h = 17$
$4g - 3h = 17$

$j = 2i - 4$
$i + j = 5$

$5k - 2l = 26$
$3k - 4l = 10$

$7m + 3n = 13$
$2m + 5n = 12$

$2p - 3q = 8$
$4p + 9q = 46$

Finishing off

Now that you have finished this chapter you should be able to:

- solve simultaneous equations graphically
- solve a pair of simultaneous equations by substitution
- solve a pair of simultaneous equations by elimination
- write down a pair of simultaneous equations to help you solve a problem.

Review exercise

1 **(a)** Copy and complete this table.

x	0	1	2	3	4
$4x$			8		
-10			-10		
$y = 4x - 10$			-2		

(b) Make a table for the line $y = 2x - 3$.

(c) Draw the lines $y = 4x - 10$ and $y = 2x - 3$ on the same axes.

(d) Use the graph to solve the simultaneous equations

$$y = 4x - 10$$
$$y = 2x - 3.$$

(e) **(i)** Add the line $y = 2x - 1$ to your graph.
(ii) Is there a solution to the equations

$$y = 2x + 1$$
$$y = 4x - 10$$
$$y = 2x - 3?$$

Explain your answer.

2 Solve these simultaneous equations by substituting one equation into the other.

(a) $y = x$
$2x + y = 9$

(b) $g = 2h$
$g + 4h = 18$

(c) $c = 3d$
$2c = 3 + 5d$

(d) $a = 2b + 1$
$2b + a = 11$

(e) $y = 3x + 5$
$y = 2x + 8$

(f) $r = 2s$
$s + 3r = 35$

3 Solve these simultaneous equations by adding the two equations together.

(a) $3f - 2g = 5$
$2f + 2g = 10$

(b) $5j + 3k = 29$
$3j - 3k = 3$

(c) $4x + 2y = 6$
$3x - y = 2$

4 Solve these simultaneous equations by subtracting one equation from the other.

(a) $3a + 2b = 11$
$a + 2b = 5$

(b) $3x - 2y = 16$
$x - 2y = 0$

(c) $5r + 2s = 47$
$5r - 3s = 42$

5 Solve these simultaneous equations.
Think carefully about whether you need to add or subtract the equations.

(a) $3s + 2t = 5$
$3s + t = 4$

(b) $4p + 3r = 11$
$2p - 3r = 1$

(c) $2g - h = 12$
$g + h = 18$

(d) $3a + 2b = 20$
$3a - b = 17$

(e) $2x - y = 5$
$x - y = 1$

(f) $4c - 2d = 30$
$4c - 4d = 20$

6 Solve these simultaneous equations.

(a) $2f + 3g = 13$
$f + g = 5$

(b) $3j - 2k = 1$
$2j + k = 3$

(c) $8m - 5n = 65$
$5m + 10n = 80$

(d) $3c + 2d = 23$
$6c + 6d = 54$

(e) $5a + b = 26$
$2a - 3b = 7$

(f) $12x - 3y = 12$
$4x + 2y = 16$

7 A family of seven people go to the cinema.
There are a adults and c children.
(a) Write down an equation for this information.
The cinema trip costs £27.
(b) Write down a second equation in terms of a and c.
(c) How many children go to the cinema?

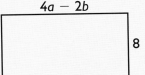

AVONFORD CINEMA

Adults £5
Children £3

8 Daniel buys four mugs and five plates for £30.
Sarah buys eight mugs and two plates for £44.

(a) Write down two equations for this information using £m for the cost of a mug and £p for the cost of a plate.

(b) Find the cost of one mug and the cost of one plate.

9 The length of this rectangle is 10 cm and the width is 8 cm.
(a) Write down two equations involving a and b.
(b) Solve your equations simultaneously.

$4a - 2b$

$a + 5b$

8

10

Investigation

I Look at these arrays. Each piece of fruit has been assigned a value.
So 3 apples + 2 bananas + 1 cherry = 13 in array (a).
Work out the value of each piece of fruit. It is different in each array.

(a)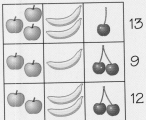

13
9
12

(b)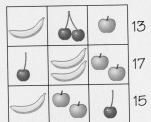

13
17
15

(c)

17
17
8

2 Solve these simultaneous equations.

(a) $3x + 2y - z = 5$
$2x + y + z = 8$
$x + 2y + 2z = 10$

(b) $x + y + z = 9$
$2x - y + 3z = 15$
$x + 2y - z = 5$

3 How many equations would you need to find the value of five unknowns?

10 Fractions

The language of fractions

cancel   common denominator   common factor   reciprocal   equivalent

lowest common denominator   numerator   lowest terms   top heavy   mixed number

These are all terms used when dealing with fractions.
Check you know the meaning of each one and explain how they can be used in the following.

1 Simplify   (a) $\frac{9}{12}$ (b) $\frac{15}{25}$ (c) $\frac{15}{4}$

2 Find the reciprocal of   (a) $\frac{2}{3}$ (b) $1\frac{4}{5}$ (c) $\frac{a}{b}$

3 Work out   (a) $\frac{2}{5}+\frac{3}{7}$ (b) $\frac{5}{6}-\frac{2}{7}$ (c) $\frac{4}{5}\times\frac{2}{9}$ (d) $\frac{2}{3}\div\frac{5}{6}$

Fractions in algebra

Miranda has written

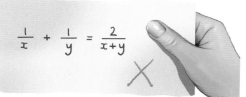

$$\frac{1}{x}+\frac{1}{y}=\frac{2}{x+y}$$

Explain Miranda's mistake.

Task

Here are some problems in algebra that involve fractions.
Copy the statements and fill in the blank spaces to solve each problem.

1 (a) $\dfrac{2a}{2b}=\dfrac{a}{\square}$ 2 is the ... ... of $2a$ and $2b$.

   (b) $\dfrac{3(x+y)}{2(x+y)}=\dfrac{\square}{2}$ The ... ... $(x+y)$ has been ... .

2 (a) $\dfrac{1}{a}+\dfrac{1}{b}=\dfrac{b}{ab}+\dfrac{a}{\square}=\dfrac{\square+\square}{ab}$ ab is the ... ... of a and b.

   (b) $\dfrac{x}{5}\times\dfrac{y}{5}=\dfrac{xy}{\square}$ The ... and denominators have been ... together.

   (c) $\dfrac{d}{5}\div\dfrac{e}{2}=\dfrac{d}{5}\times\dfrac{\square}{e}$ $\dfrac{2}{e}$ is the ... of ... .

3 Now simplify these expressions.

   (a) $\dfrac{5a}{6a}$ (b) $\dfrac{2m+2n}{m+n}$ (c) $\dfrac{2}{x}+\dfrac{1}{y}$ (d) $\dfrac{a}{5}\times\dfrac{4}{b}$

Write a set of instructions to help Miranda work out $\dfrac{1}{x}+\dfrac{1}{y}$.

Exercise

1 Work out the following.

(a) $\frac{2}{3} + \frac{1}{9}$ (b) $\frac{4}{5} - \frac{2}{3}$ (c) $\frac{4}{9} \times \frac{3}{8}$ (d) $\frac{3}{10} \div \frac{6}{14}$

2 Write a set of instructions to explain how you worked out your answers to parts (a) and (d) of question 1. You should use these words in your explanation: *common denominator*, *equivalent*, *reciprocal* and *cancel*.

3 Find the highest common factor for each pair of algebraic expressions.

(a) $5e$ and $5f$ (b) $6a$ and $12a$ (c) $(2x + 2y)$ and 4

(d) a^2b^3 and ab^4 (e) $(6m + 3n)$ and $(8m + 4n)$

4 Write each of these fractions in its lowest form. Your answers to question 3 will help.

(a) $\frac{5e}{5f}$ (b) $\frac{6a}{12a}$ (c) $\frac{2x + 2y}{4}$ (d) $\frac{a^2b^3}{ab^4}$ (e) $\frac{6m + 3n}{8m + 4n}$

5 Write down the reciprocal of each of these fractions or expressions.

(a) $\frac{4}{7}$ (b) $\frac{19}{5}$ (c) $\frac{1}{a}$ (d) $\frac{c}{d}$ (e) $\frac{1}{(a + b)}$ (f) $(x + y)$

6 Simplify each of the following expressions.

(a) $\frac{1}{x} + \frac{5}{y}$ (b) $\frac{2}{x} - \frac{1}{y}$ (c) $\frac{4}{a} \times \frac{3}{b}$ (d) $\frac{4}{a} \div \frac{3}{b}$ (e) $\frac{2a}{9b^2} \times \frac{3b}{4a^3}$

Investigation

Find out how to use the reciprocal key on your calculator.
Use it to check your answers to question 5 parts (a) and (b).

Activity

1 Change $\frac{1}{9}$ to a recurring decimal.

2 Which fraction will give the recurring decimal 0.222…?

The recurring decimal 0.131 313 … can also be written as an exact fraction.

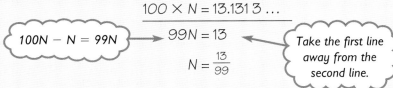

Call the fraction N then $N = 0.131\ 313\ldots$

$100 \times N = 13.131\ 3\ldots$

$100N - N = 99N$ → $99N = 13$ ←   Take the first line away from the second line.

$N = \frac{13}{99}$

? **Why does taking the first line of the calculation away from the second get rid of the decimals?**

3 Use your calculator to check that $\frac{13}{99}$ is equivalent to 0.1313 …. .

4 Use the method above to write 0.777 … as an exact fraction. Your second line should say $10 \times N$. Why?

5 Write each of these recurring decimals as exact fractions.

(a) 0.444 …   (b) 0.333 …   (c) 0.3737 …

(d) 0.4545 …   (e) 0.123 123 …

Working with mixed numbers

George wants to have this picture framed.
He wants to know how much it will cost.

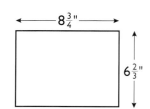

Task

Help George work out the perimeter of his picture: $8\frac{3}{4} + 6\frac{2}{3} + 8\frac{3}{4} + 6\frac{2}{3}$.

1 First add the whole numbers: $8 + 6 + 8 + 6 = ?$

2 Then choose a common denominator and add the fractions: $\frac{3}{4} + \frac{2}{3} + \frac{3}{4} + \frac{2}{3} = ?$

3 Now add your answers to parts 1 and 2. This gives: $28 + \frac{34}{12}$

Write $\frac{34}{12}$ as a mixed number. What does this cancel down to?
What is the perimeter of George's frame?

4 What is the cost of the frame for George's picture?

A length of wood $42\frac{1}{2}$ inches long is used. How much will be left?

5 Work out the whole numbers first: $42 - 30 = ?$

6 You cannot work out $\frac{1}{2} - \frac{5}{6}$ so rewrite this as $11 + \left(1\frac{1}{2} - \frac{5}{6}\right)$
Write $1\frac{1}{2}$ as a top-heavy fraction.

7 Complete the calculation. You must work out $11 + \left(1\frac{1}{2} - \frac{5}{6}\right)$.

Task

George also needs to know the area of his picture. He needs to work out $8\frac{3}{4} \times 6\frac{2}{3}$.

1 Change the mixed numbers to top-heavy fractions for George.

$8\frac{3}{4} \times 6\frac{2}{3} = \square \times \square$ ⬅ *Check to see if you can cancel before multiplying*

2 Complete the calculation and write your answer as a mixed number.

 What is the total cost of the frame and glass for George's picture?

 How could you work out $58\frac{1}{3} \div 6\frac{2}{3}$?
How does this provide a second check for the multiplication?

Exercise

1 Work out the following.

(a) $1\frac{1}{2} + \frac{3}{4}$ (b) $1\frac{1}{2} + 1\frac{3}{4}$ (c) $2\frac{1}{3} + 3\frac{4}{5}$ (d) $4\frac{5}{6} + 3\frac{2}{3}$

2 Work out the following.

(a) $1\frac{1}{2} - \frac{3}{4}$ (b) $3\frac{1}{2} - 1\frac{3}{4}$ (c) $2\frac{3}{4} - 1\frac{2}{5}$ (d) $6\frac{3}{8} - 4\frac{5}{9}$

3 Work out the following.

(a) $1\frac{3}{4} \times \frac{2}{3}$ (b) $2\frac{3}{5} \times 3\frac{1}{3}$ (c) $4\frac{1}{5} \times 1\frac{3}{7}$ (d) $3\frac{4}{9} \times 3\frac{3}{5}$

4 Work out the following.

(a) $1\frac{1}{2} \div \frac{3}{4}$ (b) $1\frac{4}{5} \div 3\frac{3}{5}$ (c) $6\frac{7}{8} \div 2\frac{3}{4}$ (d) $5\frac{1}{3} \div 1\frac{1}{7}$

5 To get to school, John walks $\frac{3}{4}$ mile to the bus stop.

He catches the bus to the station, a distance of $5\frac{1}{2}$ miles.

His train journey is $23\frac{2}{3}$ miles. Finally he walks $\frac{1}{5}$ mile to school.

What is the total length of John's journey to school?

6 Calculate the area of these shapes.

(a) 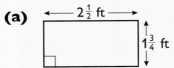   (b)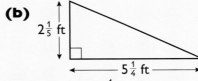

(c) 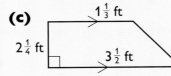   (d)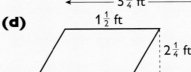

7 (a) Sometimes the mixed number $3\frac{1}{7}$ is used as an approximation of π.
Use this value to work out the circumference and area of these circles.

(i)   (ii)   (iii)

(b) Why do you think the approximation $\pi \approx 3\frac{1}{7}$ has been chosen for these calculations?

Activity

A rug measures 9 feet 6 inches by 12 feet 4 inches.
This is $9\frac{1}{2}$ feet by $12\frac{1}{3}$ feet.

(a) Calculate the area of the rug by

(i) changing the measurements to inches then converting your answer to square feet and square inches

(ii) working with the measurements as fractions.

(b) Compare your methods.

Remember there are 144 square inches in a square foot.

Finishing off

Now that you have finished this chapter you should be able to:

- understand and use the language of fractions
- cancel algebraic fractions
- simplify many algebraic expressions involving fractions
- express recurring decimals as exact fractions
- add, subtract, multiply and divide mixed numbers.

Review exercise

1 Work out the following.

(a) $\frac{2}{3} + \frac{3}{4} + \frac{5}{6}$ (b) $\frac{7}{8} + \frac{4}{5} - \frac{9}{10}$ (c) $\frac{3}{4} \times \frac{2}{3} \times \frac{4}{5}$ (d) $\frac{6}{7} \div \frac{3}{5}$

(e) $1\frac{4}{5} + \frac{3}{4}$ (f) $1\frac{1}{2} + 2\frac{3}{4} + 1\frac{7}{8}$ (g) $2\frac{4}{5} - 1\frac{7}{8}$ (h) $1\frac{5}{9} + 2\frac{5}{6} - 1\frac{2}{3}$

(i) $3\frac{1}{4} \times 1\frac{7}{8}$ (j) $1\frac{4}{5} \times 3\frac{1}{3} \times 2\frac{1}{2}$ (k) $4\frac{1}{5} \div 2\frac{1}{3}$ (l) $3\frac{2}{3} \times 4\frac{1}{2} \div 4\frac{2}{5}$

2 Cancel the following algebraic fractions.

(a) $\frac{4a}{5a}$ (b) $\frac{2a}{6b}$ (c) $\frac{a+b}{3a+3b}$ (d) $\frac{2x}{2x^2}$

3 Simplify these algebraic expressions.

(a) $\frac{1}{d} + \frac{2}{f}$ (b) $\frac{2}{b} - \frac{1}{a}$ (c) $\frac{1}{x} + \frac{1}{2x}$ (d) $\frac{1}{x} - \frac{1}{2x}$

(e) $\frac{2}{a} \times \frac{3}{b}$ (f) $\frac{1}{a} \times \frac{2}{a}$ (g) $\frac{1}{a} \div \frac{1}{b}$ (h) $\frac{a}{b} \div \frac{b}{a}$

Investigation

1 Look at this sequence involving fractions.
  (a) Work out the values of the terms.

$$1 - \frac{1}{2}, \qquad 1 - \left(\frac{1}{2} + \frac{1}{4}\right), \qquad 1 - \left(\frac{1}{2} + \frac{1}{4} + \frac{1}{8}\right) \dots$$

  (b) What is the pattern for the fractions inside the brackets?
  (c) Write down the answer to $1 - \left(\frac{1}{2} + \frac{1}{4} + \dots + \frac{1}{64}\right)$.
  (d) Explain why the sum $\frac{1}{2} + \frac{1}{4} + \frac{1}{8} + \frac{1}{16} + \dots$ is always smaller than 1.
  (e) How close does the sum get to 1? ←

*Mathematicians say that the **limit** of the series $\frac{1}{2} + \frac{1}{4} + \frac{1}{8} + \frac{1}{16} + \dots$ is 1.*

2 **(a)** Does the series $\frac{1}{2} + \frac{1}{3} + \frac{1}{4} + \dots$ ever reach 3?
  (b) Does it ever reach **(i)** 5 **(ii)** 25 **(iii)** 100?
  (c) What is the limit of this series?

3 What is the limit of the series $\frac{1}{10} + \frac{1}{100} + \frac{1}{1000} + \dots$?
  (*Hint*: How is this related to 0.111…?)

Investigation

1 Write 0.9999... as an exact fraction.

2 Does 0.9999 ... = 1?

Investigation

Professor Brown

If $\frac{1}{a} < \frac{1}{b}$ then it is possible to say that $b < a$

Joe decides to test this statement

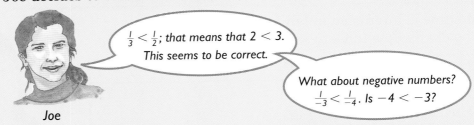

Joe

$\frac{1}{3} < \frac{1}{2}$; that means that $2 < 3$. This seems to be correct.

What about negative numbers? $\frac{1}{-3} < \frac{1}{-4}$. Is $-4 < -3$?

1 Joe decides that Professor Brown is correct. Do you agree?

2 Here are some more statements.
Test them and decide which are always true and which are sometimes true.

(a) If $\dfrac{a}{b} = \dfrac{c}{d}$ then $a \times d = b \times c$.

(b) $\dfrac{a^2 + a}{a} > a$ for all values of a.

(c) $\dfrac{1}{\frac{1}{x}} = x$ for all values of x.

Investigation

Investigate this sequence of continued functions.

$$1 + \cfrac{1}{1 + 1}, \qquad 1 + \cfrac{1}{1 + \cfrac{1}{1 + 1}}, \qquad 1 + \cfrac{1}{1 + \cfrac{1}{1 + \cfrac{1}{1 + 1}}}, \qquad 1 + \cfrac{1}{1 + \cfrac{1}{1 + \cfrac{1}{1 + 1}}}, \dots$$

Work out the value of each term as an ordinary fraction.

What do you notice?

How are your answers connected to the Golden Ratio?

Graphs

Mapping diagrams

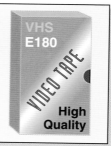

Melanie is interested in buying some video tapes.
She draws up a table to see what the various costs are:

Number of tapes	1	2	3	4	5	6
Cost of tapes (£)	2	4	6	8	10	12
Postage and packing (£)	3	3	3	3	3	3
Total cost (£)	5	7	9	11	13	15

This is the formula $y = 2x + 3$.

Melanie

? **Explain Melanie's formula.**

You can illustrate this formula or relationship with a **mapping diagram**.

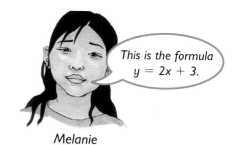

$y = 2x + 3$

This is sometimes written $x \rightarrow 2x + 3$

Not all of the arrowed lines are drawn. Some would go off the scale.

? **How can you change the y line to enable you to draw more arrowed lines?**

Task

Draw mapping diagrams to illustrate the mappings **(a)** $y = 3x + 1$ **(b)** $x \rightarrow 6 + 1.5x$.

Look at this mapping diagram. It arises from $y = x$. Every number maps on to itself. $y = x$ is called the **identity mapping**.

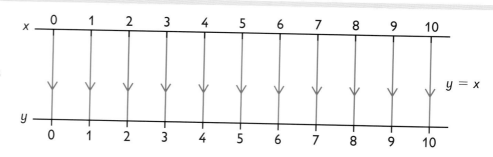

$y = x$

Exercise

1 For each of the following mappings
  (i) construct a table of values taking x from 0 to 6
  (ii) draw the mapping diagram.
  (a) $y = 5 + 2x$ **(b)** $y = 6 - x$ **(c)** $x \rightarrow 3x - 5$ **(d)** $x \rightarrow 2(x - 5)$
  (e) $y = \frac{1}{2}x + 3$ **(f)** $y = \frac{x + 2}{10}$ **(g)** $x \rightarrow \frac{x}{4} + 2$ **(h)** $x \rightarrow \frac{x - 1}{2}$

2 The height, H, metres of a bookcase depends upon
the number of shelves, S, and $H = 0.3S + 0.1$.
  (a) Copy and complete this table.

S	1	2	3	4	5
0.3S		0.6			
0.1		0.1			
H = 0.3S + 0.1		0.7			

  (b) Draw the mapping diagram.
  (c) What is the spacing, in centimetres, between shelves?
  (d) John's bedroom is 2.6 m high. How many shelves can he have?

3 The time, T minutes, to cook a joint of meat of mass
M kilograms is given by the equation $T = 20M + 30$.
  (a) Copy and complete this table.

M	1	1.5	2	2.5	3	3.5
20M		30				
30		30				
T = 20M + 30		60				

  (b) Draw the mapping diagram.
  (c) Mary has $2\frac{1}{2}$ hours for cooking. How much meat can she cook?

4 **(a)** The mapping diagram on the right
  illustrates $y = 2x$.

  Two of the mapping arrows have
  been projected backwards.
  They meet at a point on the
  zero line.
  Draw the mapping diagram and
  extend all the other mapping
  arrows backwards.
  What do you notice?

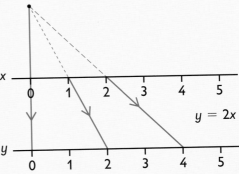

  (b) Heidi says: 'When you project them backwards,
  the mapping lines for equations like $y = 3x$
  and $y = 4x$ always meet at a point on the zero line.'
  Investigate Heidi's statement yourself. Is she right?

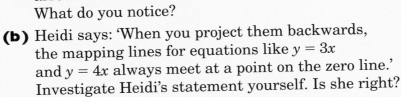

Inverse mappings

Look at these two mappings.

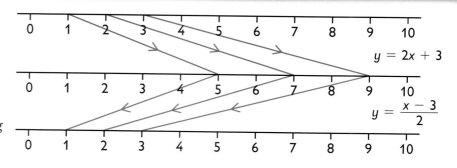

$$y = 2x + 3$$

$$y = \frac{x - 3}{2}$$

The top mapping diagram is the one that Melanie had on page 98.

The lower one is the mapping diagram for $y = \frac{x - 3}{2}$.

 What do you notice about the combined effect of both mappings?

The mapping $y = \frac{x - 3}{2}$ is called

the **inverse mapping** of $y = 2x + 3$.

Saskia

> An operation and its inverse are like a return ticket.

London to Hong Kong

Hong Kong to London

 Why does Saskia say this?

Remember about inverse operations.

Operation	Inverse operation
Add	Subtract
Subtract	Add
Multiply	Divide
Divide	Multiply
Square	Square root
Square root	Square

You can often use a flow diagram to find the formula for an inverse mapping. Look how it is done for $y = 2x + 3$.

$$x \rightarrow \boxed{\times 2} \xrightarrow{2x} \boxed{+3} \rightarrow 2x + 3 \qquad y = 2x + 3$$

> This is the formula of the mapping.

$$\frac{x - 3}{2} \leftarrow \boxed{\div 2} \xleftarrow{x - 3} \boxed{-3} \leftarrow x \qquad y = \frac{x - 3}{2}$$

> This is the formula of the inverse mapping.

 Explain this process.

Task

Find the inverse function of each of the following mappings.

(a) $y = 3x - 1$ **(b)** $y = \frac{x + 1}{3}$ **(c)** $y = 4x - 2$ **(d)** $y = \frac{x + 2}{4}$

Exercise

1 Write down the inverse function of each of the following.

(a) $y = 7x$ **(b)** $y = x + 17$ **(c)** $y = x - 9$ **(d)** $x \to \dfrac{x}{4}$ **(e)** $y = \dfrac{x}{200}$

2 Use the flow diagram method to find the formula for the inverse function of each of the following.

(a) $y = 3x + 13$ **(b)** $y = 6 + 4x$ **(c)** $y = 10 + 7x$

(d) $x \to 2x - 11$ **(e)** $x \to 7 + 10x$

3 Find the formula for the inverse of each of the following mappings.

(a) $y = \frac{1}{2}x + 15$ **(b)** $y = \frac{1}{3}x - 6$ **(c)** $y = 3(x + 4)$

(d) $x \to 5(x - 1)$ **(e)** $x \to \dfrac{4x}{7}$

4 Find the formula for the inverse of each of the following mappings.

(a) $y = \dfrac{x + 6}{2}$ **(b)** $y = \dfrac{x - 5}{3}$ **(c)** $y = 9x + 11$

(d) $y = 0.3x + 10$ **(e)** $y = \frac{4}{5}x$

5 Look at this table.
(a) Write down a formula for y in terms of x.
(b) What is the value of y when x is 50?
(c) Find the formula for x in terms of y.
(d) What is the value of x when y is 78?

x	y
1	8
2	13
3	18
4	23
⋮	⋮

Investigation

(a) Copy and extend this mapping diagram.

The diagram illustrates using the mapping $x \to 8 - x$ twice.

(b) What do each of 1, 2, ..., 8 map on to?

(c) A mapping like this is called a **self-inverse** mapping. Explain this.

$x \to 8 - x$

$x \to 8 - x$

Chi-Hoo says that any mapping of the form $y \to c - x$, where c is a constant, is a self-inverse mapping.

(d) Make another mapping diagram like the one above for the mapping $x \to 5 - x$.

(e) Is Chi-Hoo's statement true for this case?

Plotting graphs

Saskia is interested in this service for her party. She draws up this table.

Number of hours, x	1	2	3	4	5	6
Charge for music (£)	3	6				
Connection charge (£)	2	2				
Total cost, £y	5	8				

 Copy and complete the table.

The total cost, £y, and the number of hours, x, of listening are related by the formula y = 3x + 2.

Saskia

 Explain Saskia's statement.

Another way to illustrate this equation is to plot its graph.

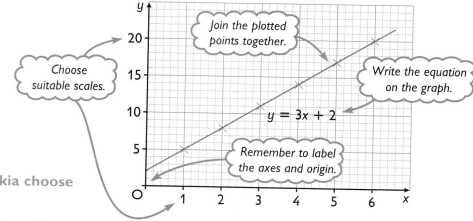

Join the plotted points together.

Choose suitable scales.

Write the equation on the graph.

$y = 3x + 2$

Remember to label the axes and origin.

? **What scale did Saskia choose on each axis?**

? **Do either of the points (1.5, 6.5), (6, 21) lie on this line?**

Task

Take values of x from −3 to 3 and plot the following lines on the same axes.

(a) $y = 2x + 6$ **(b)** $y = 2x - 6$ **(c)** $y = -2x + 6$ **(d)** $y = -2x - 6$

What shape have you drawn?

Exercise

1 (a) Taking x from -2 to 6 and y from -5 to 11, plot the lines $y = 2x - 1$ and $y = 8 - x$ on the same axes.

(b) Write down the co-ordinates of
A where these lines cross.
B where the line $y = 2x - 1$ crosses the y axis.
C where the line $y = 8 - x$ crosses the y axis.

(c) What is the area of triangle ABC?

2 The charge, y pence, to make a mobile phone call is given by $y = 15 + 3x$ where x is the duration of the call in minutes.

(a) Draw the graph of $y = 15 + 3x$ taking x from 0 to 8.

(b) Use your graph to estimate
(i) the cost of a call lasting 2 minutes and 20 seconds.
(ii) the duration of a call costing 35 pence.

3 Plot the graphs of $y = 3x + 1$ and $y = 3x + 7$ on the same axes for values of x from -2 to 6.
How are these graphs related?

4 Plot the graphs of $y = 2x + 3$ and $y = -2x + 3$ on the same axes for values of x from -4 to 4.
How are these graphs related?

5 Using the same scale on both axes and taking both x and y from 0 to 6, plot the lines $y = x + 1$ and $y = 5 - x$.
How are these lines related?

6 Which of the following points do *not* lie on the line $y = 3x - 2$?
(a) $(3, 11)$ (b) $(10, 28)$ (c) $(-5, -13)$ (d) $(t, 3t - 2)$

Investigation

The graph of the equation $2x + 3y = 12$ is a straight line.
A good way to plot lines in this form is to find where the line crosses the x and y axes.
When $x = 0$, $2 \times 0 + 3y = 12$,   so $3y = 12$ and $y = 4$.   This gives you the point $(0, 4)$.
When $y = 0$, $2x + 3 \times 0 = 12$,   so $2x = 12$ and $x = 6$ This gives you the point $(6, 0)$.

Now draw your axes and plot these two points.
Just join them together and there is your line!

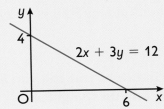

(a) Using this method, plot the graphs
(i) $4x + 5y = 40$ and (ii) $3x + 2y = 18$.

(b) What is the equation of this line?

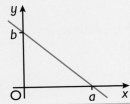

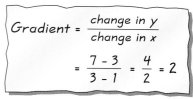

The equation of a line

Aminah draws the graph of $y = 2x + 1$ and works out the gradient.

$$\text{Gradient} = \frac{\text{change in } y}{\text{change in } x}$$

$$= \frac{7 - 3}{3 - 1} = \frac{4}{2} = 2$$

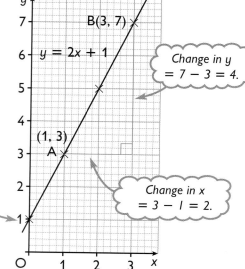

$y = 2x + 1$

B(3, 7)

Change in y
= 7 − 3 = 4.

(1, 3)
A

Change in x
= 3 − 1 = 2.

? **How does Aminah know that A(1, 3) and B(3, 7) lie on this line?**

The gradient of the line $y = 2x + 1$ is 2 and the intercept on the y axis is 1.

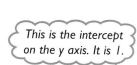

This is the intercept on the y axis. It is 1.

? **What does the gradient of a line tell you? What does the intercept tell you?**

Task

Make up three equations of the form $y = mx + c$. Draw their graphs and use them to test Aminah's theory.

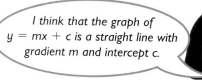

I think that the graph of $y = mx + c$ is a straight line with gradient m and intercept c.

Aminah

? **Do you think she is right?**

? **What are the gradient and intercept of the line $2y = 4x + 5$?**

? **What is the gradient of (a) a horizontal line (b) a vertical line?**

This is the graph of $y = 4 - 2x$.
The gradient of this line is −2.
The gradient of this line is a negative number.

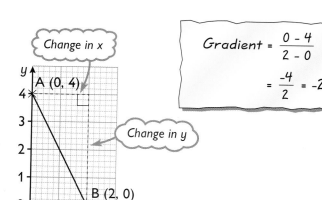

Change in x

A (0, 4)

Change in y

B (2, 0)

$$\text{Gradient} = \frac{0 - 4}{2 - 0}$$

$$= \frac{-4}{2} = -2$$

? **What does this tell you about the line on the graph?**

? **What does a positive gradient tell you about the line?**

Exercise

1 **(a)** Make out a table of values for $y = 3x + 4$, taking values of x from -3 to 5.
  (b) Draw the graph.
  (c) Calculate the gradient of the line.
  (d) Write down the co-ordinates of the intercept.

2 State the gradients and the co-ordinates of the intercepts for these lines.
  (a) $y = 5x - 2$ **(b)** $y = 7 + 8x$ **(c)** $y = 30 - 2x$ **(d)** $y = 3x$
  (e) $y = 6x + 17$ **(f)** $y = 7 - x$ **(g)** $y = 9 - 7x$ **(h)** $x + y = 4$

3 The diagram shows the lines $y = x$, $x = 6$ and $y = 3$.
  Copy the diagram and add the lines
  (a) $y = -x$ **(b)** $y = -1$ **(c)** $x = 0$ **(d)** $x = 3.5$.

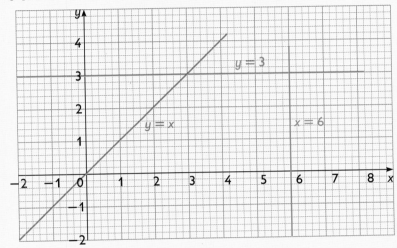

4 **(a)** Plot the line $3x + 4y = 36$ for values of x from 0 to 12.
  (b) What is the gradient?
  (c) What are the co-ordinates of the intercepts on both axes?

5 **(a)** Plot the line which passes through the points $(1, 4)$ and $(3, 10)$.
  (b) Write down the co-ordinates of the intercept.
  (c) Calculate the gradient.
  (d) Hence, write down the equation of the line.

6 Take x from -2 to 6 and draw the line with gradient 0.5 and intercept 4.

7 **(a)** Draw a set of axes from -2 to 6 and draw the quadrilateral with
    these vertices: A$(-2, -2)$, B$(-1, 5)$, C$(3, 6)$ and D$(2, -1)$
  (b) Work out the gradient of each of the lines
      (i) AB **(ii)** BC **(iii)** DC **(iv)** AD.
  (c) Describe the quadrilateral ABCD.

8 **(a)** Draw a set of axes taking x from -1 to 4 and y from -5 to 5 using the
    same scale on both axes.
  (b) Draw the lines $y = \frac{1}{2}x + 1$ and $y = -2x + 3$.
  (c) How are these lines related?

Curves

The graph of a mapping
is not always in a straight line!
Plot the graph of $y = x^2$
and you will see.

Victoria's mother

**Why is it wrong to join the points
with straight lines?**

x	-3	-2	-1	0	1	2	3
$y = x^2$	9	4	1	0	1	4	9

The points are joined
by a smooth curve.

$y = x^2$

Task

Copy and complete this table and
plot the graph of $y = x^3 + 4$.

*An equation like this
is a cubic function.*

x	-3	-2	-1	0	1	2	3
x^3	-27	-8					
$+4$	4	4					
$y = x^3 + 4$	-23	-4					

Task

Victoria says:
'I think you will always get a curve if the equation contains indices,
such as x^2, x^3 or x^4.'
Choose three simple index equations, like $y = x^2 + 7$, $y = x^3 - 5$ or $y = x^4$.
Plot their graphs.
Do you agree with Victoria's statement?

*An equation like this is
a quadratic function.*

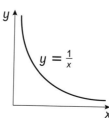

**How do you recognise a cubic function?
What about a quadratic function?**

Look at this graph of $y = \dfrac{1}{x}$ for positive values of x.
It is a curve.

$y = \frac{1}{x}$

The equation $y = \dfrac{1}{x}$ does not appear to contain any indices, but there is a hidden one!
It can be written as $y = x^{-1}$.

Exercise

1 **(a)** Copy and complete this table for $y = x^3$.

x	−3	−2	−1	0	1	2	3
$y = x^3$	−27	−8					

(b) Plot the points and join them with a smooth curve.
(c) This graph has rotational symmetry of order two.
What are the co-ordinates of the centre of rotation?

2 **(a)** Copy and complete this table for $y = 10 - x^2$.

x	−4	−3	−2	−1	0	1	2	3	4
+10	10	10	10						
$-x^2$	−16	−9	−4						
$y = 10 - x^2$	−6	1	6						

(b) Plot the points and join them with a smooth curve.
(c) This graph has a line of symmetry. What is its equation?

3 **(a)** Draw the graph of $y = 3x^2 + 7$, taking x from −1 to 3.
(b) Use your graph to estimate the value of x when $y = 15$.

Investigation

1 **(a)** On the same graph paper draw $y = x^2 + 2x + 5$ and $y = 7$.
Take values of x from −3 to 3.
(b) Use your graph to solve the equation $x^2 + 2x + 5 = 7$.

2 **(a)** Copy and complete this table for $y = (x - 3)^2$.

x	−1	0	1	2	3	4	5	6	7
$x - 3$	−4	−3	−2						
$y = (x - 3)^2$	16	9	4						

(b) Plot the points and join them with a smooth curve.
(c) On the same axes draw the line $y = x$.
(d) Use your graph to solve the equation $(x - 3)^2 = x$.

Investigation

1 On the same graph paper, draw the curves $y = x^2 + 2$ and $y = x^2 + 5$.
Take values of x from −3 to 3.
What do you notice?

2 On the same graph paper, draw the curves $y = 2x^2$ and $y = 3x^2$.
Take values of x from −3 to 3.
What do you notice?

Finishing off

Now that you have finished this chapter you should be able to:

- draw mapping diagrams
- find a formula for an inverse function
- plot the graph of a linear mapping
- recognise the equation of a straight line
- obtain the gradient and intercept of a straight line from its equation
- plot graphs which result in a curve
- tell from the equation whether a graph is a straight line or a curve.

Review exercise

1 Draw a mapping diagram for the mapping $y = x + 3$ for values of x from 0 to 7. What can you say about the arrowed lines in a mapping diagram for a mapping of the form $y = x + c$?

2 Find the inverse function of the following mappings.
  (a) $y = 8x$ **(b)** $y = 4x + 5$ **(c)** $x \to 9 + 2x$ **(d)** $x \to 7 - x$

3 **(a)** Copy and complete this combined mapping diagram for the mappings $y = \frac{x}{2} + 3$ and $y = 2(x - 3)$.

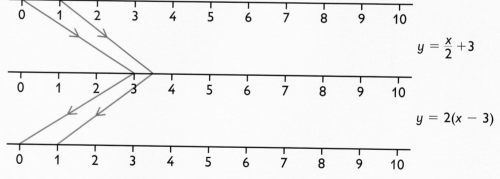

$y = \frac{x}{2} + 3$

$y = 2(x - 3)$

(b) How are the two mappings related?

4 **(a)** Plot the graph of $y = 4x^2 - 7$ for values of x from -2 to 2.
  (b) Use your graph to solve the equation $4x^2 - 7 = 0$.

5 **(a)** Draw the lines $y = x$ and $y = 2x + 1$ on the same axes. Take both x and y from -3 to 5.

  (b) What is the formula for the inverse function of $y = 2x + 1$?

  (c) Add the line $y = \frac{x - 1}{2}$ to your graph.

  (d) What do you notice?

6 **(a)** Complete this table for $y = 5x^2 + 9$.

x	-3	-2	-1	0	1	2	3
$5x^2$	45	20					
9	9	9					
$y = 5x^2 + 9$	54	29					

(b) Plot the points and join them with a smooth curve.
(c) What is the minimum value that y takes?
(d) This curve has a line of symmetry. What is its equation?

7 **(a)** Copy and complete this table and plot the graph of $y = (x - 2)(x - 4)$.

x	0	1	2	3	4	5	6
$x - 2$	-2	-1					
$x - 4$	-4	-3					
$y = (x - 2)(x - 4)$	8	3					

(b) What is the equation of the line of symmetry of this graph?
(c) Label the points A(0, 8), B(2, 0) and C(4, 0) on the curve.
(d) Draw triangle ABC and find its area.

8 **(a)** Copy and complete this table of values for $y = 6x - x^2$.

x	-1	0	1	2	3	4	5	6	7
$6x$	-6	0							
$-x^2$	-1	0							
$y = 6x - x^2$	-7	0							

This is a quadratic function.

(b) Plot the points and join them with a smooth curve.
(c) Use your graph to solve these equations.
   (i) $6x - x^2 = 0$ **(ii)** $6x - x^2 + 3 = 0$

9 **(a)** Copy and complete this table of values for $y = 2x^3 + 10$.

x	-2	-1	0	1	2
$2x^3$	-16	-2			
10	10	10			
$y = 2x^3 + 10$	-6	8			

This is a cubic function.

(b) Plot the points and join them with a smooth curve.
(c) This graph has rotational symmetry of order two.
   What are the co-ordinates of the centre of rotation?

Investigation

Look again at question 5 in this exercise.

I think if you reflect the graph of a function in the line y = x, then you obtain the graph of the inverse.

(a) Choose a few simple functions, such as $y = 3x$, $y = 2x + 3$ and $y = x^2$.

(b) Work out the inverse of each of your functions.

Victoria

(c) Plot each function and its inverse on the same axes. Use the same scales for each graph.

(d) Do you agree or disagree with Victoria's claim?

Using scale drawings

You often use maps and scale drawings.
In many real-life situations it is easier to work with a scaled down copy of the real thing.
This Task involves the site plan for a small housing estate.
Notice that the methods you use also apply to a map or a scale drawing.

Task

Look at this site plan.

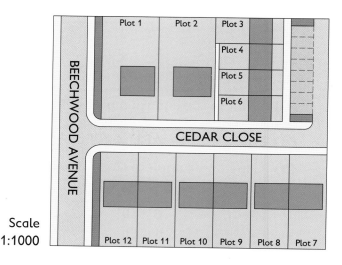

Scale
1:1000

1   How wide is Beechwood Avenue?
2   How many plots are there?
3   The edge of the road on the corner of Cedar Close with Beechwood Avenue is an arc of a circle.
   (a) What is the radius of this circle?   **(b)** How many degrees is the arc?
4   What are the dimensions of plot 3?
5   What percentage of plot 2 is covered by the house?
6   **(a)** Work out the area of plot 9.
   (b) What is the ratio, area representing plot 9 on the site plan : area of plot 9.
7   The local council want the developers to build a playground, covering an area of 1200 m², at the end of Cedar Close. What area would represent this on the site plan?

? The scale of the plan is 1 : 1000. Which questions in the Task involved using
   (a) no scale   **(b)** a scale of 1 : 1000   **(c)** a scale of 1 : 1000²?

? Do you ever need to use a scale to the power 3?

? Do you ever need to do a drawing which is scaled up rather than down?

Exercise

Use a ruler, protractor and compasses as appropriate.

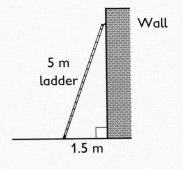

1 A ladder, 5 m long, rests against a wall.
The foot of the ladder is 1.5 m from the wall.
Make a scale drawing and use it to find

   (a) how far the ladder reaches up the wall

   (b) the angle between the ladder and the ground.

2 Abigail is finding the height of a flagpole.
She stands 60 feet from the flagpole.
From this position, the angle of elevation
of the top is 26°.
Make a scale drawing to find the height
of the flagpole.
Give your answer to the nearest foot.

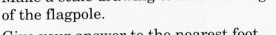

3 Robert is working out how far a
boat is from the foot of a cliff.
The cliff is 50 m high.
The angle of depression of the boat
from the top of the cliff is 19°.
Make a scale drawing and work
out how far the boat is from the cliff.

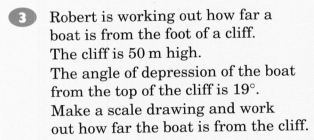

4 Lucy sets out from High Trees.
She walks 5 km south east and then
7 km north east to reach the lagoon at point P.
Make a scale drawing to find

   (a) how far point P is from High Trees

   (b) the bearing of High Trees from P.

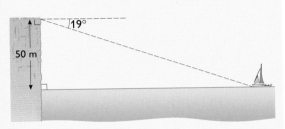

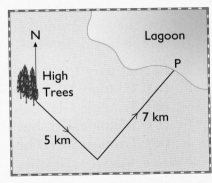

5 Andrew sees a landmark 6.5 kilometres away on a bearing of 310°.
He walks on a bearing of 070°.

   (a) Use a scale drawing to find how far he walks before he is due east
   of the landmark.

   (b) He walks at 5 kilometres per hour. How long, to the nearest five
   minutes, does he take?

6 A plot of land, ABCD, has the shape of a parallelogram.
AB = 100 m, BC = 77 m and $A\hat{B}C = 110°$.
Make a scale drawing of the plot and use it to estimate the area of the land.

Congruency and similarity

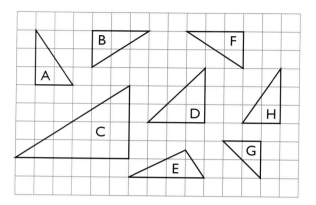

? Which of these triangles are congruent to triangle A?
What is the meaning of *congruent*?

? Which of these triangles is similar to triangle A?
What is the meaning of *similar*?

? Which other pair of triangles are similar?

? Which triangle is neither similar nor congruent to any of the others?

Task

For this Task you will need a ruler, a pair of compasses and a protractor.

Work in small groups and discuss your results together.

1 Each person in the group constructs a triangle ABC with AB = 6 cm, BC = 7 cm and AC = 5.6 cm.
Compare your triangle with the others that your group have drawn.
Are they congruent, similar or are they completely different?

2 Repeat part 1 for each of these triangles.
(a) Triangle DEF has $F\hat{D}E = 40°$, $D\hat{E}F = 65°$ and $E\hat{F}D = 75°$.
(b) Triangle GHI has GH = 6.5 cm, $I\hat{G}H = 67°$ and $G\hat{H}I = 52°$.
(c) Triangle JKL has JK = 7.5 cm, $J\hat{K}L = 30°$ and JL = 5.2 cm.
(d) Triangle MNO has MN = 5.8 cm, NO = 6.4 cm and $M\hat{N}O = 100°$.

? In each triangle in the Task you were given three measurements, either angles or lengths.
Which combinations of measurements produced congruent triangles?
Which produced similar triangles?
What about completely different triangles?

? You are going to draw a triangle ABC.
You are given the size of some of its sides and angles.
You find that the triangle is **uniquely defined**.
What does this mean?

? Can you always construct at least one triangle when you are given three measurements?

The Investigation on the opposite page looks at this question.

Exercise

1 In each case explain whether triangle ABC is uniquely defined.
   (a) AB = 7 cm, BC = 5.2 cm and AC = 8.8 cm.
   (b) AC = 8.3 cm, BC = 9.5 cm and $B\hat{A}C = 49°$.
   (c) AB = 7.3 cm, AC = 8.2 cm and $A\hat{C}B = 27°$.
   (d) AB = 14 cm, $C\hat{A}B = 54°$ and $A\hat{B}C = 71°$.

2 Daniel is 6 km south east of a hostel.
   He walks on a bearing of 250°.
   On how many occasions, if any, will he be 4.5 km from the hostel?

3 **(a)** Make a scale drawing of this triangular
       paddock using a scale of 1 cm to
       represent 10 m.
   (b) Is the paddock uniquely defined?

   A donkey, on a lead, is tied to a post at
   each corner.
   The donkey at A has a lead 20 m long.
   The donkey at B has a lead 20 m long.
   The donkey at C has a lead 30 m long.

   (c) Can every point in the paddock be reached
       by at least one of the three donkeys?
       Use suitable constructions to illustrate your answer.

4 A is a point on the circumference of a circle of
   radius 5 cm.
   Another point, B, must also be on the circumference.
   Construct a diagram showing the possible positions
   (if any) of B when the line AB is of length
   (a) 6 cm   **(b)** 10 cm   **(c)** 12 cm.

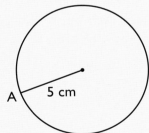

5 Ship A is 7 km due west of Ship B.
   Melanie, on Ship A, reports that there is a lighthouse on a bearing of 125°.
   Bradley, on Ship B, reports that there is a lighthouse on a bearing of 117°.
   Can these lighthouses be the same one or not?

Investigation

Explain whether or not it is possible to construct the following triangles.
(a) Triangle ABC given AB = 6.4 cm, BC = 4.9 cm and AC = 11.7 cm.
(b) Triangle LMN given LM = 9 cm, $N\hat{L}M = 132°$ and $L\hat{M}N = 50°$.
(c) Triangle PQR given PQ = 8 cm, PR = 4 cm and $P\hat{Q}R = 37°$.

Locus

What is the locus of a point P which is always 1 cm from a fixed line of infinite length?

When you are finding a locus, it is helpful to draw a diagram and mark some possible positions of the point.

Sam draws:

? Sam says it is a pair of parallel lines each 1 cm from the given line. Is he right? **What about in three dimensions?**

Task

Alison is designing a right-angled bracket BAC.

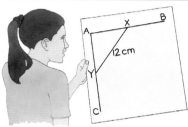

You are going to make a drawing showing the diagonal bar XY in five different positions. These positions are where AX is **1** 2 cm **2** 5 cm **3** 8 cm **4** 10 cm **5** 11.5 cm. You will mark the mid-point, M, of XY in each case. This will help you to work out the locus of M.

(a) Construct a right angle BAC.

(b) (i) Put the compass point at X_1 and draw an arc on AC. Label this point Y_1.
 (ii) Draw X_1Y_1.
 (iii) Bisect X_1Y_1 and label the mid-point M_1.

(c) Repeat step 2 starting from X_2, X_3, X_4 and X_5. (Remember the length of XY doesn't change.)

(d) Describe the locus of M, the mid-point of XY, as the position of the bar varies.

(e) For each mid-point measure the distance AM. How does this enable you to improve your answer to part (d)?

 How can you prove that AM_1 is equal to half the length of the bar X_1Y_1?

Exercise

1 **(a)** A goat is tethered by a chain 5 m long to a point P in a field. Describe the area that the goat can graze.

(b) A bird is tethered by a string 4 m long to a point Q in a farmyard. Describe the region in which the bird can fly.

2 A point P moves so that it is 2 cm from a fixed line of length 6 cm. Describe the locus P in
(a) two dimensions   **(b)** three dimensions.

3 *You must not use a protractor in this question.*

Look at this diagram. Simon is leaving the cave in a rowing boat.

He is keeping as far from the rocks as he can.

Copy the diagram and construct his path to the sea.

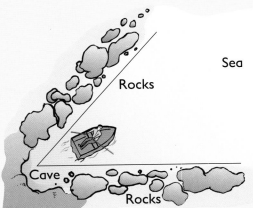

Investigation

A and B are 10 cm apart.
You have to find the locus of the point P so that $A\hat{P}B$ is 90°.

1 Draw a line AB of length 10 cm in the middle of a sheet of A4 paper.
2 Draw lines from A which make angles of 15°, 30° and 45° with AB.
3 Construct a line from B perpendicular to AC. This meets AC at P_1, as in the diagram. Only draw this part of the line otherwise your diagram will get rather crowded!

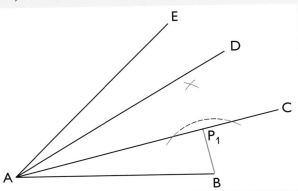

4 Repeat step 3 to obtain points P_2 on AD and P_3 on AE.
5 Construct the perpendicular bisector of AB.
6 Reflect the points P_2 and P_1 in the perpendicular bisector of AB. Label the images P_4 and P_5.

The points P_1, P_2, P_3, P_4 and P_5 are all part of the locus of P.

7 Explain how to find five more points on the locus of P.
8 Describe the locus of P.

Finishing off

Now that you have finished this chapter you should be able to:

- use maps and scale drawings to solve real-life problems
- determine whether given information defines a triangle uniquely
- describe simple loci.

Review exercise

1 Elizabeth is making a table.
The scale drawings show the front and side elevations.

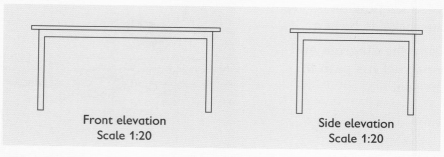

Front elevation
Scale 1:20

Side elevation
Scale 1:20

Work out
(a) the height of the table surface above the ground
(b) the thickness of the table top
(c) the area of the table top.

2 Joshua's map has a scale of 1 : 50 000.
(a) On the map the youth hostel is 5 cm from the train station.
How far, in kilometres, is it from the train station to the youth hostel?
(b) A wood is represented by an area of 3.5 cm².
Find the area of the wood in hectares (1 hectare = 10 000 m²).

3 Two ships leave port one morning.

The Arcturus leaves at 0930 and travels at 24 miles per hour on a bearing of 146°.
The Betelgeuse leaves at 0945 and travels at 28 miles per hour on a bearing of 203°.

Use a scale drawing to work out how far apart the ships are at midday.

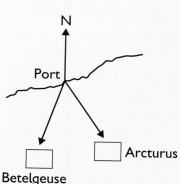

4 Three villages, Deeford, Greenbury and Crossways are located as follows.
Deeford is 6.8 km due north of Crossways.
Greenbury is on a bearing of 042° from Crossways and 5.1 km from Deeford.
  (a) Use a scale drawing to show that there are two possible locations of
  Greenbury based on this information.
  (b) Given that the bearing of Deeford from Greenbury is 339° which of your
  two locations is the correct one?

5 The line segment BC is 8 cm long.
Find the locus of the point A which moves so that
the area of triangle ABC is 16 cm².

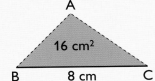

6 Dean is playing a game with his friends.
He has to run from the ash tree to the
beech tree touching the fence on the way.
Copy the diagram and construct his
shortest route.

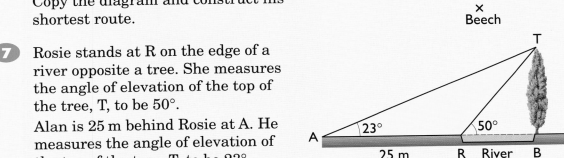

7 Rosie stands at R on the edge of a
river opposite a tree. She measures
the angle of elevation of the top of
the tree, T, to be 50°.
Alan is 25 m behind Rosie at A. He
measures the angle of elevation of
the top of the tree, T, to be 23°.
  (a) Make an accurate scale drawing of triangle ART.
  (b) Extend the line AR. Construct a perpendicular from T to this line.
  (c) Find the height of the tree.
  (d) What is the width of the river?

Investigation

1 (a) Draw an irregular quadrilateral.
  (b) Construct the mid-points of its four sides.
  (c) Join the mid-points.
What quadrilateral have you drawn?

2 What happens if you start with
  (a) a rectangle **(b)** a rhombus **(c)** a parallelogram **(d)** a square **(e)** a kite?

> **Schoolchildren eat an average of 7 packets of crisps per week.**

> **The average family goes on holiday to Spain.**

> **Children get an average of £4.00 pocket money per week.**

 What does the word **average** mean in each of the statements above?

The mean

Joe does not believe the statement about crisps.
He asks some of his friends how many packets of crisps
they ate last week.
Here are his results.

6	2	8	7	5
0	5	1	7	7
2	4	5	6	4

Joe finds the mean.

Total number of packets of crisps = 69
Number of people = 15
Mean number of bags of crisps = $\frac{69}{15}$ = 4·6

 Compare Joe's result with the statement.
Is Joe's result sensible?

Joe decides to do a bigger survey.
This time he asks 80 people.

> Joe works out the total number of packets of crisps here.

No. of packets	Frequency	Total no. of packets
0	8	0 × 8 = 0
1	12	1 × 12 = 12
2	9	2 × 9 = 18
3	4	
4	11	
5	10	
6	8	
7	15	
8	2	
9	1	
Total	80	

Task

Copy Joe's table and finish his working out.
Use this to calculate the mean.

 Do you think the statement at the top of the page is accurate?

Exercise

1   Find the mean of each of the following sets of numbers.
   (a) 6, 8, 2, 4, 10, 6, 1, 3
   (b) 0, 4, 6, 2, 3, 2, 0, 1, 2, 2, 3, 5
   (c) 11, 29, 82, 23, 44, 25, 61, 72, 55, 42

2   James and Joanne are playing ten-pin bowling.

   The number of pins they each
   knock down in each turn is
   as follows.
   (a) Find James's mean score.
   (b) Find Joanne's mean score.
   (c) Who do you think is the better bowler?

James	0	2	1	5	6	8
	4	10	4	6	5	9
Joanne	4	6	8	7	4	5
	5	2	3	6	5	

3   James thinks he can improve his bowling scores if he practises.
   After practising for several days, he records his scores over 100 turns.
   Here are his results.

Score	0	1	2	3	4	5	6	7	8	9	10
Frequency	2	4	2	6	8	7	13	23	21	9	5

   (a) Calculate James's mean score.
   (b) Has he improved?

4   A packet of toffees has the label 'Average contents 12'.
   Stuart is a quality control inspector.
   He checks the number of toffees in 50 packets.
   Here are his results.

Number of toffees	9	10	11	12	13	14	15
Frequency	1	4	9	17	12	5	2

   (a) Find the mean number of toffees in a packet.
   (b) Is the label on the packet accurate?

5   Every week, Ellie's class has a mental maths test.
   There are always 20 questions.
   After half a term (seven weeks), Ellie works out that her mean score is 14.
   These are Ellie's scores in the second
   half of the term (six weeks).

   16 15 12 14 18 16

   (a) What is Ellie's mean score for the second half of the term?
   (b) Did Ellie do better in the first or the second half of term?
   (c) What is Ellie's total score after the first half of the term?
   (d) What is her total score at the end of term?
   (e) What is Ellie's mean score for the whole term?

Median, mode and range

? What does Sam mean when he says he is average height?

Amy gets £3.50 pocket money per week.
She asks six of her friends how much pocket money they get.

I am average height.

> Anna £4.00   Emma £3.00   Jamie £3.25
> Karl £2.50   Zoe £4.00   Steve £3.80

Amy finds the **median** by writing the data in order and finding the middle value.

> Karl   Emma   Jamie   Amy   Steve   Anna   Zoe
> £2.50   £3.00   £3.25   (£3.50) £3.80   £4.00   £4.00

Median = £3.50

? What is the rule for finding the median of an odd number of data values?
What is the rule for finding the median of an even number of data values?

Task

1   Find out the shoe size of everybody in the room, including your teacher.
    (You can use the data you collected for the Task on page 30.)
2   Find the mean and the median shoe size.
3   Are the mean and the median close together?

? Do you think the mean and the median will usually be close together?
What are the advantages and disadvantages of the mean and the median?

The **mode** is the most common data value.

? What is the mode of Amy's data?
Is the mode useful in this case?

The **range** of a set of data is the difference between the greatest and the smallest data values.
The range is not an average.
It tells you how spread out the data are.
In Amy's pocket money survey, the data item with the greatest value is £4.00.
The data item with the smallest value is £2.50.
So the range is £4.00 − £2.50 = £1.50.

Exercise

1 Paul measures the heights of the boys and girls in his class.
Here are his results, in centimetres.

Boys	144	132	165	128	145	139	152
	137	161	150	148	152	141	
Girls	152	158	143	147	161	156	159
	164	143	156	138	148	157	152

(a) Find the median for the boys and the median for the girls.
(b) Find the range for the boys and the range for the girls.
(c) Who are taller, on the whole, the boys or the girls?
(d) Who have heights that are more spread out?

2 The number of times each student in Class 9C had been absent during one
term were as follows.

0	0	2	5	0	0	1	0	3	4	0
28	1	2	0	8	5	2	1	1	0	0
7	0	10	3	8	1	0				

(a) Find the median, the mean and the mode of this data.
(b) Which average do you think best describes the data?
Explain your answer.

3 Claire and Lucy are both
football fans.
They each keep a list of the
number of goals scored in
each match by their
favourite team.

Lucy's team
1 0 0 3 5 2 6 0 0 2 4
3 0 5 4 0 1 1 5 4

Claire's team
2 3 3 2 4 3 1 4 3 2 3
3 2 1 0 2 3 2 4 1 2

(a) Make a frequency table
and draw a bar chart for each team.
(b) Find the median, the mode and the range for each team.
(c) Which team do you think is better at scoring goals?
Explain your answer.

4 Alice, Ben and Charlotte are all different ages.
The range of their ages is 8 years.
The median of their ages is 7.
The mean of their ages is 9.
What are their ages?

Activity

Work with a friend.
1 Ask your friend to estimate 30 seconds, while you measure the
time with a stopwatch. Record how many seconds actually passed.
Do this 5 times.
2 Then ask your friend to time you while you estimate 30 seconds.
3 Use a suitable average to find out who was better at estimating 30 seconds.
4 Use the range to find out whose estimates were more consistent.

Stem-and-leaf diagrams

Mrs Patel teaches French in evening classes.
All her students take the same test.
Here are their results, as percentages.

Mrs Patel wants to
find the median mark.

57	82	73	64	67	41	75
33	88	79	48	66	58	71
60	64	73	52	66	35	22
81	93	52	67	70	45	56
94	51	69	49	55	71	81
56	62	50	73	85	91	47
56	64	67				

 There are 45 data values altogether.
When the data have been put in order,
which is the median?

It would be difficult to write these data in order without making any mistakes.
One way to make this easier is to put the data in a **stem-and-leaf** diagram.
This is like a grouped tally chart,
but you write down the actual data.

Here is the start of Mrs Patel's
stem-and-leaf diagram.

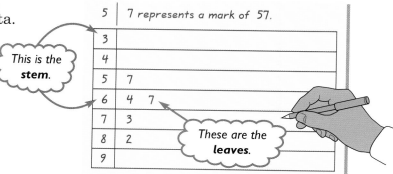

5	7 represents a mark of 57.
3	
4	
5	7
6	4 7
7	3
8	2
9	

This is the **stem**.

These are the **leaves**.

 **Task**

1 Copy the stem-and-leaf diagram above and finish filling it in.
2 Now put the data in each row in order.
   It is now an **ordered** stem-and-leaf diagram.
3 Check your diagram with a friend.

Now you can count along each row to find the median mark.

 What is the median mark?

? What advantage does a stem-and-leaf diagram have over a grouped tally chart?

? What is the mode of Mrs Patel's data?
Is the mode useful in this case?

The most common group is 60–69.
This is called the **modal class**.

? How can you find the modal class from a stem-and-leaf diagram?

Exercise

1 The ages of the people on a package holiday are as follows.

45	38	27	32	30	7	4	28	48	42	15
13	10	56	58	37	24	25	69	34	26	44
32	35	64	51	60	49	46	17	38	62	57
52	53	29	24	27	23	57	45	43	26	37
31	46	52	31							

(a) Copy and complete this stem-and-leaf diagram.

(b) Rewrite the diagram with each row sorted into order.

(c) Use your diagram to find the median age of the people on the holiday.

(d) What is the modal class?

4|5 represents age 45.

```
0
1
2  7
3  8  2  0
4  5
⋮
```

2 Here are the times a group of students took to run 100 metres.

15.5	18.3	21.2	19.4	19.5	16.2	18.1	17.4
16.2	14.1	15.8	18.5	21.7	17.6	16.2	18.3
15.6	17.4	16.8	14.7	20.0	15.1	14.9	16.3
16.1	19.8	14.6	16.1	18.4	17.0	15.5	19.2
18.7	16.4	15.2	18.5	17.1	15.8	18.6	16.4
14.9	16.3	15.7	15.9	17.8			

(a) Copy and complete this stem-and-leaf diagram.

(b) Rewrite the diagram with each row sorted into order.

(c) Use your table to find the median time taken by the students.

(d) What is the modal class?

15|5 represents 15.5 seconds.

```
14
15  5
16
⋮
```

3 40 students took a practice examination.
These are their marks (out of 60) in each of the two papers.

Paper 1

44	52	31	49	35	27	43	56	22	51	44	32	40	17
58	53	26	34	46	31	28	58	14	24	39	50	43	47
55	41	49	33	15	26	37	34	49	46	30	53		

Paper 2

28	35	17	22	59	36	24	6	42	39	44	23	16	29
13	28	37	28	24	48	42	51	31	52	40	43	37	32
19	27	31	29	35	44	38	52	41	38	22	43		

(a) Make an ordered stem-and-leaf diagram for each set of results.

(b) Find the median mark for each paper.

(c) Which paper do you think was harder on the whole?

Estimating the mean of grouped data

Abby is doing a survey on homework.
Here are her results from one of the questions on her questionnaire.
Abby has written the frequency of each response in each box.

> How long did you spend on homework last night?
> (t = no. of hours)
>
> $0 < t \leqslant 1$ `12` $1 < t \leqslant 2$ `11` $2 < t \leqslant 3$ `5`
>
> $3 < t \leqslant 4$ `2` $4 < t$ `0`

Abby wants to find the mean of the amount of homework the people
in her survey did.

 Why can't she find the mean directly?

Abby can make an estimate. She does this by assuming that everybody
who ticked the box labelled $0 < t \leqslant 1$ did 0.5 hours of homework last night, and
everybody who ticked the box labelled $1 < t \leqslant 2$ did 1.5 hours of homework, and so on.
The values 0.5, 1.5 and so on are called the **mid-interval values**.

 **Why is it sensible to use the mid-interval values to make an
estimate of the mean?**

Here are Abby's calculations.

t	Frequency	Mid-interval value	Total number of hours
$0 < t \leqslant 1$	12	0.5	$12 \times 0.5 = 6$
$1 < t \leqslant 2$	11	1.5	$11 \times 1.5 = 16.5$
$2 < t \leqslant 3$	5	2.5	$5 \times 2.5 = 12.5$
$3 < t \leqslant 4$	2	3.5	$2 \times 3.5 = 7$
Totals	30		42

Mean number of hours watched $= \dfrac{42}{30} = 1.4$

Task

1   Measure the height of each person in your class.
    (You can use the data you collected for the Task on page 28.)
2   Choose suitable class intervals and make a grouped tally and frequency chart.
3   Use this to estimate the mean of the data.
4   Also calculate the mean from the original data.

 How accurate is your estimate?

Exercise

1 This frequency table shows the number of days the students in a small village primary school were absent over one term.

Days absent	0–4	5–9	10–14	15–19	20–24	25–29
Frequency	25	38	16	4	2	1

Estimate the mean number of absences per student.

2 Anna is carrying out market research for a chain of fast-food restaurants. She wants to find out at what age groups the company should aim their advertising. Anna carries out a survey of all the customers in a town centre branch of the restaurant between 1 pm and 2 pm on a Monday. Here are her results.

Age group	0-9	10-19	20-29	30-49	50-69	70 or over
Frequency	12	14	35	28	16	2

(a) Anna uses a mid-interval value of 5 for the 0–9 group. Why does she use 5 and not 4.5?

(b) What do you think would be a suitable mid-interval value for the age group 70 or over?

(c) Estimate the mean age of the customers.

(d) Do you think Anna's survey gives a good indication of the age groups of the chain's customers? How could she improve her survey?

3 A consumer organisation wants to compare two different seed composts, A and B. 150 seeds are sown in each compost and after three weeks, the heights of the seedlings which have germinated are measured. This table shows the heights, h mm, of each set of seedlings.

	$0 < h \leqslant 10$	$10 < h \leqslant 20$	$20 < h \leqslant 30$	$30 < h \leqslant 40$	$40 < h \leqslant 50$
A	6	23	45	36	11
B	18	16	20	48	31

(a) Draw a frequency chart for each set of results.

(b) Estimate the mean height of each set of seedlings.

(c) Which compost do you think is better?

4 This frequency chart shows the ages of 60 people taking their driving test.

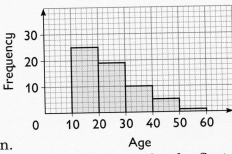

(a) Joshua makes a frequency table and uses it to find an estimate of the mean age of the 60 people. He uses the mid-interval values 15, 25, 35. ... Work out Joshua's estimate of the mean.

(b) Ben says that 15 is not a sensible mid-interval value to use for the first group. Why does Ben say this? What would be a sensible value to use?

(c) Calculate another estimate of the mean age using this new value for the first group. (Use the same mid-interval values for the other groups.)

Estimating the median of grouped data

Abby decides to carry out her homework survey on a larger sample.
She asks 180 people.

$0 < t \leqslant 1$	$1 < t \leqslant 2$	$2 < t \leqslant 3$	$3 < t \leqslant 4$	$4 < t \leqslant 5$	$5 < t \leqslant 6$
61	54	35	22	8	0

Abby wants to find the median amount of homework people did.
As with the mean, she cannot find it exactly as she does not have the actual data.
However, she can make an estimate.

 Which group is the median item in?
What would be a sensible estimate for the median?

Abby can make a better estimate of the median by using a
cumulative frequency graph.
First, she makes a **cumulative frequency table**.

> The cumulative frequency is the total of the frequencies so far.

Hours of homework	Frequency	Cumulative frequency
1 or less	61	61
2 or less	54	115
3 or less	35	150
4 or less	22	172
5 or less	8	180

> Find the cumulative frequency by adding each new frequency to the previous cumulative frequency.

Abby then plots a graph of cumulative
frequency against the number of
hours of homework.

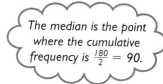
The median is the point where the cumulative frequency is $\frac{180}{2} = 90$.

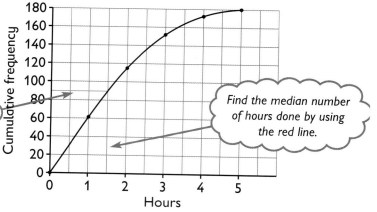
Find the median number of hours done by using the red line.

 Use the graph to find an estimate of the median number of hours of homework done.
Compare this with your earlier estimate.

Task

Use your grouped data on the heights of members of your class.
1 Draw a cumulative frequency graph and use it to estimate the median height.
2 Compare your answer with the true median.

Exercise

1 Justine has done a survey to find out how much time people spend exercising each week.
Here are her results.

Number of minutes, m	Frequency
$0 < m \le 30$	16
$30 < m \le 60$	24
$60 < m \le 90$	45
$90 < m \le 120$	38
$120 < m \le 150$	7
$150 < m \le 180$	2

(a) Make a cumulative frequency table.
(b) Draw a cumulative frequency graph.
(c) Use your graph to estimate the median amount of time spent on exercising during a week.

2 Steve is doing a survey to find out about people who visit the cinema.
He has asked all the people watching an early evening showing of a family film for their age group.
This cumulative frequency graph shows his results.

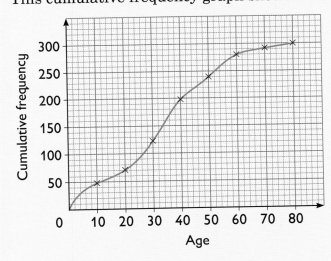

(a) Use the graph to estimate the median age of the people in the cinema.
(b) Use the graph to make a cumulative frequency table.
(c) Draw a frequency chart to show Steve's data.

3 This table shows the results, out of 50 marks, of a test given to 150 students.

Mark	0–10	11–20	21–30	31–40	41–50
Frequency	11	32	54	39	14

(a) Make a cumulative frequency table and draw a cumulative frequency graph.
(b) Use your graph to estimate the median mark.
(c) Students who got less than 15 marks had to take the test again.
Use your graph to estimate how many students had to take the test again.
(d) 20 of the students got a grade A. Use your graph to estimate the mark needed to obtain a grade A.

Estimating spread

Mr Jones is a coach in an athletics club.
He collects this data about the time taken, in seconds, by boys and girls to run 400 metres.

Time	$80 < t \leqslant 90$	$90 < t \leqslant 100$	$100 < t \leqslant 110$	$110 < t \leqslant 120$	$120 < t \leqslant 130$	$130 < t \leqslant 140$
Boys	12	39	31	17	0	1
Girls	5	29	37	18	11	0

He wants to know whether the boys' times or the girls' times are more spread out.

He cannot find the range of the times exactly, as he does not have the original data, but he can estimate the range by using the lowest value in the first class and the highest value in the last class.

Estimated range for boys = $140 - 80 = 60$

Find an estimate for the range of the girls' times.
Is the range a good way of comparing the spread in this case?

The interquartile range

A different way of measuring the spread of data is to use the **interquartile range**.
You can estimate this using a cumulative frequency graph.

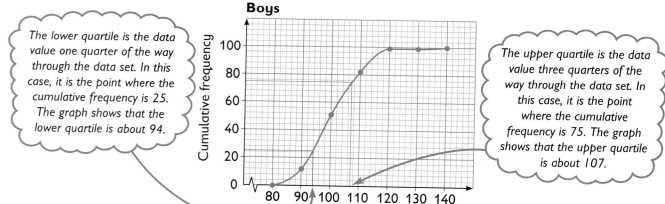

The lower quartile is the data value one quarter of the way through the data set. In this case, it is the point where the cumulative frequency is 25. The graph shows that the lower quartile is about 94.

The upper quartile is the data value three quarters of the way through the data set. In this case, it is the point where the cumulative frequency is 75. The graph shows that the upper quartile is about 107.

Boys

The interquartile range is the difference between the upper quartile and the lower quartile. It is useful because it is not affected by any unusually high or low values. It is the range of the middle half of the data, ignoring the top quarter and the bottom quarter of the data.

Estimated interquartile range for boys = $107 - 94 = 13$

Task

1 Draw a cumulative frequency graph for the girls' times at the top of the page.
2 Find the interquartile range for the girls.

From the interquartile ranges, do you think the boys' times or the girls' times are more spread out?

Exercise

1 The cumulative frequency graph shows the lengths, in seconds, of 200 chart songs.

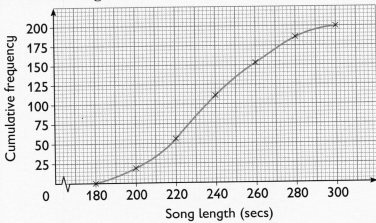

(a) Use the graph to estimate the median length of the songs.
(b) Use the graph to estimate the upper and lower quartiles.
(c) Estimate the interquartile range.

2 The table below shows the weights of all the babies born in a particular hospital one month.

Weight (kg)	Frequency (boys)	Frequency (girls)
$2.8 < w \leqslant 3.0$	2	5
$3.0 < w \leqslant 3.2$	6	9
$3.2 < w \leqslant 3.4$	11	15
$3.4 < w \leqslant 3.6$	17	18
$3.6 < w \leqslant 3.8$	24	17
$3.8 < w \leqslant 4.0$	15	12
$4.0 < w \leqslant 4.2$	8	4
$4.2 < w \leqslant 4.4$	1	0
Total	84	80

(a) Estimate the range of the boys' weights and the range of the girls' weights.
(b) Make a cumulative frequency table for each set of data.
(c) Draw a cumulative frequency graph for each set of data.
(d) Copy this table and use your graphs to complete it.
(e) What conclusions can you draw from your results?

	Boys	Girls
Median		
Upper quartile		
Lower quartile		
Interquartile range		

Finishing off

Now that you have finished this chapter you should be able to:

- find the mean, median and mode of a set of data
- find the range of a set of data
- use a frequency table to find the mean of a large set of data
- use a stem-and-leaf diagram to find the median of a large set of data
- estimate the mean of a set of grouped data
- estimate the median and interquartile range of a set of grouped data using a cumulative frequency graph
- find the modal class of a set of grouped data
- estimate the range of a set of grouped data.

Review exercise

1 55 children take a spelling test. The test has 20 words to spell.
Here are the scores of the boys and the girls.

Boys	15	12	16	19	18	11	14	13
	12	16	14	18	17	15	9	12
	11	16	15	13	17	12	10	8
	13	17	14	12	16			

Girls	14	18	16	11	20	18	5	12
	10	18	19	14	17	13	14	6
	8	20	18	13	19	16	17	16
	14	15						

(a) Find the median mark for the boys.
(b) Find the median mark for the girls.
(c) Find the range for the boys.
(d) Find the range for the girls.
(e) Who did better, the boys or the girls?
(f) Whose results were more consistent?

2 Lisa does a survey about reading.
She asks 50 Year 9 students how many books they have read in the last month.
Here are her results.

Number of books	0	1	2	3	4	5
Frequency	12	16	13	5	3	1

Find the mean number of books read.

3 Hassan is collecting data on the heights of adult men for a clothing company.
He measures the heights of 50 adult men to the nearest centimetre.

168	179	164	182	175	178	185	163	165	181
178	175	172	179	173	162	177	176	184	191
169	170	172	188	180	177	167	156	194	168
174	178	186	174	166	165	159	173	185	162
169	170	176	161	182	173	184	180	174	163

(a) Copy and complete this stem-and-leaf diagram.

```
15*
15
16*  4
16   8
17*
17   9
18*
18
19*
19
```

16 | 8 represents 168 cm.

Numbers from 150 to 154 go in the first row (*), numbers from 155 to 159 in the second row, and so on.

(b) Rewrite the diagram with each row sorted into order.
(c) Use your diagram to find the median height of the men in the survey.
(d) Use your diagram to make a grouped frequency table using the groups 155–159, 160–164, ... 190–194.
(e) What is the modal class?

4 Hassan extends his survey to 200 adult men.
Here are his results.

Height (cm)	Frequency
155–159	9
160–164	22
165–169	31
170–174	39
175–179	48
180–184	29
185–189	17
190–194	5

(a) Estimate the mean height of the men in the survey.
(b) Make a cumulative frequency table.
(c) Draw a cumulative frequency graph.
(d) Use your graph to estimate the median height of the men in the survey.
(e) Use your graph to estimate the interquartile range of the data.

Using indices

Mrs Jones

Class, what is 64×32? I will allow you 2 minutes.

That's easy. 64 is 2^6 and 32 is 2^5 The answer is obviously 2^{11}.

Brian

On page 14 you met the rules $x^a \times x^b = x^{a+b}$ and $x^a \div x^b = x^{a-b}$.

 Explain how Brian has used the multiplication rule. Write $3^6 \div 3^4$ as a power of 3.

 Use the division rule to write $2^3 \div 2^3$ as a power of 2.

Brian says

The value of 2^0 is 1.

 Explain how Brian has found this. What is the value of 10^0? What about x^0?

Task

1 **(a)** Copy and complete $2^3 \div 2^5 = \dfrac{2 \times 2 \times 2}{2 \times 2 \times 2 \dots} = \dfrac{1}{2^?}$

   (b) Use the division rule to explain why $2^3 \div 2^5$ can be written as 2^{-2}.

2 Write the answer $3^2 \div 3^5$ as

   (a) $\dfrac{1}{\text{a power of 3}}$ **(b)** a negative power of 3.

3 The rule can be written as $a^{-n} = \dfrac{1}{a^n}$.

   (a) Write 5^{-2} as $\dfrac{1}{\text{a power of 5}}$ **(b)** Write $\dfrac{1}{8}$ as a negative power of 2.

4 Copy and complete this table of powers of 10.

a	4	3	2	1	0	−1	−2	−3
10^a	10 000						$\dfrac{1}{100}$	
							0.01	

fractions

decimals

Brian says

$25^{\frac{1}{2}}$ means the square root of 25. So it is 5. $x^{\frac{1}{2}} = \sqrt{x}$.

? Use the multiplication rule to work out $x^{\frac{1}{2}} \times x^{\frac{1}{2}}$. What is $\sqrt{x} \times \sqrt{x}$? Is Brian right?

Exercise

1 Write the following in index form.
 (a) $2^7 \times 2^5$ **(b)** $5^4 \times 5^6$ **(c)** $10^{15} \times 10^7$ **(d)** $89^3 \times 89^7$
 (e) $2^5 \div 2^3$ **(f)** $7^6 \div 7^2$ **(g)** $3^4 \div 3^5$ **(h)** $10^5 \div 10^9$

2 Write each of the following as a power of 2.
 (a) 32   **(b)** 4   **(c)** 2   **(d)** $\frac{1}{32}$ **(e)** $\frac{1}{4}$ **(f)** $\frac{1}{2}$

3 Write the answer to each of these calculations in index form.

 For example $27 \times 9 = 3^3 \times 3^2 = 3^5$
 (a) 32×16 **(b)** 81×3 **(c)** 25×125
 (d) 49×343 **(e)** 8×4 (use powers of 2)
 (f) $9 \div 27$ **(g)** $\frac{1}{8} \times 2^3$ **(h)** 25×625

4 **(a)** **(i)** Use the rule for multiplying indices to work out $3^{\frac{1}{2}} \times 3^{\frac{1}{2}}$.
     (ii) Work out $\sqrt{3} \times \sqrt{3}$. What does this tell you about $3^{\frac{1}{2}}$ and $\sqrt{3}$?
 (b) Use your calculator to work out $n^{\frac{1}{2}}$ when
     (i) $n = 16$ **(ii)** $n = 9$ **(iii)** $n = 25$ **(iv)** $n = 100$
 (c) Look carefully at your answers to part (b).
     What is another way to write $n^{\frac{1}{2}}$?

5 Liam has a set of three lights.
 Each light can either be on or off.
 Liam uses these to send coded messages.

 (a) How many distinct patterns of light can Liam create?
 (b) Write your answer as a power of 2.

 Liam makes a new set of lights with four bulbs.
 (c) How many distinct patterns can he make now?
 (d) How many patterns can be made by combining both sets of bulbs?

Investigation

1 Write out all the factors of 30.

2 The prime factorisation of 30 is $2 \times 3 \times 5$.
 Complete this table to show
 how each factor is obtained
 from the prime factorisation.
 A ✓ means the prime factor is
 used, a ✗ means it is not.

Prime factors			Factor
2	**3**	**5**	
✓	✓	✓	30
✓	✓	✗	6
✗	✗	✗	1

3 30 has $2^3 = 8$ factors. Explain how this number can be obtained from the prime
 factorisation. The table should help you.

4 The prime factorisation of 21 is 3×7. How many factors does 21 have?
 Do not attempt to find the factors.

5 55 has the same number of factors as 21. How do you know this?

Writing large and small numbers

Mercury is 57 900 000 kilometres away from the sun.
Large numbers like this can be difficult to read.
This number can also be written as 5.79×10^7.

 Explain why this is the same as 57 900 000.

The probability of winning the lottery jackpot is about
$\frac{1}{14 \text{ million}}$ or 0.000 000 071.

It is easy to miscount the noughts in this number.

The number can also be written as 7.1×10^{-8}.
The numbers 5.79×10^7 and 7.1×10^{-8} are written in **standard form**.

A number in standard form is written as
(a number between 1 and 10) $\times$ (a power of 10)

*This is also known as **standard index form**.*

 32 000 000 people watched the 1966 world cup final.
In standard form this is $3.2 \times$ a power of 10. What power of 10 is needed?

 The radius of a human hair is 0.053 mm.
Write this as $5.3 \times$ a power of 10. Why do you need a negative power?

Ordering in standard form

 Which is smaller 3.46×10^7 or 9.8×10^6?
Why do you only have to look at the powers of 10 to answer this?

 Which is smaller 2.56×10^8 or 3.1×10^8?
Can you just look at the powers of 10 to answer this?

 Explain why 4.2×10^{-5} is smaller than 3×10^{-4}.

Task

1 Write these numbers in order starting with the smallest.
3.4×10^4, 4.56×10^5, 563 000, 7.4×10^6, 820 000

2 These numbers are all smaller than 1.
Write them in order starting with the smallest.
0.000 004, 6.7×10^{-6}, 0.000 002 47, 3.78×10^{-5}, 4×10^{-6}

3 Write down a number that lies between each of these pairs of numbers.
(a) 2.3×10^4 and 2.3×10^6 **(b)** 1.2×10^3 and 2.0×10^3

Beverly says

When a number is written in standard form the power of 10 tells you how big it is.

 Is Beverly right?

Exercise

1 Write these numbers in standard form.
(a) 2000   **(b)** 32 000   **(c)** 1450   **(d)** 36 000 000
(e) 0.067   **(f)** 23   **(g)** 0.003 41   **(h)** 0.000 006

2 Write these as ordinary numbers.
(a) 2×10^3 **(b)** 1.4×10^2 **(c)** 4.56×10^4 **(d)** 5.6×10^5
(e) 3.576×10^{12} **(f)** 2.7×10^{-3} **(g)** 8.32×10^{-7} **(h)** 4.9×10^{-10}

3 Write these numbers in standard form.
(a) China has an estimated population of 1 250 000 000.
(b) It takes 0.000 000 003 3 seconds for light to travel a distance of 1 metre.
(c) The world's longest river, the Nile, is 6 695 km long.
(d) An amoeba is 0.0005 metres across.
(e) Jurassic Park had a UK box office gross of £47 100 000.

4 Write these as ordinary numbers.
(a) A red blood cell has a diameter of 7×10^{-3} mm.
(b) The Gobi desert covers an area of 1.04×10^6 km^2.
(c) The total weight of fish in the world's oceans is estimated at 7.6×10^8 tonnes.
(d) The radius of a uranium atom is 8.68×10^{-15} metres.
(e) The Nou Camp stadium in Barcelona can hold 1.15×10^5 people.

5 Write these sets of numbers in order of size, starting with the smallest.
(a) 2.3×10^4, 32 000, 5.47×10^3, 1.36×10^3, 40 thousand
(b) 4×10^{-5}, 3.7×10^{-4}, 1.8×10^{-4}, 0.000 65, 0.000 03

Investigation

1 How do you know that the number 3.2×10^3 is about 3 thousand?
2 What power of 10 do you use to write 1.2 billion in standard index form?
3 What power of 10 do you use to write $\frac{4}{1000}$ in standard form?

In the number 4.12×10^6, the value of the first digit is 4 million or 4 000 000.

4 The following numbers are written in standard form. Write down the value of the first digit for each number.
(a) 6.1×10^4 **(b)** 3.62×10^4 **(c)** 2.9×10^7 **(d)** 1.352×10^7
(e) 2×10^{-2} **(f)** 1.46×10^{-2} **(g)** 5×10^{-6} **(h)** 3.21×10^{-6}

5 Fill in the missing words below.

The power of 10 in a standard form number is 10^8.
This means that the number is between ... and ... .

Standard form on the calculator

Kevin works out $300\,000 \times 60 \times 60 \times 24 \times 365$.

His calculator shows $\boxed{9.4608 \ E \ 12}$.

Light travels 300 000 km in one second. How far does it go in one year? This is called a light year.

It is showing the number 9.4608×10^{12}.

? **Use your calculator to work it out. Why is the answer in standard form?**

Do the right thing!

Entering a power of 10 on your calculator

1 To enter 3.2×10^5 into your calculator:

This tells your calculator that you are entering a number in standard form.

enter $\boxed{3.2}$, then press the $\boxed{\textbf{EXP}}$ (or $\boxed{\textbf{EE}}$) button. Now press $\boxed{5}$.

Look carefully at the display.
This is how your calculator displays 3.2×10^5.

You only enter the power. ⚠ *Do not enter 10.*

2 Now press $\boxed{=}$.

Your calculator changes 3.2×10^5 to a normal number.
$3.2 \times 10^5 = 320\,000$. Use this to check that you have entered the number correctly.

3 Enter $\boxed{7.45}$ $\boxed{\textbf{EXP}}$ $\boxed{12}$.

? **What is the standard form number that is now displayed on your calculator?**

? **Why does the** $\boxed{=}$ **button not change this number to a normal number?**

Entering a negative power of 10

1 To enter 1.6×10^{-2}

Check which sequence is needed to display a negative number on your calculator.

enter $\boxed{1.6}$ $\boxed{\textbf{EXP}}$ $\boxed{2}$ $\boxed{+/-}$

or $\boxed{1.6}$ $\boxed{\textbf{EXP}}$ $\boxed{+/-}$ $\boxed{2}$

? **Write 1.6×10^{-2} as an ordinary number.**

2 Press $\boxed{=}$ to check that you have entered the number correctly.

3 Enter $\boxed{2.07}$ $\boxed{\textbf{EXP}}$ $\boxed{15}$ $\boxed{+/-}$ (or $\boxed{+/-}$ $\boxed{15}$).

? **Write down the standard form number that is now displayed on your calculator.**

? **Write down the numbers that are shown on these calculator displays.**

$\boxed{2.45 \ E \ 3}$ $\boxed{1.567 \ E \ 23}$ $\boxed{6.5 \ E \ -6}$ $\boxed{7.36 \ E \ -10}$

? **The nearest visible star is 4.35 light years away. How many centimetres is this?**

Exercise

1 For each of these calculator displays
  (i) write the number in standard form
  (ii) enter it in standard form into your calculator.
  (a) | 1.4 E 6 | **(b)** | 2.67 E 15 | **(c)** | 5.4 E -5 | **(d)** | 8.421 E -12 |

2 Use your calculator to work out the following.
  (a) $(7 \times 10^9) \times (6.4 \times 10^8)$ **(b)** $(7 \times 10^9) \div (6.4 \times 10^8)$
  (c) $(7 \times 10^9) + (6.4 \times 10^8)$ **(d)** $(7 \times 10^9) - (6.4 \times 10^8)$

3 The problems below can be solved either by multiplying or by dividing.
  Choose the correct operation for each one and then answer the question.
  (a) A mouse weighs 1.5×10^{-2} kg.
    An owl eats 1000 mice in a year.
    What weight is this?
  (b) The speed of sound is 3.3×10^2 metres
    per second.
    How far does it travel in an hour?
  (c) A grain of salt weighs 2×10^{-5} grams.
    How many grains of salt are there in a 750 gram packet?
  (d) A packet of 500 sheets of paper is 55 mm thick.
    How thick is each sheet of paper?
  (e) The average number of clover leaves in a square metre of lawn is 1.5×10^3.
    Estimate the number of clover leaves in a park with 5×10^4 m² of lawns.

4 Find the difference between these pairs of numbers.
  Give your answer in standard form.
  (a) 1.6×10^4 and 3.1×10^5 **(b)** 4×10^{-2} and 3×10^{-1}
  (c) 6.7×10^5 and 8.2×10^5 **(d)** 4.65×10^{19} and 3.7×10^{20}

Activity

You have calculated a light year as 9.5×10^{12} km.

Our galaxy is approximately a disc. It has a diameter of
about 100 000 light years and a maximum thickness of
about 20 000 light years.

1 Estimate its volume in km³.

The galaxy contains 10^{11} stars. The sun, a typical star, is a sphere of radius 2×10^5 km.

2 Estimate the volume taken up by the stars in the galaxy.

3 Estimate the volume of empty space in the galaxy.

The formula for the volume of a
sphere of radius r is $\frac{4}{3}\pi r^3$.

Finishing off

Now that you have finished this chapter you should be able to:

- use the rules $x^a \times x^b = x^{a+b}$ and $x^a \div x^b = x^{a-b}$ to multiply and divide numbers in index form
- understand the meaning of a negative power (index)
- write and interpret large and small numbers in standard form
- use your calculator to deal with numbers in standard form.

Review exercise

1 Write the answers to the following using index notation.
(a) $2^5 \times 2^{-3}$
(b) $5^{-4} \times 5^{-5}$
(c) $7^4 \div 7^{-2}$
(d) $10^{-5} \div 10^{-3}$

2 Write the following in index form.
(a) 25
(b) $\frac{1}{2}$
(c) 81
(d) $\frac{1}{27}$
(e) $\frac{1}{16}$

3 $144 = 2^4 \times 3^2$ and $18 = 2 \times 3^2$.
(a) Use this information to write the following as products of prime factors.
(i) 144×18
(ii) $144 \div 18$
(b) Simplify the following calculations.
(i) $(2^5 \times 3^4) \times (2^4 \times 3^2)$
(ii) $(5^5 \times 3^4) \div (5^2 \times 3^2)$
(iii) $(7^2 \times 3^5) \div (7^4 \times 3^2)$

4 Write the following in standard form.
(a) 367
(b) 25 000
(c) 0.06
(d) 0.003 76
(e) 0.000 014

5 Write the following as ordinary numbers.
(a) 4×10^2
(b) 6.21×10^5
(c) 3×10^{-1}
(d) 5.32×10^{-9}

6 Write the numbers below in standard form.
(a) 36×10^2
(b) 143×10^4
(c) 0.8×10^4
(d) 45 million
(e) 2.4 billion
(f) 0.6 million
(g) $\frac{2}{1000}$
(h) 25×10^{-5}

7 Choose the larger number from each of these pairs of numbers.
(a) 2.3×10^7 and 1.9×10^8
(b) 3×10^{-4} and 2×10^{-5}
(c) 7.8 billion and 1.9×10^{10}
(d) 4.7×10^{-6} and 0.000 006 7

8 Write a number in standard form that lies between each of the following pairs of numbers.
(a) 4×10^4 and 5×10^6
(b) 1.28×10^6 and 4.6×10^6
(c) 6×10^{-3} and 5.8×10^{-5}
(d) 6.3×10^{-4} and 2.9×10^{-4}

9 Write these as ordinary numbers.
  (a) The length of a human chromosome is 5×10^{-6} m.
  (b) The CN tower in Toronto is 5.53×10^2 m tall.
  (c) The mass of an electron is 9.11×10^{-31} kg.

10 Write these numbers in standard form.
  (a) The distance between the Earth and the Moon is 239 000 miles.
  (b) A £5 note is 0.000 22 m thick.
  (c) Quartz fibre has a diameter of 0.000 001 m.

Investigation

1 **(a)** Explain how to work out 2000×300 in your head.
  (b) Now write your answer in standard form.

2 **(a)** Write the answer to $(2 \times 10^3) \times (3 \times 10^2)$ in standard form.
       Look carefully at your answer.
  (b) How is the number worked out?
  (c) How is the power of 10 worked out?

3 **(a)** Work out
       (i) $(4 \times 10^2) \times (2 \times 10^3)$ **(ii)** $(1.2 \times 10^4) \times (3 \times 10^2)$
  (b) Explain how to multiply numbers when they are written in standard form.

4 Use your method to work out $(3 \times 10^{-2}) \times (4 \times 10^{-3})$.
   Make sure you write your answer in standard form.

Investigation

Amaze your friends
Ask them to choose a number between 1 and 31 and to tell you which blocks it is in.
Now you can tell them the number they have chosen. You just add together the numbers
in the top left corner of each of the chosen blocks.

A	B	C	D	E
1 3 5 7	2 3 6 7	4 5 6 7	8 9 10 11	16 17 18 19
9 11 13 15	10 11 14 15	12 13 14 15	12 13 14 15	20 21 22 23
17 19 21 23	18 19 22 23	20 21 22 23	24 25 26 27	24 25 26 27
25 27 29 31	26 27 30 31	28 29 30 31	28 29 30 31	28 29 30 31

Explain why this trick works.

15 Formulae

Tricia is cooking a turkey.
She reads her cookery book and then writes down the formula.

$$t = 30W + 70$$

Turkey *Roasting times*

Cook at gas mk 7 for 40 minutes. Reduce the heat to gas mk 3 and cook for a further $\frac{1}{2}$ hour per kg. After that turn up the heat to gas mk 6 and cook for a further 30 minutes.

? Explain Tina's formula.
How long will it take to cook a 6 kg turkey?

? Tina cooks a turkey. It takes 400 minutes.
How heavy is it?

? To answer the last question you need to solve the **equation** $400 = 30W + 70$.
What is the difference between an equation and a formula?

Tina was able to write down her formula after reading the recipe.

Shiva's class are doing an experiment with matchsticks.

Here are the first two in a sequence of patterns. Find a formula for the number of matchsticks in pattern n.

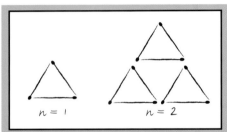

$n = 1$ $n = 2$

It is 3^n.

No, it is $6n - 3$.

It is
$$\frac{3 \times n \times (n + 1)}{2}$$

You need to draw more patterns to decide.

? One of the three formulae given is right. Which one?

? How can you explain why the formula works?

Task

You can use the triangle patterns to make hexagons.

You have to take some matches away.

Use your formula for the triangle patterns to find a new formula for the number of matches in the nth hexagon.

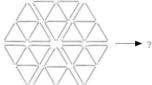

? Why are formulae useful?

Exercise

1 Use the following formulae. In each case give the unit of the answer.

(a) The area of a trapezium, $A = \frac{1}{2}(a + b)h$.
Find A, when $a = 6.4$, $b = 3.2$ and $h = 5$ (in cm).

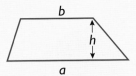

(b) Density, $d = \frac{M}{V}$.
Find d, when $M = 2.6$ (in g) and $V = 2000$ (in cm^3).
(The density of air at standard temperature and pressure.)

(c) Speed, $V = \frac{s}{t}$
Find V, when $s = 1655$ (in m) and $t = 5$ (in s).
(The speed of sound in air at room temperature.)

s is distance travelled
t is time taken

(d) The volume of a sphere, $V = \frac{4}{3}\pi r^3$.

Find V when $r = 6.2035$ cm.

2 The four parts of this question use the four formulae from question 1.
In each case substitute in the formula to form an equation.
Then solve the equation.

(a) The area of a trapezium is 25 cm^2.
The parallel sides are 15 cm and 10 cm long. How far apart are they?

(b) A block of gold of density 19.3 g cm^{-3} has volume 20 cm^3.
What is its mass?

This means grams per cubic centimetre.

(c) A car travels at 40 m s^{-1} for 25 seconds.
How far does it go?

This means metres per second.

(d) The volume of a sphere is 36π cm^3.
What is its radius?

3 The band **SPLURGE** are making a CD.
The recording company says that it will cost £350 plus £1.50 per CD plus a
further £50 per hour in the recording studio.

(a) Write this as a formula using n for the number of CDs, h for the
number of hours and £C for the cost.

(b) The band will spend five hours recording and have 200 CDs made.
How much will this cost?

(c) The band have £725 to spend and need 150 CDs.
How long can they take in the recording studio?

Investigation

The paths of the planets round the Sun are ellipses, not circles.
The formula for the area of an ellipse is $A = \pi ab$
where a and b are the lengths shown in the diagram in km.
For Pluto $a = 5.9 \times 10^9$ and $b = 5.7 \times 10^9$.

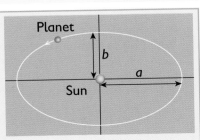

(a) Find the area inside Pluto's orbit.

(b) Compare this with the area of a circle of radius 5.8×10^9 km.

Rearranging formulae

Matt and Sue are working on polygons.

Matt

Sue

The formula for the sum of the internal angles of a ploygon is $S = (n - 2) \times 180°$.

That doesn't help. I want it as $n = \text{something}$.

Matt writes

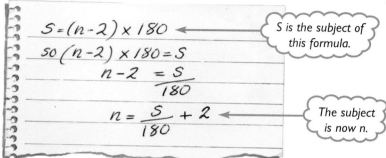

$$S = (n - 2) \times 180$$
$$\text{so } (n - 2) \times 180 = S$$
$$n - 2 = \frac{S}{180}$$
$$n = \frac{S}{180} + 2$$

S is the subject of this formula.

The subject is now n.

? Does Matt's formula work? Test it with the triangle and the quadrilateral.

? Explain each step of Matt's working.

Task

Make x the subject in each of these formulae.

(a) $y = 2x$

(b) $y = \dfrac{x}{2}$

(c) $y = x + 3$

(d) $y = x - 3$

(e) $y = 2x + 3$

(f) $y = \dfrac{x}{2} - 3$

(g) $y = ax + b$

(h) $y = \dfrac{x}{a} - b$

(i) $y = a(x + b)$

(j) $y = \dfrac{x - b}{a}$

Changing subject is just like solving an equation.

Sue

? Is Sue right?

? How do you make x the subject in $y = 6 - x$?

? The formula for the surface area of a sphere is $A = 4\pi r^2$. How do you make r the subject?

? The volume of a sphere of radius r is V, and $r = \sqrt[3]{\dfrac{3V}{4\pi}}$

How do you make V the subject of this formula?

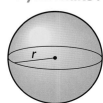

Exercise

1 Make the red letter the subject of each of the following formulae.

(a) $A = 180 - B - C$ (b) $p = 2(l + w)$ (c) $V = IR$

(d) $S = ut$ (e) $c = 2\pi r$ (f) $V = lwh$

(g) $m = \dfrac{(a + b + c + d)}{4}$ (h) $V = \pi r^2 h$ (i) $A = \frac{1}{2}(a + b)h$

(j) $A = l^2$ (k) $A = \pi r^2$ (l) $x = \sqrt[3]{V}$

(m) $t = \sqrt{\dfrac{h}{5}}$ (n) $t = 2\pi\sqrt{\dfrac{l}{g}}$ (o) $h^2 = a^2 + b^2$

What do these formulae refer to?

2 On page 140 you used the formula $t = 30W + 70$ to calculate the time, t minutes, to cook a turkey of weight W kilograms.

(a) Make W the subject of the formula.

(b) You have 2 hours 10 minutes. What weight of turkey can you cook? (Don't forget that t must be in minutes.)

3 The volume of a cylinder is given by $V = \pi r^2 h$.

(a) What is the volume of a cylinder of height 6 cm and radius 2 cm?

(b) Rearrange the formula to make r the subject.

(c) Avonford Canning Company makes cylindrical tins for tomato soup.
Each tin is 11 cm tall and holds 550 cm³ of soup.
What is the radius of a tin?

4 (a) Find x in (i) $\dfrac{1}{x} = \dfrac{1}{2} - \dfrac{1}{3}$ (ii) $\dfrac{1}{x} + \dfrac{1}{7} = \dfrac{1}{4}$.

(b) Make x the subject in $\dfrac{1}{x} + \dfrac{1}{a} = \dfrac{1}{b}$.

Activity   Look at this English sentence.

The cat is chasing the mouse.

The cat is the subject.
You can rewrite the sentence with *the mouse* as the subject.

The mouse is being chased by the cat.

Rewrite these sentences making the words in red the subjects.

(a) Mum is drinking the cup of tea.

(b) The book is being read by Kofi.

(c) Sam is chasing Matt.

(d) Romeo loves Juliet.

Finishing off

Now that you have finished this chapter you should be able to:

- construct a formula from given information
- substitute values into formulae
- rearrange formulae.

Review exercise

1 Rearrange each of these formulae to make the red letter the subject of the formula.

(a) $a = 3p + 6$

(b) $v = u + at$

(c) $y = \dfrac{x}{4} - 3$

(d) $p = 3w + d$

(e) $s = qt + p$

(f) $x = \dfrac{y}{2} + z$

(g) $v^2 = u^2 + 2as$

(h) $v^2 = u^2 + 2as$

(i) $k = \dfrac{T}{5} + 3d$

(j) $A = \frac{1}{4}\pi r^2$

2 An electrician charges £15 per hour plus a callout charge of £25.

(a) Using h to stand for the number of hours he works and £c for the charge, write a formula for the electrician's charge.

(b) (i) Calculate c when $h = 2$.

    (ii) Calculate c when $h = 3\frac{1}{2}$.

(c) Rearrange the formula to make h the subject.

(d) How many hours does he work when his bill comes to

    (i) a total of £115

    (ii) a total of £152.50

    (iii) a total of £122.50.

3 An engineer uses the formula

$$m = \frac{50wh^2}{l}$$

to find the mass, in kg, that a beam can support.

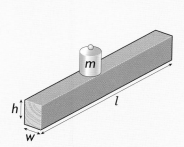

(a) Rearrange the formula to make the subject

    (i) w **(ii)** l **(iii)** h.

(b) Use the correct formula to find the value of

    (i) m when $l = 300$, $h = 15$ and $w = 20$

    (ii) l when $m = 800$, $h = 20$ and $w = 18$

    (iii) w when $m = 640$, $l = 400$ and $h = 16$

    (iv) h when $w = 20$, $l = 350$ and $m = 700$.

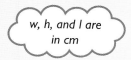

w, h, and l are in cm

4 Jenny lets out holiday flats during the summer.
The formula she uses to work out the charge is

Cost = Rate × Number of weeks + Deposit + £25 per person

The rate is £275 per week and the deposit is £150.
 (a) Write out the formula using £C to stand for the cost, W for the number of weeks and N for the number of people.
 (b) Find the cost when
   (i) four people stay for two weeks   **(ii)** two people stay for three weeks.
 (c) Three people have £1050 to spend. How long can they stay?

5 A Greek mathematician named Hero showed that the area of a triangle, of sides a, b and c, could be calculated by using the formula

$$A = \sqrt{s(s-a)(s-b)(s-c)}$$

where $s = \frac{1}{2}(a + b + c)$.
 (a) Look at these two triangles.
   The side lengths are in cm.
   (i) Use Pythagoras' theorem to check that they are right-angled.
   (ii) Use the formula $A = \frac{1}{2}bh$ to find their areas.
   (iii) Check that Hero's formula gives the same answers.
 (b) Now use Hero's formula to find the areas of these non right-angled triangles.
   (i) $a = 4$ cm, $b = 6$ cm and $c = 8$ cm
   (ii) $a = 6.7$ cm, $b = 9.3$ cm and $c = 12.9$ cm

Investigation

1 Hang a small weight on a piece of string of length l metres.
2 Move the weight to one side and let it go, so that it swings as a pendulum.
3 Copy and complete this table for different values of l.

l	time for 10 swings	time for 1 swing (t)

This means metres per second squared.

The formula that connects l and t is $t = 2\pi \sqrt{\dfrac{l}{g}}$

g stands for the acceleration due to gravity. The value of g is approximately 9.8 m s^{-2}.

4 Check if your values for t are the same as those found from the formula.
5 A pendulum takes 1 second for a complete swing. How long is it?

Robert works out the circumferences of three different circles to the nearest whole number.

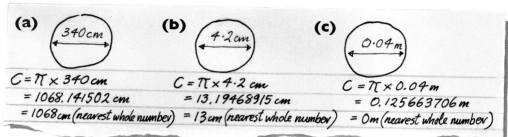

(a) 340 cm
$C = \pi \times 340$ cm
$= 1068.141502$ cm
$= 1068$ cm (nearest whole number)

(b) 4.2 cm
$C = \pi \times 4.2$ cm
$= 13.19468915$ cm
$= 13$ cm (nearest whole number)

(c) 0.04 m
$C = \pi \times 0.04$ m
$= 0.125663706$ m
$= 0$ m (nearest whole number)

? **Why are Robert's answers not all sensible?**

Numbers can be rounded to a number of **significant figures**.
The first (or most) significant figure is printed in red in each of the following numbers.

4136,   12.8,   0.523,   0.000 063 2,   4 200 000

? **Is the first significant figure always the first figure?**

In each of the following numbers the third significant figure is printed in red.

43 216,   0.654 2,   102.3,   0.000563 72,   860.32,   645 100

? **Look carefully at the zeros in the numbers above.**
When are the zeros not counted as significant figures? When are they counted?

Task

Write a sentence like Robert's to describe the
significance of the 6 in each of these numbers.
6103, 32.6, 86.12, 106.2, 0.634, 0.010 61, 1 630 000

> In the number 467, the 6 is
> the second significant figure;
> it is worth 60.

? **In which of the numbers is 6 the third significant figure?**
Does it have the same value in each number?

? **Look at these two examples of rounding.**
Explain what has happened.

679 456 = 679 000 (correct to 3 sig. figs.)
0.0027 = 0.003 (1 s.f.)

! Sometimes you have to be careful. In the next two
examples the answers don't look quite right at first sight.

> The words 'significant figures'
> are sometimes written as
> sig. fig. or s.f.

3.796 = 3.80 (3 s.f.)   **?** **Why has the zero been added?**

4973 = 5000 (2 s.f.)   **?** **Which of the zeros are significant? Why are the others there?**

? **Round Robert's answers for the circles to 3 significant figures.**
Why are your answers more sensible than Robert's?

? **Round 21.25 to 3 significant figures. What convention do you use?**

Exercise

1 Write the following numbers to the nearest 10.
(a) 254 **(b)** 1785 **(c)** 21.35 **(d)** 103.67 **(e)** 458 361

2 Write the following numbers correct to 1 decimal place.
(a) 34.43 **(b)** 12.372 **(c)** 1.567 **(d)** 0.432 **(e)** 0.256

3 Copy the following numbers and underline the second significant figure in each number.
(a) 45.3 **(b)** 127 **(c)** 0.6351 **(d)** 0.000 845 **(e)** 587 210

4 Write each of the numbers in question 3 correct to 2 significant figures.

5 Write the following numbers correct to the number of significant figures in the bracket.
(a) 18.34 (2) **(b)** 41.359 (3) **(c)** 1246 (3) **(d)** 0.015 (1)
(e) 460 (1) **(f)** 4986 (2) **(g)** 0.0204 (2) **(h)** 0.1096 (3)

6 Each of these statements contains a mistake.
(i) Rewrite the statement correctly. **(ii)** Explain the mistake.
(a) 354 = 35 correct to 2 significant figures.
(b) The 4 is the second significant figure in the number 20 453.
(c) 2135 = 2130 correct to 3 significant figures.
(d) 0.4196 = 0.42 correct to 3 significant figures.
(e) 0.23 is exactly the same as 0.230.

7 Peter has rounded 41.45 to 2 significant figures: Explain Peter's mistake.

$41.45 = 41.5$ (3 sf)
$41.5 = 42$ (2 sf)

8 Use your calculator to work out the following.

Give your answers correct to 3 significant figures.
(a) $\sqrt{4.9 + 18.73}$ **(b)** $56 \times (23 + 14)$ **(c)** $\dfrac{3 + 4 + 2.5 + 5.5 + 6 + 1.5}{6}$
(d) $\pi \times 4.7$ **(e)** $\pi \times 3.5^2$ **(f)** $\sqrt{(3.4^2 + 1.6^2)}$

Activity

750 is accurate to 2 significant figures.

1 Explain why 746 = 750 correct to 2 significant figures.
2 What is the smallest number that will give 750 when rounded to 2 significant figures?
3 Write down the largest number that will give 750 when rounded to 2 significant figures.
4 0.30 is accurate to 2 significant figures. Why is the second zero significant?
5 Explain the difference betweeen 0.24 and 0.240.

Range of values

A penny has a diameter of 21 mm
(to the nearest mm).

? How many pennies are needed to
make a line 1 km long?

? How much money can be raised this way?

Avonford High School only raised £465.11.

? Why is this different from the answer
you have just calculated?

Avonford High School
CHARITY DAY
Help us to lay a kilometre of pennies.
Add your spare pennies to the end of the line.

Any measurement is really a range of possible measurements.

20.5 mm ≤ 21mm to the nearest mm < 21.5 mm

Why is the symbol < used here?

The distance of 1 kilometre was measured
to the nearest metre.

999.5 m ≤ 1000 m (= 1 km) < 1000.5 m

1000.5 m = 1 000 500 mm

? The calculation 1 000 500 ÷ 20.5 will give the largest possible number of pennies
in a kilometre of pennies. Work this out.

? Work out the smallest number of pennies.

Task

1 **(a)** Measure the thickness of your *Formula One Maths* textbook.
  (b) How accurate is your measurement?
  (c) Write your measurement as a range of values.
  (d) Work out
    (i) the greatest height of a pile of ten *Formula One Maths* books.
    (ii) the smallest height of a pile of ten *Formula One Maths* books.
  (e) Place ten books in a pile. Measure the height of the pile.
  (f) Compare your measurement with your answers to part (d).

2 **(a)** Measure the height and width of your *Formula One Maths* book.
  (b) Write each measurement as a range of values.
  (c) Work out the smallest and largest possible area for the front cover of your
    textbook.

Errors

The measurement 21 mm (to the nearest mm) can also be written as 21 ± 0.5 mm.
0.5 mm is the largest possible error when measuring to the nearest mm.

? Ben is 167 cm tall. How accurate is this measurement?
What is the largest possible error in this measurement?
Write Ben's height as a range of values.

Exercise

1 Brian weighs 67 kilograms to the nearest kilogram.
  (a) What is the largest possible error when measuring to the nearest kilogram?
  (b) Write down the smallest possible value for Brian's weight.
  (c) Write down the largest possible value for Brian's weight.
  (d) Write Brian's weight as a range of values.

2 Write each of the following measurements as a range of values and state the largest possible error for each measurement.
  (a) 45 cm (to the nearest cm)
  (b) 124 litres (to the nearest litre)
  (c) 58 grams (to the nearest gram) ⟨ *Change 4.1 cm to mm first.* ⟩
  (d) 4.1 cm (to the nearest mm) ←
  (e) 2.5 km (to the nearest metre) ← ⟨ *Change 2.5 km to metres first.* ⟩

3 Explain why it might not be safe for these people to travel together in the lift.

  David 65 kg, Brian 92 kg, Bronwen 74 kg, Pat 54 kg,
  Peter 86 kg, Bruce 95 kg, Ahmed 89 kg, Mark 93 kg

> **Lift**
> **Maximum safe load**
> **8 persons or**
> **650 kg**

4 Mary has 64 CDs. Each CD is 1 cm wide to the nearest mm.
  She needs a shelf to store her CDs.
  How long should she make her shelf?

5 **(a)** Write the following numbers correct to 2 significant figures.
      (i) 1.24 **(ii)** 1.237 **(iii)** 1.1652 **(iv)** 1.151 **(v)** 1.249 **(vi)** 1.249 99
  (b) The number 1.2 is given correct to 2 significant figures.
      Write this as a range of numbers.

6 Write each of the following as a range of numbers.
  (a) 230 (correct to the nearest 10)   **(b)** 5.62 (correct to 2 decimal places)
  (c) 200 (correct to 1 significant figure) **(d)** 200 (2 significant figures)
  (e) 0.4 (correct to 1 significant figure) **(f)** 0.40 (2 significant figures)

7 Explain why 0.40 is not always the same as 0.4.
  Use your answers to question 6 parts (e) and (f) to help you.

8 The measurements of this photograph are accurate to the nearest mm.
  (a) Work out the perimeter and area of the photograph.
  (b) Work out the smallest and largest values for the perimeter and area.
  (c) Write the perimeter and area as ranges of possible values.
  (d) What are the largest possible errors in your answers to part (a)?

←— 6.3 cm —→

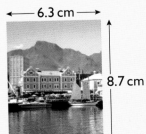

8.7 cm

Estimating answers

Mirna measures the trolley and a tin of dog food.
She calculates

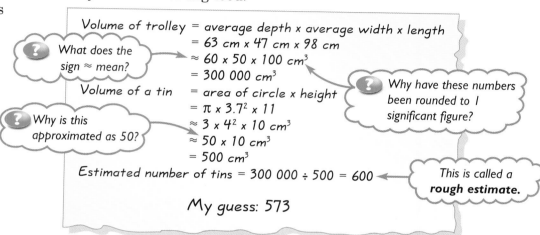

? What does the sign ≈ mean?

Volume of trolley = average depth x average width x length
= 63 cm x 47 cm x 98 cm
≈ 60 x 50 x 100 cm³
= 300 000 cm³

? Why have these numbers been rounded to 1 significant figure?

Volume of a tin = area of circle x height
= π x 3.7² x 11
≈ 3 x 4² x 10 cm³
≈ 50 x 10 cm³
= 500 cm³

? Why is this approximated as 50?

Estimated number of tins = 300 000 ÷ 500 = 600

? This is called a **rough estimate.**

My guess: 573

? Why has Mirna chosen a guess that is less than her estimate?

? Do you think that Mirna's estimate is a good one? Explain your answer.

Task

For each of these calculations

(a) round all the numbers to 1 significant figure

(b) use the rounded values to estimate the answer to the calculation

(c) do the calculation and compare your answer with your estimated value.

1 $47 \times 123 \times 87$ **2** $2.35 \times (8.2 + 1.78)$ **3** $(735 + 209) \div 32$

4 $\pi \times 2.7^2$ **5** $10.7^2 + 4.2^2$ **6** $0.53 \times 1.87 \times 82$

? Describe some situations when you would want to make a rough estimate.

Estimating square roots and cube roots

? What are the first ten square numbers?
What are the first ten cube numbers?
Explain why $\sqrt{39} \approx 6$ and $\sqrt[3]{69} \approx 4$.
Give approximate values for $\sqrt{97}$ and $\sqrt[3]{120}$.

? Estimate the answer to $\sqrt{39 \times 22}$

Exercise

1 Round the numbers in the following calculations to 1 significant figure to find an approximate answer for each one.

(a) 87.9×2.97 **(b)** $487 \div 5.23$ **(c)** $(67 + 32) \div 1.78$

(d) $\sqrt{35}$ **(e)** $\sqrt{119}$ **(f)** $\sqrt[3]{340}$

(g) $\sqrt{(52 \times 1.9)}$ **(h)** $2.8^2 + 7.13^2$ **(i)** $\sqrt{(4^2 + 5^2)}$

(j) $(12.7 + 108) \div 8.7$ **(k)** $\pi \times 4.8$ **(l)** $\pi \times 2.7^2$

2 Use your calculator to evaluate the calculations in question 1.
Give your answers correct to
3 significant figures.

3 Show how you would estimate the
number of sweets in this jar.

4 Select the correct answer for each of these calculations.
Explain your choice.

(a) $385^2 =$ **(i)** $164\,025$ **(ii)** $148\,225$ **(iii)** 1425 **(iv)** 1615

(b) $45.6 \times 8.1 =$ **(i)** 412.36 **(ii)** 305.26 **(iii)** 369.36 **(iv)** 402.46

(c) $3.9^2 + 2.1^2 =$ **(i)** 17.52 **(ii)** 36.3 **(iii)** 12.44 **(iv)** 19.62

(d) $\dfrac{12.3 + 18.9}{7.2} =$ **(i)** 4.33 **(ii)** 6.33 **(iii)** 15.33 **(iv)** 20.33

5 **(a)** Estimate the cost of 2.3 m of cloth at £4.75 per metre.
(b) The distance from London to Aberdeen is 480 miles.
Estimate the journey time at an average speed of 58 miles per hour.
(c) Estimate the number of seconds in a day.
(d) A bicycle wheel makes 456 turns in a distance of 1 kilometre.
Estimate the circumference of the wheel.

Activity

1 Write the prices on this bill correct to the nearest
pound (£).

2 Use your answers to estimate the total of the bill.
Why does this not give a very good estimate?

3 A better way to estimate the bill is
(a) to add up all the complete pounds
(b) then look at the pence and group these in amounts
that are roughly equal to £1.
For example: $79p + 24p \approx £1$
(c) add any complete pounds to the total in part (a).

Use this method to find a better estimate of the total bill.

4 Find some old shopping bills. See how quickly you can estimate the total of each bill.

Corn flakes	£1.49
Milk	£0.79
Bacon	£2.24
Apples	£1.14
Bananas	£1.39
Frozen peas	£2.35
Coffee	£4.49
Chicken	£1.99

Finishing off

Now that you have finished this chapter you should be able to:

- understand significant figures
- round numbers and measurements to decimal places, significant figures or the nearest unit
- understand that any measure is really a range of possible values
- understand that any measurement contains an error
- provide efficient estimates to many calculations.

Review exercise

1 Write the following to the number of significant figures stated in the brackets.

   (a) 12.1 (1)   **(b)** 1.35 (2)   **(c)** 103.6 (3)   **(d)** 999 (1)

   (e) 0.352 (2)   **(f)** 0.6045 (3)   **(g)** 0.0017 (1)   **(h)** 0.509 (2)

2 **(i)** Round the numbers to 1 significant figure to find a rough estimate for each of the following calculations.

   (ii) Use the calculator to give the answer correct to 3 significant figures.

   (a) 4.77×23.8 **(b)** $82.8 \div 14.6$ **(c)** 56.3×0.573 **(d)** $7.65 \div 6.345$

   (e) 675×256 **(f)** $45.6 \div 14.76$ **(g)** 0.32×0.127 **(h)** $537.8 \div 34.7$

   (i) 3.45^2 **(j)** 127.5^2 **(k)** $\sqrt{(34.5 + 18.23)}$ **(l)** $\sqrt{(12 \times 2.34)}$

   (m) $\frac{3.793 \times 0.458}{4.89}$ **(n)** $\frac{43.8 \times 3.62}{4.83}$ **(o)** $\frac{975 \times 0.838}{41.9}$ **(p)** $\frac{57.8}{5.45 \times 11.35}$

3 The 1995 populations of a number of countries are given in the table. The figures are accurate to the nearest 1000. Write each number as a range of possible values.

Country	Population
Australia	18 107 000
Denmark	5 229 000
France	58 286 000
Japan	125 156 000
United Kingdom	58 306 000
United States	263 563 000

4 State the largest possible error for each of these measurements.

   (a) 78 cm (to the nearest cm)   **(b)** 10.4 cm (to the nearest mm)

   (c) 67 °C (to the nearest °C)   **(d)** 18 g (to the nearest g)

5 Give the possible error for each of these measurements.

   (a) The area of the room is 1570 m².

   (b) The winning time for the 100 m swim is 53.48 seconds.

   (c) The average speed for a car journey is 1023.5 km per hour.

   (d) I am 867 450 days old.

Activity

Guess the number of balloons in the car and win the car!

15 cm
25 cm
1.2 m
1.4 m
3.7 m

Estimate the number of balloons needed to fill the car.

Investigation

Freda is confused by the comment written on her homework.

1 Write the measurement 3.7 cm as a range of possible values.

2 Use your answer to question 1 to calculate the largest and smallest values for the circumference of the circle.

3 Write each of your answers to question 2 and Freda's answer correct to 3 significant figures. Do these answers agree?

4 Look carefully at your answers to question 3.
What do you think is a sensible answer to Freda's calculation?

Investigation

1 **(a)** How accurately are the measurements given in this diagram?
   (b) Write down the possible error for each measurement.
   (c) Find the total possible error when the following are calculated.
   The perimeter of **(i)** the rectangle **(ii)** the square.
   The area of **(i)** the rectangle **(ii)** the complete shape.

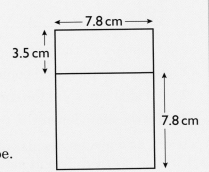

7.8 cm
3.5 cm
7.8 cm

17 Three dimensions

Viewing solids

Kayleigh is the quiz show host for 'The Strongest Link'.
A team are playing a game about solids.

? What is the mathematical name
for the top view of a solid?
Who is right?
Do they need more information?

Kayleigh gives the team more clues.

? What mathematical names are used for
the front view and side view of a solid?

? Do they now have enough information?
What is the solid?

Task

Work in small groups. Look at these plans of different solids.

  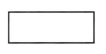 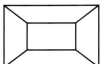

Each person in the group

1 picks one plan and copies it

2 decides one solid for their plan

3 draws sketches of the front and side elevations of their solid.

Then, as a group, discuss each plan.
Find as many different solids as you can for each plan.

Exercise

1 In each case identify the solid shape.

(a) Plan   **(b)** Plan   **(c)** Plan   **(d)** Plan

Front   Side   Front   Side   Front   Side   Front   Side
elevation elevation elevation elevation elevation elevation elevation elevation

2 A cube is sliced to give a square cross-section.
   (a) Copy the diagram.
   (b) Draw the cube again. Show another way of slicing the cube to give a square cross-section.
   (c) Draw the cube once more. Show a way of slicing the cube to give a rectangular cross-section.

Square cross-section

3 Use squared paper to draw the plan and two elevations of these shapes.

(a) 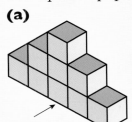   **(b)** 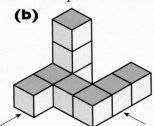   **(c)**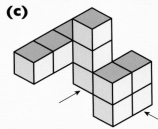

4 Look at these views of a solid.
   (a) Copy them on squared paper.   **(b)** Work out what the solid looks like.
   Draw it on isometric paper.

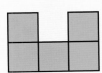   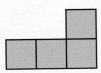   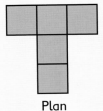

Front elevation   Side elevation   Plan

Investigation

Different-shaped triangles can be made by joining three vertices of a cube.
AEG is a right-angled triangle.

How many different-shaped triangles can be made by joining three vertices of the cube.

How many are there of each type?
What about for a cuboid?

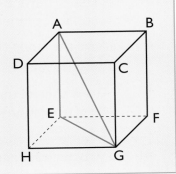

Planes of symmetry

Ruth cooks a meal for her family.
The recipe uses 125 g of butter.
She cuts a 250 g rectangular block of butter in half.

 In how many ways can she do this?

Here are three ways.

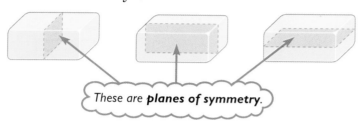

These are **planes of symmetry**.

A plane of symmetry cuts a solid into two equal parts; one part is a reflection of the other.
A plane of symmetry is like a flat mirror.

 Why does a diagonal cut not give a plane of symmetry?
How many planes of symmetry does this cuboid have?

Task

Here is a net of a prism. Its cross-section is a regular hexagon.

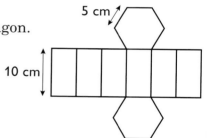

5 cm

10 cm

1 Draw this net and cut it out.
Make sure that the base and top are *regular*
hexagons.

2 Using flaps, stick the sides together to make a
hexagonal prism.
Label the prism as shown in the diagram.

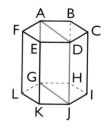

3 Stand your prism on one end.
This regular hexagonal prism has a vertical plane of
symmetry ADJG.

(a) Use a coloured pencil to draw this plane.
(b) Look for other vertical planes of symmetry.
Use different coloured pencils to draw all the
vertical planes of symmetry.

4 Look at the lines that you have drawn on the top face of the prism.
Explain how this can help you find vertical planes of symmetry.

 Does this hexagonal prism have any horizontal planes of symmetry?
If so, how many?

 **Do prisms with regular and irregular cross-sections have the same number of planes
of symmetry? Explain.**

Exercise

1 Look at this square-based pyramid.
Vertex V is directly above the middle
of the base ABCD.

> *E, F, G and H are
> the mid-points of the
> edges of ABCD.*

(a) Sketch and label the pyramid as shown.

(b) The plane of symmetry EGV is shown.
Using letters, identify the three other
vertical planes of symmetry.

(c) Explain why this solid has no
horizontal plane of symmetry.

(d) How many planes of symmetry
does this pyramid have?

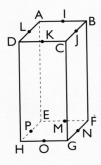

2 Look at this cuboid. It has a square base.

(a) Sketch and label the vertices and mid-points of the
edges of cuboid as shown in the diagram.

(b) Draw a *horizontal* plane of symmetry on your sketch.

(c) Identify all the *vertical* planes of symmetry.

(d) How many planes of symmetry does this cuboid have in all?

3 Name and sketch the solid in each case.

(a) A prism has ten faces and nine planes of symmetry.
Its cross-section is a regular polygon.

(b) A pyramid has seven faces and six planes of symmetry.
Its base is a regular polygon.

4 Look at this regular octahedron.
It is made by joining two equal square-based
pyramids at their square bases.

> *E, F, G and H are
> the mid-points of the
> edges of ABCD.*

(a) Sketch and label the octahedron as shown.

(b) Identify all the vertical and horizontal
planes of symmetry.

(c) Using separate sketches, show
each plane of symmetry.

(d) Describe the shape of the horizontal
plane of symmetry in this octahedron.

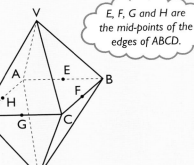

(e) Describe the shape of the vertical planes of symmetry in this octahedron.

(f) Which planes of symmetry have identical shapes?

Investigation

Look at this cube. The red line AB goes through the centre of the
top and bottom of the cube. The cube is rotated 90° clockwise
about this line.
The line AB is called an **axis of rotation**.

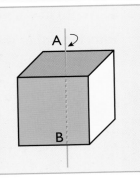

 What colour is the front face of the cube now?
How could you rotate the cube so that the top face is red?
Where would the axis of rotation be?

Cylinders

Do you remember?

Area of a circle = πr^2
Circumference of a circle = $2\pi r$

 What is the approximate value of π? What does r represent?

Volume of a prism = Area of cross-section $\times$ length

A **cylinder** is a prism which has a circle as its cross-section.

 How can you use the information above to find the volume and surface area of a cylinder?

Task

You will need a tin can for this task.
You are going to estimate its volume and surface area.

1 Measure the diameter of the can and so find the area of its top.

2 Measure the height of the can. What is the volume of the can in cm³?

3 Work out the volume of the can in millilitres (ml).
Remember that 1 cm³ is equal to 1 ml.

 Why is your answer only an estimate?

The net of a cylinder looks like this.

 Why is the width of the rectangle equal to the circumference of the circle?

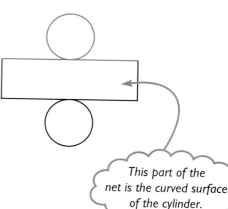

This part of the net is the curved surface of the cylinder.

 Do **not** attempt to cut open your tin can!

4 Use this diagram to help you
   (a) find the area of the curved surface
   (b) find the total surface area of the can.

5 Write down *formulae* for the volume and surface area of a cylinder.
Your formulae will contain π, r and h.

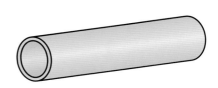 How can you find the volume of metal in a pipe?

Exercise

1 Find the volume and surface area of each of these cylinders.

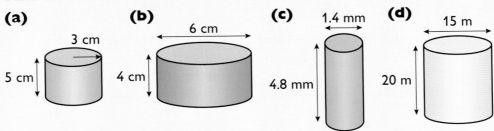

(a) 3 cm, 5 cm

(b) 6 cm, 4 cm

(c) 1.4 mm, 4.8 mm

(d) 15 m, 20 m

2 Samantha has two cylindrical mugs.
The first has diameter 6 cm and
height 8 cm.
The second has diameter 8 cm and
height 4.5 cm.
Both are filled with tea.

Which mug holds the more tea and
by how much?

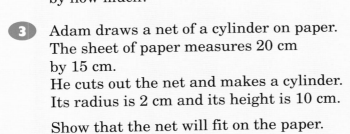

3 Adam draws a net of a cylinder on paper.
The sheet of paper measures 20 cm
by 15 cm.
He cuts out the net and makes a cylinder.
Its radius is 2 cm and its height is 10 cm.

Show that the net will fit on the paper.

4 A cylinder has volume 125π cm^3 and surface area 100π cm^2.
Show that the radius and height can both be 5 cm.

5 Lisa has made a wedding cake with three
cylindrical layers.
The radii are 6 cm, 10 cm and 20 cm.
The heights of the layers are 5 cm, 6 cm and
8 cm respectively.
She covers the top and sides of each layer
with icing.
(a) Find the total volume of the cake.
(b) What is the total area covered with icing?

6 A copper pipe has inner and outer radii of 2.6 cm and 3 cm. It is 500 cm long.
Find the volume of copper in the pipe.

7 A cylindrical candle has diameter 6 cm and height 15 cm.
Carlos packs it into a box in which it just fits.
Find the volume of air in the box.

Finishing off

Now that you have finished this chapter you should:

- know and understand the terms *plan*, *front elevation* and *side elevation*
- understand the term *plane of symmetry*
- be able to find and identify planes of symmetry
- be able to work out the volume and surface area of cylinders
- be able to work out the volume and surface area of prisms involving cylinders.

Review exercise

1 Copy and complete these tables.

Prisms

Shape of cross-section of prism	Number of planes of symmetry
Equilateral triangle	
Square	
Regular pentagon	
Regular hexagon	
Regular heptagon	
Regular octagon	

Pyramids

Shape of base of prism	Number of planes of symmetry
Equilateral triangle	
Square	
Regular pentagon	
Regular hexagon	
Regular heptagon	
Regular octagon	

2 Look at these views of a solid.
Identify the solid and sketch it.

Front elevation   Side elevation   Plan

3 Ann is a scientist.
She pours 50 ml of acid into a measuring cylinder of diameter 3 cm.
Find the depth of the acid in the cylinder.

4 Look at this sweet.
Its inner and outer radii are 5 mm and 1 cm.
Its thickness is 4 mm.
Show that

(a) its volume is 300π mm^3.   **(b)** its surface area is 270π mm^2.

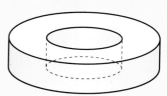

5 Fatima measures rainfall for a geography project.
The rain is collected into a cylindrical tray which has radius 25 cm.
It then flows into a measuring cylinder underneath which has diameter 10 cm.
What is the depth of water in the measuring cylinder after 0.4 cm of rain has fallen into the tray?

6 This is the side view of a wooden skirting board.
It is a rectangle with a quadrant (quarter-circle) on top.
The length of the skirting board is 14m.
The front of the skirting board and its ends are
painted white.

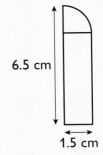

6.5 cm

1.5 cm

(a) Find the volume of wood.

(b) What is the area covered with white paint?

7 This solid is a pyramid. Its base is a regular pentagon.
The mid-points of the edges of ABCDE are F, G, H, I
and J in that order. V is directly above the middle
of the base.

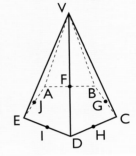

(a) Identify all the vertical planes of symmetry.

(b) Explain why this solid has no horizontal plane
of symmetry.

Activity

Draw the net of a cube and include flaps. Cut it out and make it.

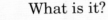

(a) Choose one vertex.
Draw, in red, the diagonals of the three square faces that
meet at that vertex.
These diagonals go to three new vertices.
Draw, also in red, the diagonals from these vertices.
Your red lines are the edges of a new three-dimensional shape.
What is it?

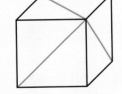

(b) Now choose another vertex, one that you have not used so far.
Repeat the procedure, but this time draw your lines in blue.
Do you get the same three-dimensional shape again?

(c) Mark the points where red and blue lines cross.
These points are the vertices of a regular polyhedron.
What is it?

Investigation

Look at these crystals. Describe their shapes.
Find out about the shape of other crystals.

Shapes of graphs

Michael is a window cleaner and often fills his bucket with clean water.
He wonders how the water level rises with time. He draws this sketch graph.

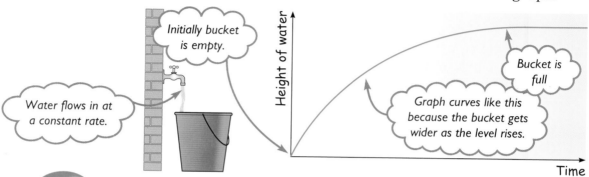

Task

Each of these situations can be represented by a graph.
Match the situations 1 to 5 with the graphs (a) to (e).

1 The temperature, y, of a cup of coffee left to cool in a room, plotted against time, x.

2 The number, y, of litres of fuel left in the tank of a car moving at constant speed, plotted against time, x.

3 The distance, y, travelled by an accelerating racing car, plotted against time, x.

4 The number, y, of harmful bacteria left in the body as it responds to treatment, slowly at first, then more rapidly, plotted against time, x.

5 The number of dollars, y, you can buy for a number of pounds sterling, x.

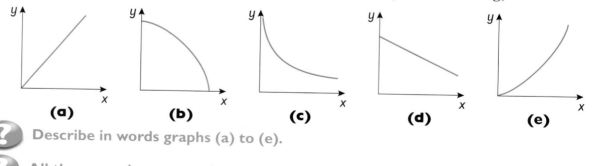

(a)   **(b)**   **(c)**   **(d)**   **(e)**

? Describe in words graphs (a) to (e).

? All these graphs use x and y. Suggest other suitable letters for each one.

Milk is poured into this one-litre carton at a constant rate.
Copy and complete the sketch graph to show how the milk level rises with time as the carton is filled.

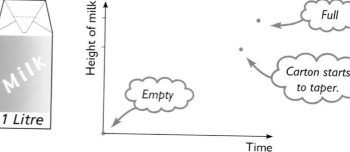

Exercise

1 The table shows the hourly temperature at Palma on a particular day.

Time	9 am	10 am	11 am	12 noon	1 pm	2 pm	3 pm	4 pm
Temperature (°C)	10	15	29	30	35	33	30	28

(a) Show this information as a smooth curve on a graph.
(b) Between which times does the temperature rise most quickly?
(c) Between which times does the temperature fall most rapidly?
(d) Estimate for how long the temperature exceeds 29 °C.

2 The graph shows the income tax paid on
different salaries in a certain country.
(a) Annette's salary is £3900.
How much tax does she pay?
(b) Sam's salary is £12 000.
Estimate how much tax he pays.

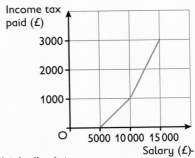

3 The graph shows the height of a basketball
plotted against time after throwing.
(a) What happens to the height of the ball
in the interval when it is rising?
(b) Give a reason for the shape of the
graph when *t* is greater than 3.

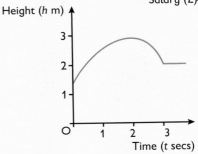

4 Perfume is poured into each of these containers at a constant rate.
Sketch graphs showing how the perfume level rises with time.

(a)　　　　　　**(b)**　　　　　　**(c)**　　　　　　**(d)**

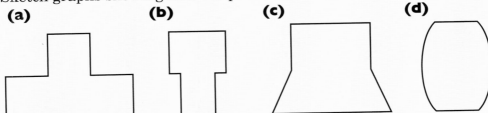

5 The table shows the depth of water in a harbour during one day.

Time of day	0900	1000	1100	1200	1300	1400	1500	1600	1700	1800	1900	2000	2100
Depth (metres)	1.00	1.27	2.00	3.00	4.00	4.73	5.00	4.73	4.00	3.00	2.00	1.27	1.00

(a) Show this information as a smooth curve.
Use 2 cm for one hour and 2 cm for one metre.
(b) Estimate the depth of water at 11.30 am.
(c) A certain ship requires a depth of at least 2.5 m of water to enter the
harbour. Between which times is it safe for the ship to enter?

Working with equations of graphs

John is playing in the Open Golf Championship. He scores a 'hole in one'.
A newspaper publishes this picture.
It shows the position of the ball at one-second intervals, $t = 0, 1, 2, ..., 7$. (t is in seconds.)

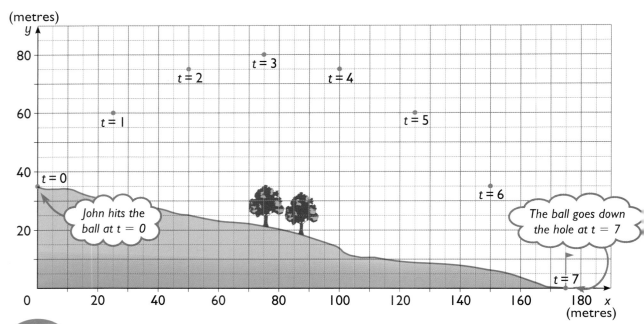

Task

(a) Copy and complete this table with the positions of the golf ball.

t	0	1	2	3	4	5	6	7
x	0							
y	35							

(b) (i) Draw a travel graph for the horizontal motion of the ball (x against t).
(ii) Find a formula for x in terms of t.

(c) (i) Draw a travel graph for the vertical motion of the ball (y against t).
(ii) Show that for all the points on the graph, $y = 35 + 30t - 5t^2$.

 Where does the 35 come from in the last formula?

John's playing partner is Sanjay.

The equation of the flight of Sanjay's golf ball is $y = 35 + \dfrac{5x}{6} - \dfrac{x^2}{180}$.

? **How can you tell whether Sanjay's shot is too short, too long or just right? Compare the two shots.**

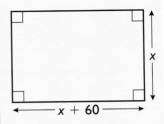

Exercise

1 A company makes rectangular rugs.
The lengths of the rugs are 60 centimetres
greater than their widths.
   (a) Show that the area, A cm^2, of a rug is $A = x^2 + 60x$.
   (b) Copy and complete this table.

Width, x	0	20	40	60	80	100
x^2		400				
$60x$		1200				
$A = x^2 + 60x$		1600				

   (c) Take x from 0 to 100 and plot a graph of A against x.
   (d) Estimate the dimensions of a rug which has an area of 14 000 cm^2.

2 The flight of a football during a free-kick is given by the equation $h = 4t - t^2$,
where h is the height of the ball, in metres, after t seconds.
   (a) Plot a graph of this information for values of t from 0 to 4 seconds.
   (b) What is the greatest height of the ball?
   (c) The ball reaches the goal-line at time $t = 3.8$ seconds.
   The goals are 2 metres high.
   Could this free kick result in a goal?

3 The formula for the volume, V cm^3,
of a square-based pyramid is

   $$V = \tfrac{1}{3}b^2h$$

where b cm is the base length and h cm
is the perpendicular height.

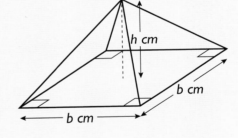

   (a) A toy company produces wooden
   square-based pyramids with
   perpendicular heights of 6 cm.
   Find a formula for V in terms of b.
   (b) Plot the graph of V against b for values of b from 0 to 4 cm.
   (c) Use your graph to estimate the value of b when $V = 20$.
   (d) How could you have found the answer to part (c) without drawing
   a graph?

4 Sue is putting a fence round her vegetable garden.
It is a rectangle of area 60 m^2, x m long
and w m wide
She uses 30 metres of fencing.
She uses an existing wall as one side of the rectangle.

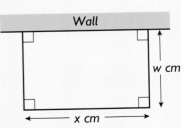

   (a) Show that w cm $= \dfrac{30 - x}{2}$.
   (b) Show also that $120 = 30x - x^2$.
   (c) Draw a suitable graph and use it to estimate x.
   What are the possible dimensions of Sue's vegetable garden?

Finishing off

Now that you have finished this chapter you should be able to:

● interpret a range of straight line (linear) graphs arising from real situations
● interpret a range of curved (non-linear) graphs arising from real situations
● draw and sketch graphs to illustrate real situations
● obtain information from graphs of real situations.

Review exercise

1 For each of the following distance–time (or travel) graphs
    (i) describe the motion
    (ii) state the distances travelled, times and speeds in the different sections.

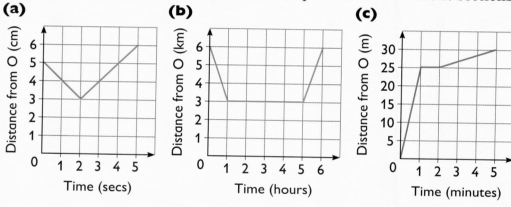

(a)   **(b)**   **(c)**

2 Paul has shares in Avonford Pharmaceuticals. He draws this graph to show the share price at the end of each day for ten working days.

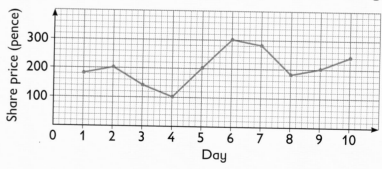

(a) What is the difference between the initial and final prices of a share?
(b) During which periods is the price of a share increasing?
(c) When is the best time to buy shares in Avonford Pharmaceuticals plc?
(d) When is the best time to sell shares?
(e) Paul says 'The share price halved between the end of the second and fourth days.' Is this statement true or false?

3 The table shows Brian's height from birth until the age of 24.

Age	0	4	8	12	16	20	24
Height (cm)	31	92	128	158	174	179	180

(a) Plot these points on a graph and join them with a smooth curve.
(b) In which 4-year interval does he grow most rapidly?
(c) Estimate his height when he was 10 years old.

4 The speed, v m s^{-1}, of a spacecraft t seconds after take-off is given by

$$v = 50 + 60t - t^2 \quad \text{for } 0 < t < 30$$
$$v = 950 \quad \text{for } t \geqslant 30.$$

(a) Copy and complete this table.

t	0	5	10	15	20	25	30	35	40
50	50	50	50				–	–	–
60t	0	300	600				–	–	–
$-t^2$	0	−25	−100				–	–	–
$v = 50 + 60t - t^2$	50	325	550					950	950

(b) Plot a graph of v against t. Use 2 cm for 5 seconds on the horizontal axis and 1 cm for 50 m s^{-1} on the vertical axis.
(c) What is the initial speed of the spacecraft?
(d) What is the maximum speed?
(e) Estimate the time when the velocity reaches 500 m s^{-1}.
(f) Why do you think the velocity remains constant after 30 seconds.

5 Water is pumped out of a swimming pool at a constant rate.
Copy and complete the sketch graphs to show how the volume and height of water remaining in the pool changes with time.

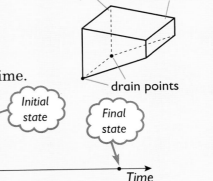

(a) Volume / Time — Initial state, Final state

(b) Height / Time — Initial state, Final state

Activity

Sketch graphs to show how
(a) the value of a sum of money invested in a savings account changes over a number of years
(b) the temperature of a hot drink changes when it is left to cool for a long time
(c) the value of a new car changes over a number of years
(d) the length of this spring varies with the weight, w.
(e) the number of hours of daylight in London changes over the year.
(The shortest day is usually 21st December.)

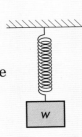

Do you remember?

 What is a **transformation**?

Here are three types of transformation.
The **translation** which maps A to B is 5 in the
x direction and -2 in the y direction.
It is written $\begin{pmatrix} 5 \\ -2 \end{pmatrix}$.

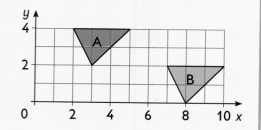

? Describe the translation which maps B to A.

? Here are some **reflections**.

(a) 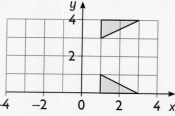 **(b)** 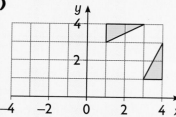 **(c)**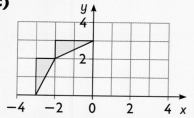

 Where is the mirror line in each of these reflections?

In the diagram the green triangle (the **object**) is **rotated**
to form the orange triangle (the **image**).

? Describe this rotation fully.

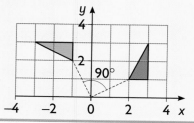

Task

Sally designs tiles. Here are some of her designs.

(a) **(b)** 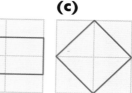 **(c)** **(d)** 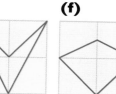 **(e)** **(f)** **(g)**

1 How many different types of tiles does she need to make each of these shapes?
2 How many different types does she need in total?
3 Now suppose Sally is designing glass panes rather than tiles.
How does this affect your answers to parts 1 and 2?

In translations, reflections and rotations the object and image are **congruent**.

 What does congruent mean?

Exercise

1 Describe fully the transformations which map

(a) G → D   (b) B → I
(c) F → I   (d) A → B
(e) D → J   (f) I → A
(g) I → H   (h) F → B
(i) E → I   (j) A → D
(k) E → A   (l) G → C

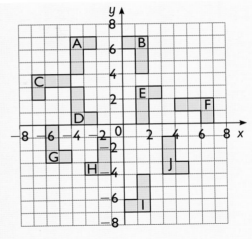

2 Look at the shapes on the grid in question 1.
For each of these transformations find a shape and its image.

Example: Reflection in $x = 1$.
Answer: H → J.

(a) A translation of $\begin{pmatrix} 9 \\ -1 \end{pmatrix}$.

(b) A rotation through 180° about $(-2, 2)$.
(c) A reflection in $y = -x$.
(d) A rotation through 90° anticlockwise about $(-1, 1)$.

3 (a) (i) Draw and label x and y axes from -6 to 6.
(ii) Plot the following points and join them to form a trapezium.
Label it T. $(1, 6), (3, 5), (3, 4), (1, 4)$

(b) (i) Rotate T through 90° clockwise about the origin. Label the image A.
(ii) Translate A by $\begin{pmatrix} -7 \\ 1 \end{pmatrix}$. Label the image F.

(c) (i) Rotate T through 90° clockwise about $(0, 3)$. Label the image B.
(ii) Describe the translation which maps B to F.

In parts (b) and (c) T has been mapped to F by a combination of a rotation followed by a translation.

(d) Describe a third combination of a rotation followed by a translation which maps T to F.
(e) Describe a translation followed by a rotation which maps F to T.

Investigation

1 You are going to create the outline of a four-pointed star.
Find three points on a grid so that
Step 1 joining them with two lines, and
Step 2 carrying out a number of reflections
gives you the outline of your star.
Write down the steps you take.

2 Repeat the investigation to obtain an eight-pointed star.

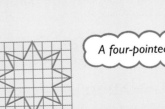

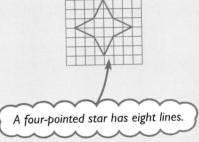

A four-pointed star has eight lines.

Enlargement and similar figures

Look at the diagram. A′B′C′D′ is the image of ABCD under enlargement, centre E, scale factor 3.

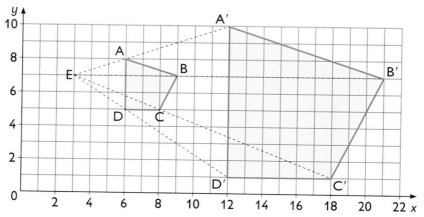

? **What are the values of ratios (a) EB′ : EB (b) EA′ : EA?**

? **What are the values of (a) $\dfrac{D'C'}{DC}$ (b) $\dfrac{A'B'}{AB}$?**

*AB and A′B′ are **corresponding** sides.*

? **What other pairs of corresponding sides can you find? What about corresponding angles?**

You have met 'corresponding angles' with parallel lines. This is a different meaning of the term.

? **How do the angles in ABCD compare with those in A′B′C′D′?**

Shapes ABCD and A′B′C′D′ are **similar**.

- Corresponding sides have the same ratio.
- The ratio of the sides is the same as the scale factor of the enlargement.
- Corresponding angles are equal.

Task

1 Draw *x* and *y* axes from 0 to 16, and the triangle K: (5, 9), (7, 9) and (7, 10).
2 L is the image of K under enlargement centre P(2, 11), scale factor 2. Draw L.
3 M is the image of K under enlargement centre Q(3, 8.5), scale factor 3. Draw M.
4 Triangle M is an enlargement of triangle L.
   (a) Find the co-ordinates of the centre of enlargement, R.
   (b) What is the scale factor?
5 What do you notice about the points P, Q and R?

? **In triangles ABC and PQR, ∠A = ∠P, ∠B = ∠Q and ∠C = ∠R. Are the triangles definitely similar?**

? **In quadrilaterals ABCD and PQRS, ∠A = ∠P, ∠B = ∠Q, ∠C = ∠R and ∠D = ∠S. Are the quadrilaterals definitely similar?**

Exercise

1 Explain whether or not each of the triangles below is similar to triangle T.

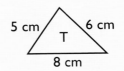

(a)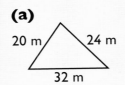

(b)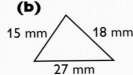

(c)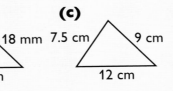

(d)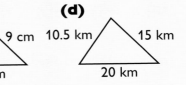

2 On centimetre squared paper draw and label a set of axes from 0 to 15.
  (a) Draw the trapezium with vertices A(12, 7), B(12, 8), C(13, 8) and D(13, 6).
  (b) Using (14, 7) as the centre of enlargement
    (i) enlarge ABCD by scale factor 2 to form A′B′C′D′.
    (ii) enlarge A′B′C′D′ by scale factor 3 to form A″B″C″D″.
  (c) Describe the single transformation which maps ABCD on to A″B″C″D″.

3 The photograph shows a bacterium seen through a microscope and enlarged by a scale factor of 10 500.
  (a) What is the actual length of the bacterium?
  (b) Explain why the area of the bacterium, as seen in the photograph, is not increased 10 500 times.

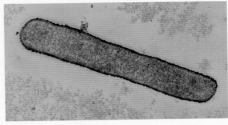

4 Draw an x axis from 0 to 18 and a y axis from 0 to 12.
  (a) Plot the points A(2, 9), B(6, 6) and C(2, 6). Join them to form a triangle.
  (b) Using (1, 8) as the centre of enlargement, enlarge triangle ABC by a scale factor of 3 to form triangle A′B′C′.
  (c) Work out the following ratios.
    (i) Perimeter of triangle ABC : Perimeter of triangle A′B′C′
    (ii) Area of triangle ABC : Area of triangle A′B′C′
  (d) When a shape is enlarged by scale factor k, what is the effect on
    (i) the perimeter   **(ii)** the area?
  (e) A solid is enlarged by scale factor k. What is the effect on its volume?

Investigation

1 Draw an x axis from 0 to 20 and a y axis from 0 to 15.
2 Draw the following triangles.
  (a) A: (1, 8), (4, 14), (7, 8) **(b)** B: (7, 6), (9, 10), (11, 6) **(c)** C: (11, 9), (12, 11), (13, 9).
3 Find the centres of enlargement of **(a)** A from B **(b)** A from C **(c)** B from C.
4 What do you notice about these three centres of enlargement?
5 For any three similar triangles of different size and the same orientation do the centres of enlargement always lie on a straight line?

Fractional enlargements

These triangles are similar.

The scale factor from A to B is 3.

The scale factor from B to A is $\frac{1}{3}$.

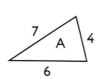 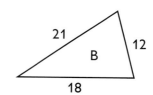

> ### Task
>
> Look at this Christmas card.
> The main picture (picture 1) contains a reduced version of itself (picture 2), which contains a reduced version (picture 3), ...
>
>
>
> **1** **(a)** Measure the height of the trees in pictures 1, 2, 3 and 4.
>
> **(b)** What is the scale factor of the enlargement from picture 1 to picture 2?
> What about picture 2 to picture 3?
> And picture 3 to picture 4?
>
> **(c)** Measure the heights of the snowmen in picture 1.
> Use your answers to part (b) to *calculate* the heights of the snowmen in pictures 2, 3 and 4.
>
> **2** **(a)** Measure the length and height of pictures 1, 2, 3 and 4.
>
> **(b)** Explain why these pictures are similar shapes.
>
> **3** **(a)** The area of picture 1 = k × area of picture 2.
> Work out the value of k.
>
> **(b)** The area of picture 1 = c × area of picture 3.
> Work out the value of c.
>
> **(c)** What fraction of picture 1 is covered by picture n?

Exercise

1 On centimetre squared paper draw a set of axes.
Draw the x axis from 0 to 16 and the y axis from 0 to 8.

   (a) Draw the trapezium whose vertices are

        P(2, 8), Q(8, 8), R(5, 2), S(2, 2).

   (b) Using (14, 5) as the centre

      (i) enlarge PQRS by scale factor $\frac{1}{3}$ and label the image P′Q′R′S′.

      (ii) enlarge PQRS by scale factor $\frac{2}{3}$ and label the image P″Q″R″S″.

   (c) P′Q′R′S′ is an enlargement of P″Q″R″S″.

      (i) What are the co-ordinates of the centre of enlargement?

      (ii) What is the scale factor?

2 The enlargement reading on a photocopier
is 100% when the copy is to be the same
size as the original.
When the reading is 120% then each
length is increased by 20%.

   (a) What enlargement reading do you
use if you want

      (i) each length decreased by 10%

      (ii) a 5 cm line increased to 7 cm

      (iii) a 6 cm line reduced to 4.5 cm?

   (b) A shaded area on the original is 12 cm^2.
What is the shaded area on the copy when the enlargement reading is

      (i) 141%

      (ii) 71%?

   (c) The ratio 141 : 71 is approximately 2 : 1.
Explain why the answers to parts (b)(i) and (b)(ii) are not in the ratio
2 : 1 approximately.

3 A rectangular park is 2.5 km by 1.5 km.
On a map the longer side of the park measures 5 cm.

   (a) (i) What is the scale of the map?

      (ii) On the map how long is the shorter side?

The area of a housing estate is 2 km^2?

   (b) (i) How is area affected by the scale of a map?

      (ii) Work out the area on the map covered by the housing estate.

Investigation

Find a breakfast cereal which is packaged in two different sizes.
(a) Measure the boxes.
(b) (i) Is the larger box similar to the smaller box?
    (ii) If so, are the contents of the boxes in the ratio $1 : n^3$
    where n is the scale factor of enlargement?

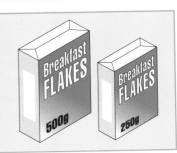

Finishing off

Now that you have finished this chapter you should be able to:

- work with translations, reflections and rotations and combinations of these
- enlarge simple shapes using a centre of enlargement with a positive scale factor greater or less than 1
- know the relationship between corresponding sides, angles and areas in similar figures.

Review exercise

1 Describe fully the following transformations
   (a) E → A
   (b) C → D
   (c) G → C
   (d) J → G
   (e) I → A
   (f) C → J
   (g) F → C
   (h) B → H

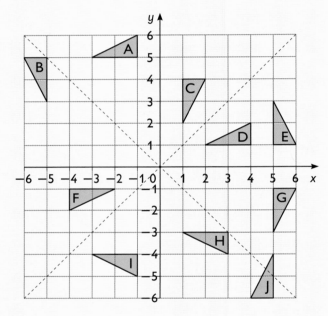

2 Look at the diagram in question 1.
Describe fully the following combinations of mappings.
   (a) A translation and reflection mapping J → F.
   (b) A reflection and translation mapping H → A.

3 Look at the diagram in question 1.
Describe fully the shape formed by the object and the image when
   (a) I is reflected in $y = -4$ **(b)** C is reflected in $y = 2x$.

4 Draw an x axis from -8 to 8 and a y axis from -6 to 6.
   (a) Plot triangle T whose vertices are (2, 4), (2, 6) and (3, 6).
   (b) Rotate triangle T through 90° clockwise about (0, 3) and label the image A.
   (c) Rotate triangle A through 90° clockwise about (1, 0) and label the image B.
   (d) Describe the single transformation which maps triangle T to triangle B.
   (e) The mappings in parts (b) and (c) are applied in reverse order to triangle T.
   How does this affect the outcome?

5 **(a)** Draw and label x and y axes from 0 to 15.
   (b) Plot these points and join them to form the quadrilateral Q.

   (9, 3), (9, 9), (13, 11) and (15, 9)

   (c) Plot the following points and join them to form the quadrilateral Q'.

   (6, 8), (6, 11), (8, 12) and (9, 11)

   (d) Explain why Q' is an enlargement of Q.
   (e) Write down the co-ordinates of the centre of enlargement.
   (f) Work out the scale factor of enlargement.
   (g) Explain how this enlargement affects
      (i) the angles
      (ii) the perimeter
      (iii) the area of the quadrilateral Q.

Activity

You need two sheets of A4 paper, a ruler and a pair of scissors for this Activity.

1 Copy the table and fill in your results as you work through the Activity.

2 Measure the sides of a sheet of A4 paper. Work out the ratio longer side ÷ shorter side.

Size of paper	Longer side	Shorter side	Longer ÷ shorter
A4			
A5			
A6			

3 Cut the second sheet of A4 paper in half (see diagram).
   Each half is an A5 sheet.
   Measure the sides and work out the ratio for an A5 sheet.

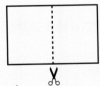

4 Cut the second A5 sheet in half (see diagram) to make two A6 sheets.
   Measure the sides and work out the ratio for an A6 sheet.

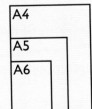

5 What do you notice about the three ratios that you have worked out?

6 Place the three sheets on top of one another.
   What do you notice?

7 The length and width of an A0 sheet are l cm and w cm. When it is cut in half down the middle, two A1 sheets are formed.

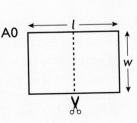

   (a) Write down the length and width of an A1 sheet in terms of l and w.

   (b) A0 and A1 sheets are similar. Show that $\dfrac{l}{w} = \dfrac{w}{0.5l}$

   (c) The area of an A0 sheet is 1 m². Find the values of l and w.

20 Inequalities

The Eiffel Tower is larger Avonford
than Clock Tower

£2   is less   £20
than

? **What are the correct inequality signs to go between these pairs of numbers?**

(a) 2 kg   2100 g   (b) $3\frac{3}{4}$ 3.7   (c) 10^2 1000

(d) 2.6 m   26 cm   (e) 6.25 $6\frac{1}{3}$ (f) 3^2 2^3

There are two other inequality signs that you need to know, they are:

$\geqslant$ and $\leqslant$

? **What do these two signs mean?**

Task

Match these words with the correct inequality sign.

$\leqslant$ $<$ $>$ $\geqslant$

(a) Less than ☐   (b) At least ☐   (c) More than ☐
(d) At most ☐   (e) Less than or equals ☐   (f) More than or equals ☐
(g) No more than ☐   (h) No less than ☐

? **What does the newspaper report actually tell you about the number of people that attended the match?**

The club's director wrote down this inequality

$3500 \leqslant$ number at match < 3800

? **Explain why both inequality signs face the same way.**

Avonford United Win

At Saturday's match police said that at least 3500 fans attended. Football officials said that there were definitely less than 3800 people present.

Task

Look at this report on a riot after the match.
1 Write the information given in the report using inequalities.
   Use f for the number of fans, £d for the cost of the damages, p for the number of police officers and t hours for the time.
2 Give three possible values for each of these variables.
3 Now make up your own report and give it to your partner to write out using inequalities.

Report from the officer on duty to the Chief of Police

- Between 150 and 200 fans rioted after Saturday's match.
- At most £25 000 of damage was caused.
- During the riot there were never less than 120 police officers on duty.
- The rioting lasted over 2 hours but everything was back to normal in under 3 hours.

Exercise

You may find this number line useful for some of these questions.

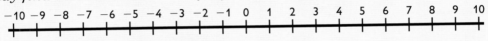

1. Copy the following pairs of values and put the correct inequality sign between them.
   (a) 2 kg ☐ 2500 g
   (b) 1500 mm ☐ 1.4 m
   (c) £6.50 ☐ 600p
   (d) $6\frac{1}{3}$ ☐ 6.3
   (e) 2.6 cm ☐ 30 mm
   (f) 5 years ☐ 100 million seconds

2. Copy the following pairs of numbers and put the correct inequality sign between them.
   (a) 5.6 ☐ 6.5
   (b) −6 ☐ −8
   (c) 0.3 ☐ 0.2
   (d) −2.5 ☐ −5.2
   (e) −2 ☐ 5
   (f) −3 ☐ 7
   (g) 3 ☐ −7
   (h) −3.1 ☐ −3.15
   (i) 10^2 ☐ 30

3. Write the following statements using inequalities.
   (a)
   > **IMPORTANT NOTICE**
   >
   > Max load 12 people

   Let n stand for the number of people in the lift.

   (b)
   > **MANAGER REQUIRED**
   > salary from £22 000 to £25 000
   > depending on experience

   Let £s stand for the manager's salary.

   (c)
   > **SUPER ROLLER COASTER**
   > **Admit one**
   > **All riders must be over 1.65 m tall.**

   Let h m stand for the height of a rider.

   (d)
   > **Young Person Required**
   > to help at Avonford Youth Club
   > Applicant must be over 18 and up to 25 years old

   Let a stand for a person's age.

4. In each part of this question, work out the values of the two expressions. Then replace the ... by one of these signs: $<$, $=$ or $>$.
   (a) $3y + z \ldots 2y - x$
   (i) $x = 2, y = 3, z = -4$
   (ii) $x = 3, y = -2, z = 4$
   (iii) $x = -1, y = 0, z = -2$
   (b) $x^2 \ldots 2yz$
   (i) $x = 2, y = 3, z = 1$
   (ii) $x = -4, y = 3, z = 5$
   (iii) $x = -1, y = 0, z = -2$

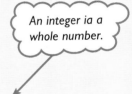

An integer ia a whole number.

5. For each of the following expressions, list all the possible integer values.
   (a) $2 < x < 10$
   (b) $3 \leqslant x \leqslant 8$
   (c) $0 < x < 9$
   (d) $-5 < x \leqslant 1$
   (e) $-9 \leqslant x \leqslant -4$
   (f) $-1 < x < 1$

Inequalities on the number line

The information given about the roller
coaster can be written as

$$1.65\text{ m} \leqslant \text{height} < 2.2\text{ m}$$

ROLLER COASTER
Minimum height:
1.65 m
Low tunnel!
You MUST be
under **2.2 m**

? Can you write down all the possible
heights for people allowed to ride on
the roller coaster?

*The filled in circle shows that
1.65 m is included.*

*The heavy line shows
all the possible values.*

height $\geqslant 1.65$ m

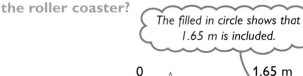

*The arrow means the
values go on forever.*

height < 2.2 m

1.65 m $\leqslant$ height < 2.2 m

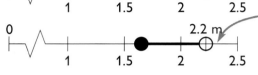

*The empty circle means
that 2.2 m is not included.*

Look at this diagram.

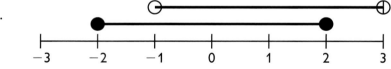

? Explain how this shows that when the variable x satisfies

$$\left. \begin{array}{l} -2 \leqslant x \leqslant 2 \\ \text{and} \\ -1 < x < 3 \end{array} \right\} \text{then } -1 < x \leqslant 2$$

*This is called **solving
simultaneous inequalities.***

? What does simultaneous mean?

Task

1 Show the following inequalities on number lines from -6 to 6.
   (a) $x \geqslant 3.5$ **(b)** $x < -2$ **(c)** $x > 0$ **(d)** $x \leqslant 5\frac{1}{2}$ **(e)** $0 < x \leqslant 4$ **(f)** $-3.5 \leqslant x < 3$

2 Draw number lines to solve these simultaneous inequalities.
   (a) $-3 < x < 5$ *and* $-2 \leqslant x \leqslant 4$ **(b)** $4.5 < x \leqslant 6$ *and* $-2 \leqslant x < 3$

⚠ Look at this number line.
Indira and Ela try to write it as an inequality.

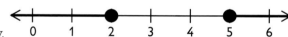

Indira

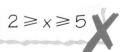

$2 \geqslant x \geqslant 5$ ✗

Ela

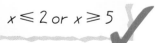

$x \leqslant 2$ or $x \geqslant 5$ ✓

? Explain why Indira is wrong.

Exercise

1 To play for Avonford Youth Club table
tennis team you need to be at least 12,
but less than 20 years old.
  (a) Write this information as an inequality
  and represent it on a number line.
  (a) List all the ages you could be
  (in whole years) to play for the team.

2 Write down the inequalities represented by the following number lines.

(a)
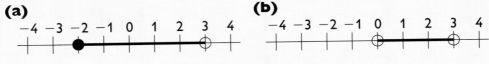

(b)
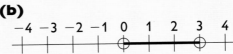

(c)

(d)
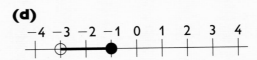

3 Draw and label number lines from -4 to 4 and show the following
inequalities, each on a separate number line.
  (a) $x > 1$ **(b)** $x \leqslant 1$ **(c)** $x \geqslant -1$
  (d) $x < -1$ **(e)** $x < 3$ **(f)** $-2 < x \leqslant 3$
  (g) $-3 \leqslant x < -2$ **(h)** $-1 < x < 4$ **(i)** $-4 < x \leqslant -1$

4 Write the information in these situations using inequality symbols.
  (a) The number of people, p, who went to Pat's party was less than 22.
  (b) Bob buys l litres of petrol for his car. The minimum amount that he can
  buy is 5 litres and his car has a 45 litre tank.
  (c) Each house on an estate has either 2, 3, 4 or 5 bedrooms.
  Mr and Mrs Hajba buy a house with b bedrooms.
  (d) An RSPCA shelter has enough space to keep 25 stray pets.
  One day they have x stray dogs and y stray cats.

5 Solve the following simultaneous inequalities.
  (a) $-3 < x \leqslant 5 \text{ and } -4 \leqslant x < 6$ **(b)** $-6 \leqslant x < 0 \text{ and } -2 \leqslant x \leqslant 3$
  (c) $0 < x \leqslant 4 \text{ and } 2 < x < 5$ **(d)** $-1 < x < 2 \text{ and } -4 \leqslant x \leqslant 3$

Activity

Steve makes kitchen tables. He always tries to make them
1500 mm long and 800 mm wide, but sometimes he does
not cut the wood very accurately. He measures all the table
tops, in millimetres, to check the measurements.
He writes down what he finds as inequalities.

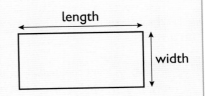

$1495 \leqslant length \leqslant 1505$
$795 \leqslant width \leqslant 805$

Find the maximum and minimum area a table can be in **(a)** mm^2 **(b)** m^2.

Solving inequalities

Jane is going on holiday with three suitcases.
One of them weighs 8 kg. The other two are an
unknown weight, but both the same as each other.
She is told that she is over the weight limit of 30 kg.

I will write the problem as an inequality.

Jane

She writes

$$2x + 8 > 30$$

? **What does x stand for?**
   What does the inequality tell you?

Jane then writes

	$2x + 8 > 30$
Subtract 8	$2x > 22$
Divide by 2	$x > 11$

The weight of each suitcase is still unknown but Jane does know that each one is more than 11 kg.

Task

Solve these inequalities. Write what you have done at each step.
(a) $3x + 5 \geqslant 20$ **(b)** $4x - 9 < 2x + 11$ **(c)** $3(x + 1) > x - 7$ **(d)** $8(x + 1) \leqslant 3(x + 6)$

⚠ Be careful with inequalities like $-2x > 8$

? **Which of these values of x satisfy the inequality $-2x > 8$?**
   (a) 5   **(b)** -5 **(c)** 3   **(d)** -3 **(e)** 10   **(f)** -10

Boris and Lara
try to solve the
inequality.

Boris

$$-2x > 8$$

add 2x }
Take away 8 } $-8 > 2x$

Divide by 2 $-4 > x$

So $x < -4$ ✓

Lara

$$-2x > 8$$

Divide by -2 $x > -4$

✗

? **What has Lara done wrong?**

Lara says

So I can multiply or divide an inequality by a negative number, but I must change the direction of the inequality sign.

Lara: Correction

$$-2x > 8$$

Divide by 2 $-x > 4$

Multiply by -1 $x < -4$ ✓
change the inequality sign

? **Is Lara right?**

Exercise

1 Write each of these statements as inequalities and solve them.

(a) Peter and Margaret are twins. When they add their ages together and add 10 the total is less than their sister Ruth's age.
Ruth is 31 years old.
Let a stand for Peter and Margaret's age.

(b) Jasmine buys five identical cakes.
She receives change from £2.
Let c stand for the cost of each cake.

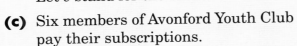

(c) Six members of Avonford Youth Club pay their subscriptions.
The leader collects the money and puts it with £20 taken from the Tuck Shop.
He notices that altogether he has less than £50.
Let s stand for the cost of the subscription.

(d) The manager of Avonford Cars fills six identical new cars with diesel.
He also puts 90 litres into the car transporter.
When he checks the pump, he sees that he has used more than 350 litres.
Let l stand for the number of litres of diesel in each car.

2 Solve the following inequalities.

(a) $3x + 4 \geqslant 16$ **(b)** $5x + 7 < 32$ **(c)** $4x - 3 > 29$
(d) $8x + 6 \geqslant 38$ **(e)** $3(2x - 3) > 6$ **(f)** $4(3x + 2) < 44$

3 Solve these inequalities. Be careful about the directions of the signs.

(a) $5 - 6x < 29$ **(b)** $8 - 3x \geqslant 14$ **(c)** $12 - 5x \geqslant 3$
(d) $8 + \frac{x}{2} > 11$ **(e)** $5(x - 2) < 10$ **(f)** $6x + 7 > 8x + 15$

Investigation

The shaded region is formed by the lines $x = 4$, $y = 6$ and $y = x$.

(a) Write three inequalities to describe it.

(b) Shade a region of your own.
Ask a friend to write down the inequalities.

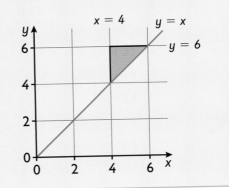

Finishing off

Now that you have finished this chapter you should be able to:

- know and use the symbols $<$, $>$, $\leqslant$ and $\geqslant$
- write information as inequalities
- show inequalities on a number line
- solve simultaneous inequalities
- solve inequalities
- describe regions using inequalities.

Review exercise

1 Write the information in the following articles using inequalities.

(a)

Avonford Electric Company shares collapse

From a maximum of 175p, shares dropped to an all time low of 63p today.

Let S stand for the share price.

(b)

Angling News

Bob Dace recently caught 37 fish in the National Angling Competition, this was his best ever catch. Bob said later that the least he ever caught was 13.

Let F stand for the number of fish.

(c)

Avonford Striker breaks Club Record

Henry Wilson, Avonford's star striker, scored 39 goals this season. His lowest ever total was 11 in the 1995 season.

Let G stand for the number of goals.

(d)

Avonford Youth Club Age of Admission

To be a member of the club you must be at least 12 but less than 21 years of age.

Let A stand for the admission age.

2 Put the correct inequality sign between each pair of values.

(a) 7 cm ☐ 6 m

(b) 1.5 kg ☐ 1000 g

(c) £6.74 ☐ 675p

(d) 25 mm ☐ $2\frac{1}{4}$ cm

(e) 5.6 cm ☐ 500 cm

(f) 10^3 ☐ 35

(g) 2^2 ☐ 3^3

(h) $2\frac{1}{2}$ km ☐ 2300 m

3 Here are six inequalities. For each one write down four possible values of x.

(a) $7 \leqslant x \leqslant 15$

(b) $0 < x \leqslant 4$

(c) $-2 \leqslant x \leqslant 2$

(d) $-7 \leqslant x < -1$

(e) $-5 \leqslant x \leqslant 0$

(f) $17 < x \leqslant 23$

4 Write down the inequalities represented on each of these number lines.

(a)
$$-5 \quad -4 \quad -3 \quad -2 \quad -1 \quad 0 \quad 1 \quad 2 \quad 3 \quad 4 \quad 5$$

(b)
$$-5 \quad -4 \quad -3 \quad -2 \quad -1 \quad 0 \quad 1 \quad 2 \quad 3 \quad 4 \quad 5$$

(c)
$$-5 \quad -4 \quad -3 \quad -2 \quad -1 \quad 0 \quad 1 \quad 2 \quad 3 \quad 4 \quad 5$$

(d)
$$-5 \quad -4 \quad -3 \quad -2 \quad -1 \quad 0 \quad 1 \quad 2 \quad 3 \quad 4 \quad 5$$

(e)
$$-5 \quad -4 \quad -3 \quad -2 \quad -1 \quad 0 \quad 1 \quad 2 \quad 3 \quad 4 \quad 5$$

(f)
$$-5 \quad -4 \quad -3 \quad -2 \quad -1 \quad 0 \quad 1 \quad 2 \quad 3 \quad 4 \quad 5$$

(g)
$$-5 \quad -4 \quad -3 \quad -2 \quad -1 \quad 0 \quad 1 \quad 2 \quad 3 \quad 4 \quad 5$$

(h)
$$-5 \quad -4 \quad -3 \quad -2 \quad -1 \quad 0 \quad 1 \quad 2 \quad 3 \quad 4 \quad 5$$

5 Draw number lines from -6 to 6 to show each of these inequalities.

(a) $-5 < x < 3$ **(b)** $0 \leqslant x \leqslant 5$ **(c)** $-3 < x \leqslant 0$

(d) $-4 \leqslant x < 4$ **(e)** $2\frac{1}{2} < x < 5$ **(f)** $-2 \leqslant x \leqslant 3\frac{1}{2}$

(g) $-6 \leqslant x < -4$ **(h)** $0 < x \leqslant 5$ **(i)** $-1 \leqslant x < 1\frac{1}{2}$

6 Solve these inequalities. Show all your working clearly.

(a) $2x + 6 < 15$ **(b)** $3x + 12 \leqslant 30$ **(c)** $4x + 1 \geqslant x + 8$

(d) $9x + 4 < 5x - 8$ **(e)** $9 - 2x > 3$ **(f)** $2(x - 5) \leqslant 0$

(g) $13 - 4x < 5$ **(h)** $5(x - 2) < 6x$ **(i)** $1 - \frac{1}{2}x \leqslant 3$

7 In each part of this question, work out the values of the two expressions.
Then replace the ... by one of these signs, $<$, $=$ or $>$.

(a) $b^2 + a \ldots 7a + 2b$ **(i)** $a = 3, b = -2$ **(ii)** $a = 4, b = 4$
(b) $3b + 5c \ldots 5a + c$ **(i)** $a = 2, b = 5, c = -2$ **(ii)** $a = 5, b = 8, c = -1$
(c) $abc \ldots 15b$ **(i)** $a = 3, b = -2, c = 5$ **(ii)** $a = 2, b = 0, c = 7.5$

8 Solve the following pairs of simultaneous equations and show each solution on a number line.

(a) $-4 < x < 3 \ and \ -5 \leqslant x < 5$ **(b)** $-2 \leqslant x < 5 \ and \ 0 < x \leqslant 6$
(c) $-3 < x < 0 \ and \ -1 < x < 0$ **(d)** $0 \leqslant x \leqslant 4 \ and \ 0 < x < 5$

Activity

1 Draw a graph with x values from -4 to 4 and y values from 0 to 16.

2 Draw **(a)** the curve $y = x^2$ **(b)** the lines **(i)** $y = 9$ **(ii)** $y = 14$ **(iii)** $y = 3x$.
Your graph has five different enclosed regions.

3 Number each region and shade them using different colours.

4 Describe each region using inequalities.

21 Probability

Calculating probabilities

Alison has a bag of 20 sweets.
There are toffees, strawberry creams and mints.

The probability of picking a strawberry cream is $\frac{1}{4}$.

The probability of picking a toffee is $\frac{2}{5}$.

? How many of each type of sweet are there in the bag?

? What is the probability of picking a mint?
Add up the three probabilities.
Explain your answer.

When Alison picks a sweet out of her bag, there are three
possible **outcomes**, a toffee, a strawberry cream, or a mint.
These are called **mutually exclusive** outcomes, because
only one of them can happen.

? What do you get when you add up
the probabilities of all the mutually
exclusive outcomes of an experiment?

The probability of picking a toffee from my bag is $\frac{1}{3}$, and the probability of picking a mint is $\frac{1}{2}$.

Alison's friend Sarah also has a bag of
the same three types of sweet.

? What is the probability of picking a strawberry cream from
Sarah's bag?

? Sarah has 12 toffees in her bag.
How many sweets does she have altogether?
How many mints and how many strawberry creams does she have?

Task

Try this game with a friend.

1. Your friend puts five cubes in a bag. Some cubes should be red and some blue.
2. You take a cube out, write down its colour and put it back.
3. Repeat this 10 times.
4. Now guess how many red and how many blue cubes are in the bag.
   Your friend must not tell you if you are right or wrong.
5. Continue picking cubes out of the bag, and after every ten goes make another guess.
6. When you are reasonably sure that you know the numbers of cubes, ask your
   friend to tell you if you are right.

? Discuss your results with the rest of the class.
How many experiments did it take to guess?
How sure could you be?

Exercise

1 Sophie is playing an arcade game. Each turn costs 50p.
Each time she plays, one of four symbols appears.
She wins £5 if she gets a star.
She loses if she gets an apple, a banana or a pear.
(a) What is the probability of getting a star?
(b) Sophie plays the game 40 times.
How much does she spend?
(c) How many times should she expect to win £5?

Probabilities:
Apple   0.3
Banana   0.4
Pear   0.25
Star   ?

2 Lynne has three bags containing red, green and blue balls.

A 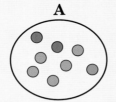 B 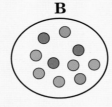 C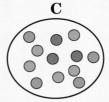

(a) Copy and complete this table.

	A	B	C
Probability of picking red			
Probability of picking green			
Probability of picking blue	$\frac{1}{8}$		

(b) Lynne wants to pick a green ball.
Which bag should she pick from?

(c) For two of the bags, the probability of picking red is the same.
Which two bags are these?

3 Steve has a bag containing red, black and white counters.
The probability of picking a red counter is $\frac{3}{8}$.
(a) From this information, what is the smallest number of counters there could be in the bag?
The probability of picking a black counter is $\frac{2}{5}$.
(b) What is the probability of picking a white counter?
(c) What is the smallest number of counters there could be in the bag?
(d) In fact there are 45 red counters.
How many black counters and how many white counters are there in the bag?

4 James has a biased die.
The probability of scoring six is twice the probability of scoring one.
The probability of scoring each of the numbers 2, 3, 4 and 5 is $\frac{1}{8}$.
Find the probability of scoring six.

Combined outcomes

Robert is playing a fruit machine.
The machine has two windows.
Each window can show an orange, a banana or a pear.
Each fruit is equally likely to appear.

Robert wins 50p if he gets two bananas.
Robert wants to work out how likely he is to win.

He makes this list of possible outcomes.
Each of the outcomes on the list is equally likely.

Window 1	Window 2
orange	orange
orange	banana
orange	pear
banana	orange
banana	banana
banana	pear
pear	orange
pear	banana
pear	pear

 What is the probability of getting two bananas?

 Robert plays nine games. How much profit or loss would he expect to make?

Robert writes

$P(\text{winning}) = \frac{1}{9}$

$P(\text{losing}) = \frac{8}{9}$

This is a quick way of writing 'The probability of winning'.

 Task

Another fruit machine has three windows, each of which can show one of the same three fruits: orange, banana or pear.
Each fruit is equally likely to appear in each window.
You win if you get three bananas.

1 Make a list of all the possible outcomes and use it to find P(winning).

2 This machine also costs 10p per go. The owner wants it to make about the same amount of profit per game as Robert's machine.

 How much should the prize money be?

 How many outcomes would there be if there were
(a) four windows
(b) three windows but four different fruits?
Find a rule for working out the number of possible outcomes if you know the number of windows and the number of fruits.

Exercise

1 Mark throws two ordinary dice, one red and the other green. He adds the scores together.

(a) Copy and complete this table to show all the possible outcomes.

(b) Use your table to find
   (i) P(4)
   (ii) P(7)
   (iii) P(11)
   (iv) P(more than 8)
   (v) P(5 or less)
   (vi) P(prime number).

Die 1 (Red)

	1	**2**	**3**	**4**	**5**	**6**
1	2	3	4			
2	3					
3						
4						
5						
6						

Die 2 (Green)

2 Helen takes 5 tops and 3 pairs of shorts on holiday.

Helen chooses a top and a pair of shorts at random one day.
(a) Make a list of all the possible combinations she could choose.
(b) What is the probability that she chooses a top and a pair of shorts which are the same colour?

3 Darren spins these two spinners.
He finds his score like this.

The score is   Larger number – Smaller number
If the numbers are the same, the score is zero.

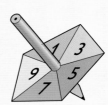

(a) Make a table or list to show all the possible outcomes.
(b) Find
   (i) P(0)   **(ii)** P(1)   **(iii)** P(more than 4)
   (iv) P(10)   **(v)** P(even number)

4 **(a)** List all the possible outcomes of tossing two coins.
(b) Find P(one head and one tail).
(c) List all the possible outcomes of tossing three coins.
(d) Find P(two heads and one tail).
(e) List all the possible outcomes of tossing four coins.
(f) Find P(two heads and two tails).
(g) What is the rule for working out the number of different outcomes when you toss n coins?

Estimating probabilities

The number 10 hasn't come up in the National Lottery for several months, so it will probably come up in the next few weeks.

I have three sons already, so my next baby will probably be a boy as well.

Tomorrow it could rain or be fine, so there is a 50% chance of rain.

 Are these statements correct? Explain your answers.

 In which of the situations above can the probability be calculated? In which can the probability only be estimated?

Right-handed	24
Left-handed	4

Justin wants to find out the probability that a person selected at random is left-handed.

He asks everybody in his class whether they are right-handed or left-handed.
Justin can use these results to find the relative frequency of left-handedness.

$$\text{Relative frequency of left-handedness} = \frac{4}{28} = 0.14$$

Relative frequency can be used as an estimate of probability.
From Justin's results, P(left-handedness) = 0.14.

 Do Justin's results mean that the probability that a new baby will be left-handed is exactly 0.14?

Justin finds this article in a magazine.

Are you right-eyed or left-eyed?

Look at a mark on the far wall. Make your thumb and forefinger into a circle and look at the mark through it, at arm's length.

Now close your left eye. Is the mark still in the circle? If it is, you are right-eyed.
Open your left eye and close

your right eye. Is the mark still in the circle? If it is, you are left-eyed.

 Task

1   Use the instructions above to find out whether each person in your class is right-eyed or left-eyed.

2   Also find out whether they are right-handed or left-handed.

3   Write your results in a two-way table like this.

4   Use your results to estimate the probability that somebody selected at random is

	Right-handed	Left-handed
Right-eyed		
Left-eyed		

(a) left-eyed   (b) left-handed   (c) both.

Exercise

1 Gemma carries out a survey of the colours of cars passing her house one morning.
Here are her results.

Red	Blue	Green	Black	White	Other
43	32	19	14	26	16

(a) How many cars are there in Gemma's survey?

(b) Estimate the probability the next car that passes Gemma's house is
   (i) red   (ii) blue   (iii) black.

(c) There are 500 cars in a car park near Gemma's house.
   How many of these cars would you expect to be
   (i) red   (ii) blue   (iii) black?

2 Jamie is practising ten-pin bowling.
He keeps a record of the number of pins he knocks down on each turn.

Number of pins	0	1	2	3	4	5	6	7	8	9	10
Frequency	7	2	3	8	5	11	14	10	12	5	3

Estimate the probability that on his next turn Jamie scores

(a) 6   (b) 10   (c) 4 or less   (d) more than 7.

3 Ian is a football fan.
He keeps a record of his team's results one season.

(a) From Ian's results, estimate the probability
   that in the next match his team play they will
   (i) win   (ii) draw.

Win	27
Lose	14
Draw	9

(b) Do you think your answers are good estimates?
   Explain your answer.

Activity

1 Throw a drawing pin ten times.
Record how many times it lands 'point up'.
Use these results to estimate the probability that the pin will land point up.

2 Repeat the experiment another 10 times.
Use all 20 results to estimate the probability again.

3 Continue to repeat the procedure, estimating the
probability after every 10 throws, until you have
done 100 throws altogether.

4 Plot your results on a graph like this.

5 What do you notice?

Relative frequency of 'point up'

Number of throws

Finishing off

Now that you have finished this chapter you should be able to:

- know that the probabilities of all mutually exclusive outcomes add up to 1
- identify all the possible mutually exclusive outcomes of two or more events
- use relative frequency to estimate probabilities from an experiment
- compare experimental and theoretical probabilities.

Review exercise

1 Michelle keeps a record of the number of goals scored by her hockey team in each match.

Based on her results, Michelle estimates these probabilities.

P (scoring no goals) = 0.15
P (scoring 1 goal) = 0.3
P (scoring 2 goals) = 0.25
P (scoring 3 goals) = 0.2

(a) What is the probability of her team scoring more than 3 goals?

(b) Michelle's records show that the team scored more than 3 goals in four matches.
How many matches have they played?

(c) How many times did they score no goals?

2 Parvinda takes a card from an ordinary pack. She writes down its suit, Hearts, Diamonds, Clubs or Spades.
She then puts the card back, shuffles the pack and takes out another card. She writes down which suit this card is.

(a) Make a table or list to show all the possible outcomes.

(b) Find

(i)   P(both cards are the same suit)

(ii) P(both cards are red)

(iii) P(the cards are different colours)

(iv) P(the cards are a Heart and a Spade).

3 A die is biased so that P(1) = 0.3 and P(6) = 0.1
The probabilities of getting 2, 3, 4 or 5 are equal.

(a) Find P(2).

(b) Joe throws the die 200 times.
How many times would you expect him to get

(i) 1   (ii) 6   (iii) 5?

4 Michael and Joe are playing a game.

Michael puts some counters in a bag.
The counters are a mixture of red, yellow, green and blue.

Joe picks a counter out of the bag, records its colour, and puts it back.
Joe does this 50 times. Here are his results.

Red	Yellow	Green	Blue
15	12	5	18

(a) From Joe's results, estimate the probability of getting
    (i) a blue counter   **(ii)** a green counter   **(iii)** a red counter.

(b) Michael tells Joe that here are 20 counters in the bag altogether.
Use Joe's results to estimate how many counters there are
of each colour.

5 In a game, Sue throws a red die and a blue die,
each numbered 1 to 6.

She uses this rule to find her score.

$$Score = 2 \times number\ on\ red\ die - number\ on\ blue\ die$$

(a) What is Sue's score if she gets
    (i) a 3 on the red die and a 2 on the blue die
    (ii) a 2 on the red die and a 3 on the blue die?

(b) Copy and complete this table to show all the possible outcomes.

Red die

	1	2	3	4	5	6
1	1	3				
2	0					
3	−1					
4						
5						
6						

Blue die

(c) What is the probability that Sue's score is
    (i) 0   **(ii)** negative   **(iii)** 4   **(iv)** −1   **(v)** −5?

Activity

(a) Throw a die 100 times and record your results.
Use your results to estimate the probability of getting each number.
Compare your results with the theoretical probabilities.

(b) Collect together the results from the whole class.
Use the combined results to estimate the probability of getting each number.
Compare these probabilities with the theoretical probabilities.

Right-angled triangles

Craig and Jess each sketch a triangle. They mark some lengths and angles.

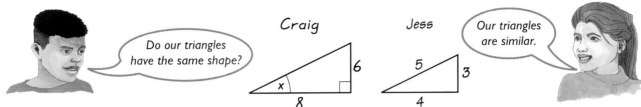

? **How can Craig find the length of his missing side?**
Jess thinks her triangle has a right angle. How can she check?

? **What does similar mean? How can you tell that the triangles are similar?**
What can you say about the angles in similar triangles?

Each side in a right-angled triangle has a name.
● The longest side is called the **hypotenuse**.
● The side opposite the marked angle is called the **opposite**.
● The remaining side, next to the marked angle, is called the **adjacent**.

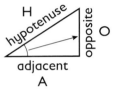

Craig and Jess work out the three *ratios* for their triangles: $\dfrac{O}{H}, \dfrac{A}{H}$ and $\dfrac{O}{A}$.

? **What do they find?**

Task

Look at these sketches.
1 Use Pythagoras' theorem to
   (a) find the missing length in triangle ①
   (b) show that triangle ② is right-angled.
2 Redraw both triangles to show this information.
3 Explain carefully why the triangles are similar.
4 For each triangle, work out the three ratios: $\dfrac{O}{H}, \dfrac{A}{H}$ and $\dfrac{O}{A}$. What do you notice?

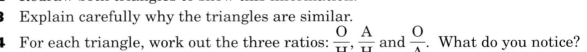

P and Q are two right-angled triangles.
The ratios, $\dfrac{O}{H}$ and $\dfrac{A}{H}$, are equal for both triangles.

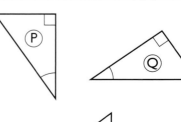

? **What can you say about the triangles?**

Look at this triangle.

? **What are the values of O and A for angle *a*?**
What are the values of O and A for angle *b*?

Exercise

1 Sketch each of these triangles.
Label the hypotenuse, opposite and adjacent sides using H, O and A.

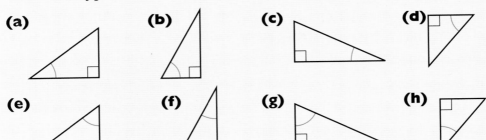

(a)   (b)   (c)   (d)

(e)   (f)   (g)   (h)

2 For each of these triangles
(i) use Pythagoras' theorem to show that it is right-angled
(ii) work out the three ratios, $\dfrac{O}{H}$, $\dfrac{A}{H}$ and $\dfrac{O}{A}$.
Which of the triangles are similar to each other?

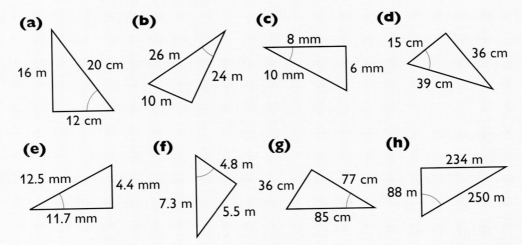

(a) 16 m, 20 cm, 12 cm

(b) 26 m, 24 m, 10 m

(c) 8 mm, 10 mm, 6 mm

(d) 15 cm, 36 cm, 39 cm

(e) 12.5 mm, 4.4 mm, 11.7 mm

(f) 4.8 m, 7.3 m, 5.5 m

(g) 36 cm, 77 cm, 85 cm

(h) 234 m, 88 m, 250 m

3 For each of these triangles
(i) use Pythagoras' theorem to work out the missing side
(ii) find the three ratios, $\dfrac{O}{H}$, $\dfrac{A}{H}$ and $\dfrac{O}{A}$.
Which of the triangles are similar to each other?

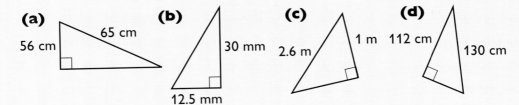

(a) 56 cm, 65 cm

(b) 30 mm, 12.5 mm

(c) 2.6 m, 1 m

(d) 112 cm, 130 cm

Trigonometrical ratios

Emily draws this triangle. It has hypotenuse 5 cm.
She measures the other two sides.

She finds the three ratios, $\dfrac{O}{H}$, $\dfrac{A}{H}$ and $\dfrac{O}{A}$,

for the angles 30° and 60°.

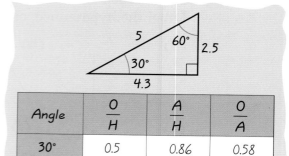

Angle	$\dfrac{O}{H}$	$\dfrac{A}{H}$	$\dfrac{O}{A}$
30°	0.5	0.86	0.58
60°	0.86	0.5	1.72

 Explain how Emily has got these answers.

 The value of each ratio depends on the size of the angle. How can you tell?

These three ratios have special names.

This is the greek letter theta. It is often used to show an angle.

$$sin\ \theta = \frac{O}{H} \qquad cos\ \theta = \frac{A}{H} \qquad tan\ \theta = \frac{O}{A}$$

'sin', 'cos' and 'tan' are short for sine, cosine and tangent.

You can remember this by the mnemonic:
Some Old Horse Cracked All His Teeth On Apples

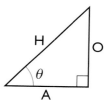

You can use a calculator to work out these ratios.
Your calculator must be in degrees (DEG) mode.
To work out sin 30°, press

| 3 | 0 | sin | on a scientific calculator *or* | sin | 3 | 0 | EXE | on a graphic calculator.

Task

You will need a ruler, protractor and calculator.

1 (a) Draw a horizontal line of any length.
(b) Draw an angle, θ, of 20° from the left end and make a right-angled triangle.
(c) Measure H, O and A.
(d) Use your measurements to work out sin θ, cos θ and tan θ.

 **Do you all get the same answer? Why?**
What does this have to do with similar triangles?

2 Now use a calculator to find sin θ, cos θ and tan θ.

3 Compare your answers to parts 1 and 2.

Which method is more accurate?
Which method is better? Why?

Exercise

1 For each of these triangles, write down
   (i) the names (using H, O or A) of the two sides which are given
   (ii) the name and value of the trigonometrical ratio that involves these
   two sides.

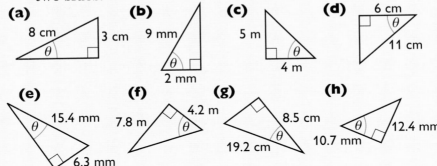

(a) 8 cm, 3 cm, θ
(b) 9 mm, 2 mm, θ
(c) 5 m, 4 m, θ
(d) 6 cm, 11 cm, θ
(e) 15.4 mm, 6.3 mm, θ
(f) 7.8 m, 4.2 m, θ
(g) 8.5 cm, 19.2 cm, θ
(h) 12.4 mm, 10.7 mm, θ

2 For each of these triangles, work out the value of sin θ, cos θ and tan θ.

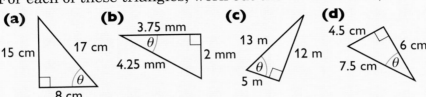

(a) 15 cm, 17 cm, 8 cm, θ
(b) 3.75 mm, 4.25 mm, 2 mm, θ
(c) 13 m, 12 m, 5 m, θ
(d) 4.5 cm, 6 cm, 7.5 cm, θ

3 For each of these triangles
   (i) use Pythagoras' theorem to find the missing side
   (ii) find the value of the three trig. ratios, sin θ, cos θ and tan θ.

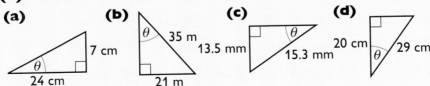

(a) 7 cm, 24 cm, θ
(b) 35 m, 21 m, θ
(c) 13.5 mm, 15.3 mm, θ
(d) 20 cm, 29 cm, θ

Investigation

1 Look at these triangles.
   (a) Use Pythagoras' theorem to find x and y.
   (b) Use triangle A to find sin 45°, cos 45° and tan 45°.
   Use triangle B to find sin 60°, cos 60° and tan 60°
   and also sin 30°, cos 30° and tan 30°.
   (c) Copy the table. Use your results to complete it.

Use square root signs in your answers when you need to.

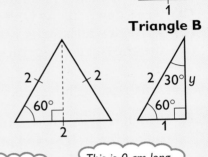

Triangle A
x, 45°, 1, 1

Triangle B
2, 30°, y, 60°, 1

2, 2, 60°, 2

θ	30	45	60
sin θ			
cos θ			
tan θ			

2 (a) Use this 'triangle' to work out sin 0°, cos 0°
   and tan 0°.
   (b) What does it tell you about sin 90° and cos 90°?
   (c) There is a problem with tan 90°. What is it?

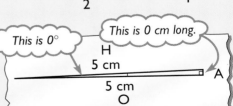

This is 0°
This is 0 cm long.
H, 5 cm, A, 5 cm, O

Finding lengths

John is a window cleaner. His ladder is 6 m long.
The angle between the ladder and ground is 70°.

John wants to find the height that his ladder reaches.

*I will start by drawing
the triangle and labelling
the sides H, O and A.*

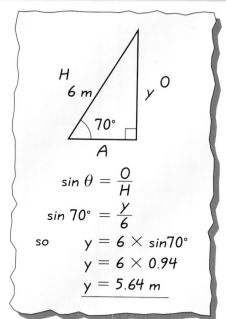

$$\sin \theta = \frac{O}{H}$$

$$\sin 70° = \frac{y}{6}$$

so $\quad y = 6 \times \sin 70°$

$$y = 6 \times 0.94$$

$$y = 5.64 \ m$$

He writes *y* for the length that he wants to find.

? **You know the length of one side. Which is it?**
You want to know the length of another side.
Which is it?
Which trig. ratio involves these two sides?

John also wants to find the distance of the bottom
of the ladder from the wall.

? **Which trig. ratio does he need to use?**

Task

Look at these right-angled triangles.

1

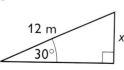

2

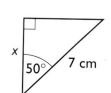

3

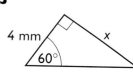

For each triangle,
(a) make a sketch and label the sides O, A and H
(b) write down (using O, A or H) which side you know and which side you want to find
(c) write down the trig. ratio that involves these two sides
(d) use the correct trig. ratio and your calculator to find the side length that you want.

Look at this regular hexagon.

? **Which trig. ratios would you use
to find the height and base of
triangle OAM?**

? **How can you find the area of
the hexagon?**

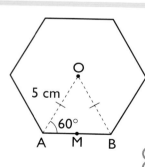

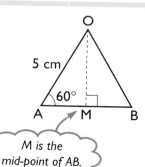

*M is the
mid-point of AB.*

Exercise

1 For each of these triangles, find the length labelled x.

(a)
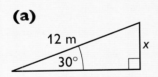
12 m
30°
x

(b)
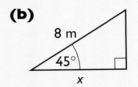
8 m
45°
x

(c)
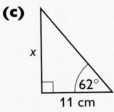
x
62°
11 cm

(d)
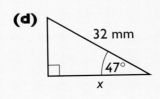
32 mm
47°
x

(e)
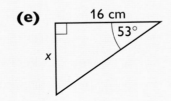
16 cm
53°
x

(f)
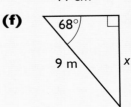
68°
9 m
x

2 For each of these triangles, find the lengths labelled x and y.

(a)
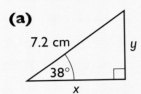
7.2 cm
y
38°
x

(b)
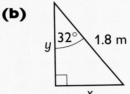
32°
1.8 m
y
x

(c)
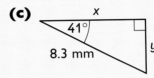
x
41°
8.3 mm
y

(d)
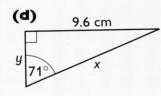
9.6 cm
y
71°
x

(e)
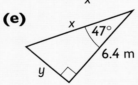
x
47°
6.4 m
y

(f)
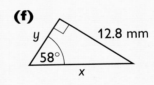
y
12.8 mm
58°
x

3 Look at the picture.
Amy is flying a kite.

What is the height of the kite above
Amy's hand?

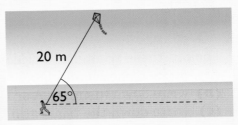
20 m
65°

4 Look at the picture.
Kamil is standing 12 m away from a tree.

Find the height of the tree.

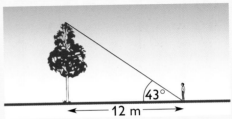
43°
12 m

5 A ship sails 8 km from port on a
bearing of 036°.
How far north and how far east
has it travelled?

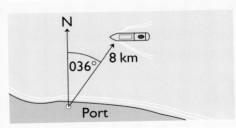
N
8 km
036°
Port

Finding angles

Nelson plays golf at Avonford Golf Club.
He wants to work out the angle of the hill.

I know the length of the opposite and hypotenuse.

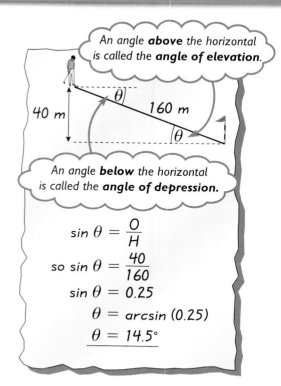

*An angle **above** the horizontal is called the **angle of elevation**.*

*An angle **below** the horizontal is called the **angle of depression**.*

You can find an angle in a right-angled triangle if you know two lengths.

 Which two lengths does Nelson know?
Which trig. ratio links these two sides?

 Nelson wrote arcsin (0.25). It means the angle whose sin is 0.25.
There are other ways of writing this, besides 'arcsin'. What are they?

$$\sin \theta = \frac{O}{H}$$
$$\text{so } \sin \theta = \frac{40}{160}$$
$$\sin \theta = 0.25$$
$$\theta = \arcsin (0.25)$$
$$\underline{\theta = 14.5°}$$

Nelson found sin θ = 0.25.
To find θ, you press

| . | 2 | 5 | = | INV | sin | on a scientific calculator

or   SHIFT | sin | . | 2 | 5 | EXE   on a graphic calculator.

Task

Look at these triangles. For each of them
(a) make a sketch and label the sides O, A and H
(b) write down (using O, A or H) which two sides you know
(c) write down the trig. ratio that involves these two sides
(d) use the correct trig. ratio and your calculator to find the marked angle

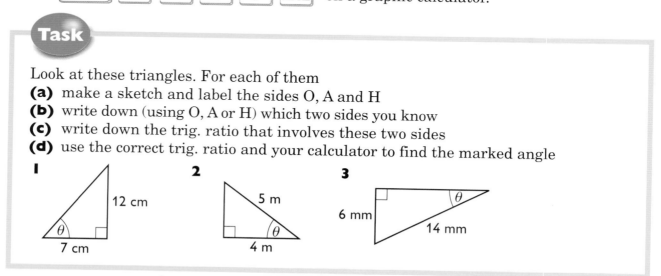

1
12 cm
θ
7 cm

2
5 m
θ
4 m

3
6 mm
θ
14 mm

Jayne, Paul and Laura each use a different trig. ratio to work out angle θ in this triangle.

 How do they do their calculations?
Show they all get the same answer for θ.

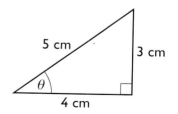

5 cm
3 cm
θ
4 cm

Exercise

1 Use your calculator to find θ.
   (a) $\sin \theta = 0.5$ **(b)** $\cos \theta = 0.707$ **(c)** $\tan \theta = 1.732$
   (d) $\sin \theta = 0.866$ **(e)** $\cos \theta = 0$ **(f)** $\sin \theta = 1$
   (g) $\cos \theta = 0.5$ **(h)** $\tan \theta = 0.577$ **(i)** $\tan \theta = 0.5$

2 Find angle θ in each of these triangles.

   (a)   **(b)**   **(c)**

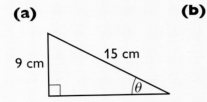 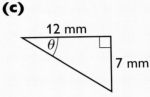

   (d)   **(e)**   **(f)**

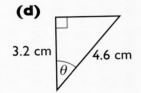 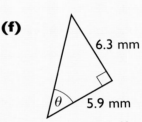

3 Steve is in a small boat. It is 1500 m away from the bottom of a cliff.
The height of the cliff is 230 m.
Find the angle of elevation of the top of the cliff from the boat.

4 A ladder leans against a wall. It is 7 m long.
The bottom of the ladder is 2.5 m away from the wall.
   (a) Find the angle of elevation of the ladder.
   (b) How high up the wall does the ladder reach?

5 Danielle cycles from Abbotville to Bradbury
along a straight road.
Bradbury is 4 miles north and 3 miles east of Abbotville.
   (a) Find the bearing of her journey.
   (b) How far does she cycle?
   (c) What is the return bearing?

6 Look at this diagram.
It shows a circle with a chord AB of length 8 cm.
The radius of the circle is 5 cm.
Find θ.

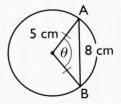

Activity

Look at this diagram.

(a) Use trigonometry to find the value of $A + B + C$.
(b) Use your answer to part (a) to prove that $B = D$.

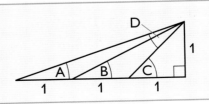

Finishing off

Now that you have finished this chapter you should:

- be able to recognise the hypotenuse, opposite and adjacent sides of a right-angled triangle
- know the three trigonometrical ratios: $\sin \theta = \dfrac{O}{H}$, $\cos \theta = \dfrac{A}{H}$ and $\tan \theta = \dfrac{O}{A}$
- be able to calculate lengths given one side and one angle of a right-angled triangle
- be able to calculate angles given two sides of a right-angled triangle
- know how to use a calculator to find angles.

Review exercise

1   Find the missing length in each of these triangles.

(a)

y
x
$37°$
15 m

(b)

8 mm
y
$72°$
x

(c)

9 cm
x
$43°$
y

2   Use your calculator to find θ to 1 decimal place.
   (a) $\cos \theta = 0.296$ **(b)** $\tan \theta = 0.545$
   (c) $\sin \theta = 0.741$ **(d)** $\cos \theta = 0.118$

3   A rectangular field is 160 m long and 120 m wide.
   A straight path along one diagonal cuts across it.
   (a) Find the angle the path makes with the longer side.
   (b) Work out the length of the path.

4   Hazel is surfing the internet.
   (a) What height are her eyes above the centre of the screen?
   (b) Find the horizontal distance from her eyes to the centre of the screen.

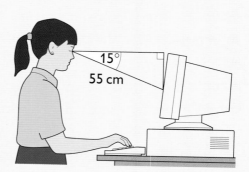

$15°$
55 cm

5   **(a)** Draw x and y axes using the same scale for each.
   (b) Using values of x from 0 to 4, draw the line $y = 2x - 3$.
   (c) Find the angle that the line $y = 2x - 3$ makes with the x axis.

6 Find the lengths of the marked sides in the following diagrams.

(a)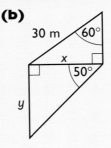

(b)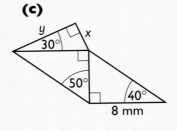

(c)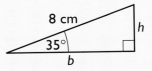

7 Look at this triangle.
(a) Find h. **(b)** Find b. **(c)** Find its area.

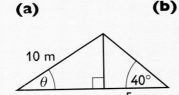

8 In each case, find the angle marked θ.

(a) **(b)** 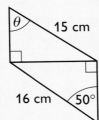 **(c)**

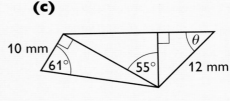

Activity

1 Use a calculator to complete this table.

$\theta°$	0	10	20	30	40	50	60	70	80	90
$\sin \theta$										
$\cos \theta$										
$\tan \theta$										

2 Plot points of $\sin \theta$ against θ. Join your points using a smooth curve.
3 Repeat for $\cos \theta$ and $\tan \theta$.
4 Describe each trigonometrical graph.

Activity

The diagram shows a form of spiral.
It continues with more triangles.
(a) Work out the lengths of **(i)** OB **(ii)** OC **(iii)** OD.
Use square root signs in your answers when you need to.
(b) How many triangles are needed to complete
(i) 180° of the spiral **(ii)** 360° of the spiral?

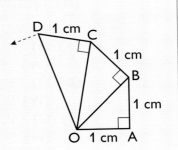

Investigation

There are three *other* trigonometrical ratios: cosec θ, sec θ and cot θ.
Find out more about these ratios and what their graphs look like.

23 Review

This chapter consists of questions.
You covered the work for them in previous years.
Answering the questions will help you to check that you have not forgotten that work.

Numbers and the number system

 Do not use your calculator for the questions on this page.

1 Write each of these sets of numbers in order of size, smallest first.
   (a) $\frac{5}{6}$, 82%, 0.85, $\frac{4}{5}$ **(b)** 0.28, 25%, $\frac{1}{5}$, $\frac{2}{7}$

2 In a triathalon race it takes Peter $4\frac{1}{2}$ minutes to complete the swimming section of the race, 2 minutes 45 seconds to complete the cycling, and 3 minutes 10 seconds to complete the running.
How long did Peter take altogether?

3 Marie cuts a slice of cake. She takes one-sixth of the cake.
What fraction is left?
Sarah cuts the remainder in half and takes it for her picnic.
What fraction is left now?
Simon eats a quarter of the original cake. How much is left finally?

4 Calculate: **(a)** $\frac{1}{2} + \frac{1}{3}$ **(b)** $\frac{2}{11} + \frac{3}{5}$ **(c)** $\frac{3}{8} - \frac{1}{4}$ **(d)** $\frac{7}{10} - \frac{2}{5}$
   (e) $\frac{2}{3} \times \frac{9}{10}$ **(f)** $\frac{7}{11} \times \frac{1}{21}$ **(g)** $\frac{2}{3} \div 10$ **(h)** $\frac{4}{5} \div \frac{1}{5}$

5 Carry out these calculations:
   (a) Add 0.32, 4.8 and 7.14   **(b)** Add 13, 6.4 and 3.12
   (c) Take 0.82 from 1.08   **(d)** Subtract 5.41 from 7.3
   (e) 4.6×0.01 **(f)** 7.6×0.2 **(g)** 3.7×2.3
   (h) $6.5 \div 0.05$ **(i)** $0.47 \div 0.2$ **(j)** $63 \div 0.03$

6 **(a)** Write the following in order of size, smallest first. $\frac{1}{4}$, -2, $-\frac{1}{2}$, 0, 4
   (b) Illustrate the numbers in part (a) on a number line.

7 Calculate:
   (a) **(i)** $4 - 7$ **(ii)** $9 - 14$ **(iii)** $(+6) + (-3)$
      (iv) $(+4) + (-9)$ **(v)** $21 - 30$
   (b) **(i)** $6 - 4$ **(ii)** $7 - (-1)$ **(iii)** $-4 - (-3)$
      (iv) $20 - 39$ **(v)** $-5 - (-11)$
   (c) **(i)** $2 \times (-3)$ **(ii)** $(-5) \times (-7)$ **(iii)** $(-5)^2$
      (iv) $(-3)^2$ **(v)** $(-2)^3$
   (d) **(i)** $-8 \div 2$ **(ii)** $(-32) \div (-4)$ **(iii)** $40 \div (-5)$
      (iv) $(+48) \div (+3)$ **(v)** $\frac{(-4) \times (-3)}{(-6)}$

8 Write the following numbers correct to 2 decimal places.
   (a) 4.318   **(b)** 11.622   **(c)** 0.515   **(d)** 6.929
   (e) 7.988   **(f)** 13.996   **(g)** 0.09624

Algebra

1 **(a)** Find the value of $a + 2b - 3c$ when

    (i) $a = 1, b = 3, c = 2$ **(ii)** $a = 3, b = 0, c = 1$

    (iii) $a = b = c = 4$ **(iv)** $a = -2, b = -3, c = -5$

  (b) Find the value of $a^2 + bc$ when

    (i) $a = 1, b = 3, c = 2$ **(ii)** $a = 3, b = 4, c = 0$

    (iii) $a = 0, b = 2, c = -1$ **(iv)** $a = -4, b = -3, c = -1$

  (c) Find the value of $\dfrac{3x^2}{6 - x}$ when

    (i) $x = 1$ **(ii)** $x = 2$ **(iii)** $x = 3$ **(iv)** $x = 4$.

2 Penny is making a patchwork quilt.

    Stage 1   Stage 2   Stage 3

  (a) Draw the next two stages.

  (b) How many patches will there be in stage:

    (i) 4   **(ii)** 5   **(iii)** 10   **(iv)** n?

  (c) Penny sews around the edge of each patch.

    Find an expression for the number of edges will she have to sew in stage n.

3 Solve the following equations.

  (a) $x + 5 = 6$ **(b)** $x - 5 = 6$ **(c)** $11x - 5 = 6$

  (d) $3x + 4 = 4$ **(e)** $3x + 6 = x + 12$ **(f)** $14x - 1 = 2x + 35$

  (g) $2(x - 6) = 8$ **(h)** $2(x - 6) = (x - 6)$ **(i)** $5(3x + 4) = 7(x + 4)$

4 Look at this parallelogram.

  (a) Write down the co-ordinates of three points that lie on:

    (i)   side AB

    (ii)   side BC

    (iii) side CD

    (iv) side DA of the parallelogram.

  (b) Use your co-ordinates to help you find the equation of each line.

  (c) What are the co-ordinates of the mid-point of the diagonal:

    (i)   AC   **(ii)**   BD?

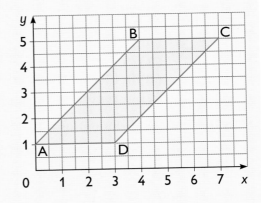

Space, shape and measures

1 Calculate the size of each lettered angle in these diagrams.

(a)

(b)
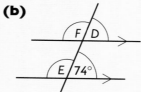

(c)
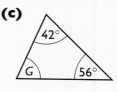

(d)

(e)
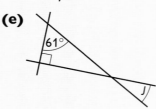

(f)
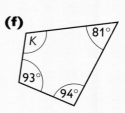

2 Find angle *x* in each of these diagrams.

(a)
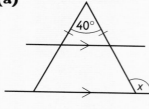

(b)
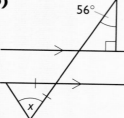

(c)
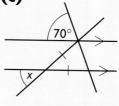

3 An aircraft travels on a bearing of 047° for 74 miles, then on a bearing of 207° for a further 107 miles.
(a) Show this information on a scale diagram.
(b) What is the aircraft's distance and bearing from the starting point?

4 Write down the names of all quadrilaterals which have:
(a) equal length diagonals
(b) the diagonals bisecting each other
(c) the diagonals intersecting at right angles
(d) the diagonals bisecting each other at right angles
(e) just one diagonal bisecting the other.

5 How many lines of symmetry do the following shapes have?
(a) a parallelogram   **(b)** a rectangle   **(c)** an equilateral triangle
(d) a kite   **(e)** a rhombus   **(f)** a square
(g) a regular heptagon   **(h)** a scalene triangle

6 Find the volume and surface area of each of these solids.

(a)
(b)
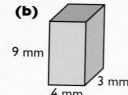
(c)
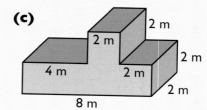

Data handling

1 Mr Brown's class of 30 students take a mental maths test each week.
There are 20 questions in each test.
Mr Brown wants to know if the students' scores have improved.
Here are the scores from the first week of term.

12	16	8	11	15	6	5	10	14	8
16	13	10	13	18	12	3	7	14	11
16	8	9	13	11	16	14	15	10	12

Here are the scores from the first week of term.

10	15	17	12	13	6	11	18	8	12
19	15	16	12	20	18	7	9	11	14
13	15	7	12	8	14	16	15	18	6

(a) What is the median score for the first week of term?
(b) What is the median score for the last week of term?
(c) Calculate the mean score for the first week of term.
(d) Calculate the mean score for the last week of term.
(e) Find the range of the scores for the first week of term.
(f) Find the range of the scores for the last week of term.
(g) Do you think the class has improved?
(h) What does the range of each set of scores tell you?

2 James is playing a game with this spinner.
(a) What is the probability that James scores
   (i) 1   **(ii)** 2   **(iii)** 3?
(b) James spins the spinner 30 times.
How many times would he expect to get each number?

Sally is also using a spinner with the numbers 1, 2 and 3 on it.
Sally's spinner has 5 sides, all the same size.
She spins it 50 times.
Here are her scores.

1	8 times
2	23 times
3	19 times

(c) Draw Sally's spinner.
(d) Sally spins her spinner another 50 times.
Do you think she will get the same results?

3 Sarah gets £40 pocket money per month and has to buy her own clothes.
One month, Sarah spends her pocket money like this.

Sarah wants to draw a pie chart to show
how she spends her money.
(a) How many degrees should Sarah use
to represent £1?
(b) Draw Sarah's pie chart.

Clothes	£15
Magazines	£3
Sweets	£4
CDs	£12
Other	£6

Proof

These numbers are a magic square.

Alka

6	4	9	15
13	11	2	8
3	5	16	10
12	14	7	1

 What makes a magic square magic?

 Task

Prove Alka's square is magic.

Sometimes you can prove a result by looking at *all* the possibilities.
This is called **proof by exhaustion**.

 **Explain how you used proof by exhaustion for the magic square.
How many checks did you need?**

 Often there are too many possible cases to look at all of them.
You cannot prove something by taking just a few of the possible cases.

I have made a great discovery in my coursework!

Malik

You have not proved it.
You have to show it works for all values of n.

That is impossible. It would take forever.

Malik writes:

$n^2 + n + 1$ is always a prime number if n is a prime number.

n	$n^2 + n + 1$	Prime?
2	7	Yes
3	13	Yes
5	31	Yes
17	307	Yes
101	10 303	Yes

It always works, even for large numbers. ✗

This is Malik's **conjecture**.

 **Who is right, Alka or Malik?
What would you need to do to prove Malik's conjecture?**

Anyway, I have found a value of n it doesn't work for.

Oh dear!
That means it is false.

 **Find a value of n for which Malik's conjecture does not work.
This is called a counter-example.**

To prove something is true you must either consider all possible cases *or* give a correct argument (for example using algebra).
To prove it is false all you need is one **counter-example**.

Exercise

1 Prove this square is magic.

4	3	8
9	5	1
2	7	6

2 This map shows the various routes from village X to village Y. Distances are in km.

Prove that the shortest route from X to Y is 22 km.

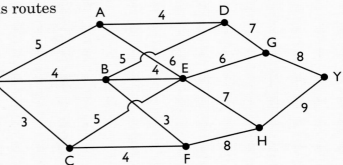

3 **Goldbach's Conjecture**
The number 28 can be written as the sum of two prime numbers.

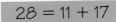

$$28 = 11 + 17$$

Goldbach (1690 – 1764) was a famous Prussian mathematician.

Goldbach's Conjecture says: 'You can split every even number from 4 onwards into the sum of two prime numbers'.

(a) Show that Goldbach's Conjecture is true for all even numbers from 4 to 50.

(b) Fame awaits you. Nobody has ever proved Goldbach's Conjecture is true for **all** even numbers. If you can do so you will be world famous *and* rich.

(i) Explain why proving it up to even ten million is not a general proof.
(ii) How many counter-examples would you need to disprove it?

4 All these statements are false. Give a counter-example for each.
(a) All planets are lifeless.
(b) All prime numbers are odd.
(c) All angles greater than 90° are obtuse.
(d) All right-angled triangles are scalene.
(e) All parallelograms have two diagonals of different lengths.
(f) All fractions can be converted into *exact* decimals.
(g) All numbers can be written exactly as fractions.

5 **(a)** Find the interior angles of the following *regular* polygons.
(i) triangle
(ii) quadrilateral
(iii) hexagon
(iv) 20-sided polygon

The interior angle of a regular polygon is always a whole number of degrees.

Conrad

Look at Conrad's conjecture.
(b) Prove or disprove Conrad's conjecture. Explain your reasoning.

Using algebra for proof

Odd and even numbers

 What makes a number even? What makes it odd?

Your answers are conjectures.

 What sort of number do you get if you add
(a) two even numbers **(b)** two odd numbers **(c)** an odd and an even number?
Are your conjectures true in *all* cases?

You can use algebra to **prove** your conjectures.
Let n be any whole number.

*Proving something means showing it **must** be true in all cases.*

 When you say 'Let $n = ...$' you are taking a **general case**. What does this mean?

Look at this table.

n	0	1	2	3	4	5	6	7	...	All whole numbers
$2n$	0	2	4	6	8	10	12	14	...	All even numbers
$2n + 1$	1	3	5	7	9	11	13	15	...	All odd numbers

All even numbers can be written as $2n$ for some value of n. For example, $46 = 2 \times 23$.

All odd numbers can be written as $2n + 1$ for some value of n.

 What is the value n for these odd numbers? **(a)** 29 **(b)** 83 **(c)** 657 **(d)** 1827

 *Erika, prove that the sum of two even numbers is always an even number.*

Here is Erika's proof:

Let x and y be two even numbers.
Let $x = 2m$ and $y = 2n$
where m and n are whole numbers.
$x + y = 2m + 2n = 2(m + n)$.
$(m + n)$ is a whole number
so $2(m + n)$ must be an even number.
So $x + y$ must be an even number.

 Why does Erika say $2(m + n)$ must be an even number?

Task

Use algebra to prove that
(a) the sum of an odd number and an even number is always odd.
Start like this: Let x be odd and y be even.
Let $x = 2m + 1$ and $y = 2n$ where m and n are whole numbers.
...

(b) the sum of two odd numbers is always even.

Activity

1 Find the sum of each of these sets of consecutive numbers.
   (a) 6, 7, 8, 9, 10   (b) 52, 53, 54, 55, 56
   (c) −12, −11, −10, −9, −8   (d) −3, −2, −1, 0, 1
   (e) 1 000 004, 1 000 005, 1 000 006, 1 000 007, 1 000 008

2 What do your answers to question 1 have in common?

3 Let x be an integer. The next integer is $x + 1$.
   Write down an expression for the integer after $x + 1$.
   Write down expressions for the next two integers.

An integer is a whole number.

4 Prove that the sum of five consecutive integers must be divisible by 5.

Activity

1 Calculate the products of these pairs of even numbers.
   (a) 8×6 (b) 34×22 (c) 16×10

2 Here is a proof that the product of two even numbers must be even.

   Let $2m$ and $2n$ be even numbers, where m and n are integers.
   $2m \times 2n = 4mn$
   $4mn$ is even, so $2m \times 2n$ must be even.

   (a) Explain why the last line must be true.
   (b) How does the proof show that the product of *any* two even numbers is even?

3 Prove that the product of an odd number and an even number must be even.

4 Prove that the product of two odd numbers must be odd.

Investigation

1 (a) Think of an even number and square it.
   (b) Divide your answer by 4 and write down the remainder.
   (c) Repeat parts (a) and (b) for five more even numbers.
   (d) What do you notice?
   (e) Write down a proof that the square of an even number is always divisible by 4.

2 (a) Think of an odd number and square it.
   (b) Divide your answer by 4 and write down the remainder.
   (c) Repeat parts (a) and (b) for five more odd numbers.
   (d) What do you notice?
   (e) Expand $(2n + 1)^2$.
   (f) Write down a proof that when the square of an odd number is divided by 4, the remainder is always 1.
       Use the result of your expansion in part (e) in your proof.

Proof in geometry: angles

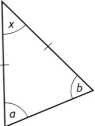

In this triangle *x* is 50°.
Why are *a* and *b* both 65°?
Suppose *x* was 100°.
What would the other two angles be?

When you solve angle problems you must be able to *explain* your answer.
You should write down your explanation so that another person can follow your reasoning.

Task

Angle FED is also written FÊD.

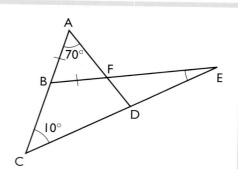

Copy this diagram.
You are going to prove that angle FED is 30°.

Copy the table below.
Complete the table by adding the reasoning for each step.

Each time you find the value of an angle, write it on your diagram.

Working	Reasoning
AFB = 70°	△AFB is isosceles (Two sides equal). ∴ Base angles are equal.
ABF = 40°	
FBC = 140°	
FED = 30°	

Each step in your working is made using angle facts.
What fact can you use to miss out ABF = 40° in the steps above?

Task

Copy this diagram.

Write down the steps to prove that SQR = 22°.

Show your reasoning at each step.

Is there only one way to prove the result?

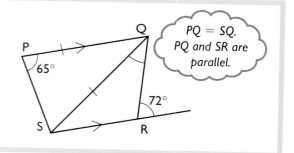

PQ = SQ. PQ and SR are parallel.

Exercise

In this exercise you are asked to **prove** some results.
That means you must set out your reasoning properly.

- Each step should be written on a new line.
- Every line must end with a reason.

1 Angle ABC is a right angle.
Lines BCD and EFG are parallel. FE = FH.
$B\hat{A}C = 64°$.
Prove that $F\hat{H}E = 13°$.

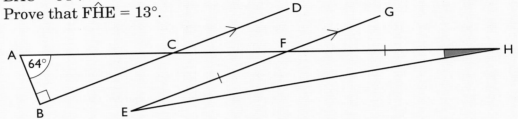

2 CE = CD.
Lines DEF and GHI are parallel.
$A\hat{C}B = 28°$.
$H\hat{G}J = 32°$.
Prove that $G\hat{J}K = 136°$.

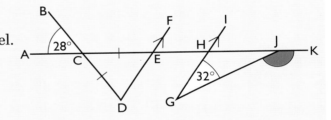

3 AB = AC
DE = DF.
Lines AB and CDE are
parallel.
$C\hat{A}B = 88°$.
$C\hat{B}D = 100°$.
Prove that $D\hat{E}F = 73°$.

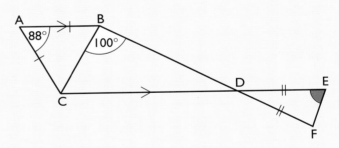

4 **(a)** ABCDE is a regular pentagon.
Prove that $B\hat{F}C = 36°$.

(b) What sort of triangle is BFC?
Explain your answer.

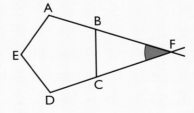

5 Lines ABF and ED are parallel.
$A\hat{C}B = 81°$ and $C\hat{B}F = 132°$.
Prove that $x = 129°$.
Give your reasoning at each step.

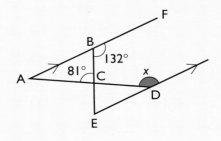

Proof in geometry: circles

Task

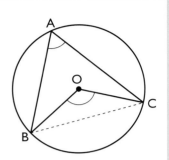

1 Draw a circle of radius approximately 6 cm.
2 Mark the centre O and add a chord BC.
3 Mark a point A on the circumference on the *larger* arc BC.
4 Measure and write down BÂC and BÔC.
5 Repeat the steps above for three other circles with different radii.

BÂC is called the angle at the circumference.
BÔC is called the angle at the centre.

They both stand on the chord BC.

 What does the Task above suggest about the angle at the centre and the angle at the circumference?

Form a conjecture.

Task

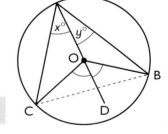

Copy the diagram with line AOD.

 **Why are lengths OC, OA and OB all equal?
What does this tell you about triangles ABO and ACO?**

You are going to prove that:

The angle at the centre is twice the angle at the circumference.

Let CÂO = $x°$ and BÂO = $y°$.
Then CÂB = $x° + y°$.

 Why do you need to show that CÔB = $2(x + y)°$?

Copy and complete the table below.
Add information to your diagram as you go along.

Working	Reasoning	
Triangles ABO and ACO are isosceles.	Lengths OA = OB and lengths OA = OC.	
AĈO = $x°$ and AB̂O = $y°$	Base angles of an isosceles triangle are equal.	
CÔD = ... and BÔD = ...		
CÔB = CÔD + BÔD = ...		
CÂB = $x° + y°$		
So CÔB is twice CÂB		

Your proof has used angle facts and algebra.

Exercise

In this exercise the centre of the circle is labelled O.

1 AĈB = 51°.

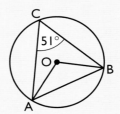

(a) Write down the value of AÔB.

(b) Prove that OB̂A = 39°.

2 PÔR = 124° and OR̂Q = 33°.

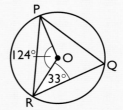

(a) Write down the value of PQ̂R.

(b) Prove that PR̂O = 28°.

(c) Prove that OP̂Q = 29°.

3 Chord XZ passes through the centre O.
It divides the circle into two semicircles.

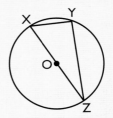

(a) What other name can be given to XZ?

XŶZ is called the angle in a semicircle.

(b) What is the size of XÔZ?

(c) Write down the value of XŶZ

(d) Explain why **the angle in a semicircle is always a right angle.**

Activity

Look, AD̂B and AĈB are both 61°.

Bethany

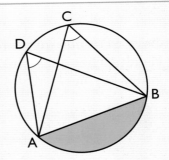

Chord AB divides the circle into two segments.
AD̂B and AĈB are called **angles in the same segment.**
They both stand on AB and they are on the same side of it.

1 Draw a circle of your own with a chord and five angles
in the same segment. Measure the angles.
Do you find the same result as Bethany?

2 Explain why you cannot prove a result by measuring.

3 In this diagram AÔB = 154°.
Explain why AD̂B and AĈB are both 77°.

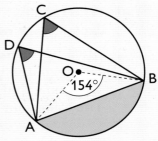

4 Complete this proof that **angles in the same segment
are equal**.
AD̂B = ½AÔB.   Also AĈB = ...
So AD̂B = ...

5 Part 4 is a proof but parts 1 and 3 are not proofs. Explain why.

Logic

Look at these two arguments.

A
All cats have tails.
Jimmy has a tail.
Therefore Jimmy is a cat.

B
All cats have tails.
Jimmy is a cat.
Therefore Jimmy has a tail.

 One of the arguments is correct, the other is wrong. Which is correct? Explain why the other is wrong.

Your explanation can be illustrated with a **Venn diagram**.
T is the set of animals with tails.
C is the set of cats.

 Why must set C be entirely inside set T?

The three statements in argument B are an example
of correct **logic**.
The last line can be **deduced** from the two lines above it.

Task

Five boys were playing football. *One* of them kicked the ball through a window.
The Headteacher questions each boy. The four innocent boys tell the truth.
The guilty boy lies.

*It wasn't Brian.
He is innocent.* — Andrew

It was Conrad. — Brian

It wasn't me. — Conrad

*Andrew is
innocent.* — Ewan

*I was tying
my boots.* — David

 **Who is guilty?
Explain your reasoning as a logical argument.**

Hint: Start by **assuming** that *all* the boys are telling the truth.
Do any of the boys' statements **contradict** each other?
You know that just one boy is lying.
The other four are all telling the truth.

There is no single way of presenting an argument. You must find the best way.
Diagrams and tables are often helpful.

Exercise

For each question you are given five answers to choose from.
Only one of the answers is correct.
(a) Decide which is the correct answer.
(b) Present your argument clearly and logically.

1 This is an extract from a commentary on a football match.
"It was an exciting game. Eight goals were scored. The hero was Richards.
He scored three goals for the losing team in the last six nail-biting
minutes…". What was the score?
(a) 8–0   **(b)** 7–1   **(c)** 6–2   **(d)** 5–3   **(e)** 4–4

2 Five schools had a games meeting, with knock-out competitions.
Each school won one and only one competition.
Only Borley and Eastfield played in the cricket.
Dapton beat Coleridge in the first round of the football.
Abbey Grove won the athletics easily.
Neither Dapton nor Coleridge entered the tennis.
Who won the hockey?
(a) Abbey Grove   **(b)** Borley   **(c)** Coleridge   **(d)** Dapton   **(e)** Eastfield

3 There are three roads between two towns.
Only one of them is a dual carriage-way.
Two of the roads go over bridges; the other one goes through a tunnel.
Two cyclists, Roisin and Sarah, travel between the two towns by different
roads.
Four of the following statements are true, one is false. Which one is false?
(a) At least one cyclist does not go on a dual carriage-way.
(b) If Sarah goes through a tunnel, Roisin goes over a bridge.
(c) At least one cyclist goes over a bridge.
(d) If Roisin goes over a bridge, Sarah must go on a dual carriage-way.
(e) Roisin and Sarah cannot both go through a tunnel.

4 Among the three one-Euro coins, A, B and C, there is
a forged one which may be too heavy or too light.
The other two are the same weight,
as is a fourth one, D, which is known to be good.

● A and B together are heavier than C and D together.
● A and C together are lighter than B and D together.
● A and D together are lighter than B and C together.

You can deduce that
(a) A is too heavy.   **(b)** A is too light.   **(c)** B is too heavy.
(d) B is too light.   **(e)** C is the forged coin.

5 A girl once said: "My mother's mother's only daughter's eldest daughter
died just a few minutes after her only sister was born". The family called
the baby Hope, for a new beginning. What relation was Hope to the girl?
(a) Her mother   **(b)** Her daughter   **(c)** Her sister
(d) Her aunt   **(e)** Herself

Finishing off

Now that you have finished this chapter you should be able to:

- prove a statement is true by exhaustion and by using algebra
- prove a statement is false by finding a counter-example
- prove geometrical results
- present an argument logically.

Review exercise

An integer is a whole number.

1 **(a)** Prove that the sum of seven consecutive integers is always divisible by 7.
  (b) Prove that the sum of six consecutive integers is *not* divisible by 6.

2 Two angles positioned like x and y are called **allied angles**.
Copy the diagram.
Prove that allied angles add up to 180°.

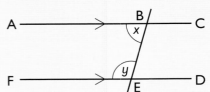

3 Here is a magic circle.
  (a) Find the sum of the numbers on one of the diameters.
  (b) Find the sum of the numbers on one of the circles.
  (c) What do you think is magic about the circle?
  (d) Prove that the circle is magic.
  (e) What sort of proof have you used?

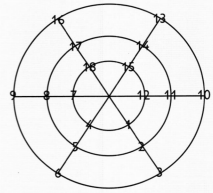

4 ABC is the pantograph of a tram which carries electric current from the overhead wire, XY.

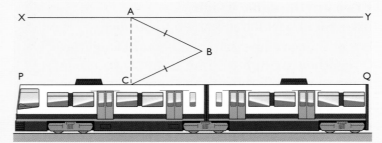

The two arms of the pantograph are the same length so that AB = BC.
The wire and the top of the tram are both horizontal. AC is vertical.
A$\hat{B}$C can vary from 30° to 110°.

  (a) Prove that B$\hat{A}$Y varies from 15° to 55°.
  (b) Prove that B$\hat{C}$Q = B$\hat{A}$Y.

5 Complete this proof that PT and QS are parallel.

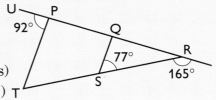

R$\hat{Q}$S = 88°   (Exterior angle of a triangle
= sum of opposite interior angles)

S$\hat{Q}$P = ...   (.....................................)

....

6 **(a)** Show by substituting numbers for a and b that $(a + b)^2$ does not equal $a^2 + b^2$.

(b) What does $(a + b)^2$ equal?

(c) The lengths in this figure are as shown.
Find the area of JKLM in two ways:

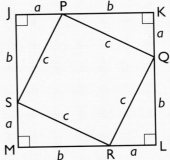

  (i) as a square (in terms of a and b)

  (ii) as square PQRS (in terms of c) and four triangles.

(d) Make an equation by putting your answers to part **(c)** equal to each other and simplify it.

(e) What well-known theorem have you proved?

7 An event B can occur if and only if a previous event A has occurred.
Similarly, event C can only occur if event A has occurred.
Event D can only occur if events B and C have occurred.

For each of these statements
(a) state whether it is true or false
(b) present your argument clearly and logically (diagrams may help).

  (i) If A occurs, B, C and D must occur.

  (ii) D cannot occur unless A has occurred.

  (iii) B cannot occur if C does not occur.

  (iv) C cannot occur if B occurs.

Investigation   Look at this solid shape.

1 Find the number of
  (a) vertices
  (b) edges
  (c) faces.

2 What does this tell you about Euler's Rule?

3 Now form extra edges and faces by joining AP, BQ, CR and DS. What can you say about Euler's Rule now?

25 Investigations

In real life, you come across mathematics problems in all sorts of forms. Often they don't look like maths at all to start with.

Here is a general procedure for investigating such problems.

1 Find the simplest possible case to get started. This will help you see what is going on.

2 Then look at the next most simple case, and the next, so that step-by-step you get into more complicated cases.

3 When you think you can see what is happening, form a conjecture.

4 Test your conjecture with harder cases.

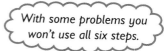

With some problems you won't use all six steps.

5 If possible prove your conjecture.

6 Ask yourself whether you can extend the work to other situations.

Task

Here is a problem.

> In a family everybody gives everybody else a present at Christmas.
> The total number of presents is over 100.
> What can you say about the number of people in the family?

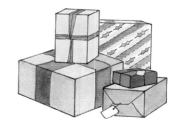

Work through the problem using the six steps listed above.

Write out your solution. In the margin write down where each new step begins.

 In the Task, the question asked was 'What can you say about the number of people in the family?', but first you had to answer another question. What was that question?

 You will often find that you must answer other questions before you can answer the one you are being asked.

1 Paying your debts

Ama, Beatrice and Charmian go on a camping holiday together. They agree to share their expenses equally.

Every time anybody spends money it is entered into a notebook.

At the end of the holiday they add up the total spent by each person.

How do they then work out who owes whom what?

2 Noughts and crosses

Is there a winning strategy for the player who goes first in a game of noughts and crosses?

3 Darts

Penny is playing darts but she is not a very good shot. She is quite likely to miss the number she is aiming for and to get one of those nearby instead.

Where should Penny aim to get the highest score?

4 Traffic control

Design Plans for Chellbury New Town: Specification for Traffic Speed Control

The map shows the town's central box. There will be traffic lights at each intersection. The speed limit will be 40 kilometres per hour. A motorist who enters the box on a green light and then proceeds at this speed will not be held up at all. By contrast somebody who exceeds this speed will have to wait at a red light.

How can the traffic lights be timed to achieve this specification?

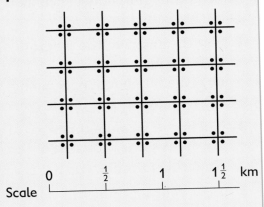

5 Goldbach numbers

On page 207 you met Goldbach's conjecture. It says that, from 6 upwards, any even number can be written as the sum of two prime numbers.

So, for example, 14 can be written as the sum of 3 and 11, both of which are prime.

$14 = 3 + 11$

There is another way of splitting 14.

$14 = 7 + 7$

> Remember: 1 is not a prime number.

Because there are two ways of splitting 14 into two prime numbers, 14 is said to have Goldbach number of 2.

> Investigate whether, as you take larger even numbers, their Goldbach numbers increase, decrease or stay about the same.

How can you use a spreadsheet to help you with this investigation?

6 Pick's theorem

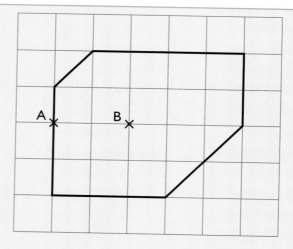

Look at the diagram. It shows an irregular polygon drawn in a 1 cm grid.
Some of the grid-points, such as A, are on the edge of the polygon.
These are called *edge-points*.
Some of the grid-points, such as B, are inside the polygon.
These are called *inside-points*.

1 For the shape in the diagram, find
   (a) the area
   (b) the number of edge-points
   (c) the number of inside-points.

2 There is a formula (known as Pick's theorem) giving the area of a polygon, drawn on a grid like this, in terms of the numbers of edge-points and inside-points.
   Find this formula. (Do not try to prove it.)

3 Does your formula still work for shapes with holes in them?

7 ⟩ Weights

Throughout this investigation you should assume that any object to be weighed is a whole number of units.

1 Robin has three weights and some scales. The weights are 1, 2 and 4 units and they go on the right of the scales. The object Robin is weighing hangs on the hook on the left.

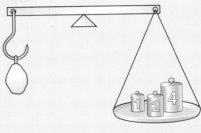

> Show that Robin can weigh any object up to 7 units.

2 Robin now replaces the hook in the left by a pan. He can now put weights on either side and so he can weigh an object of 5 units in two different ways, as shown.

> Show that Robin can now weigh an object of 3 units in three different ways.

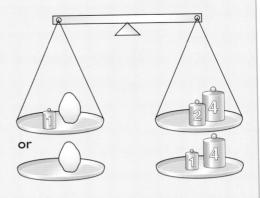

or

3 Robin gets a new set of three weights. He can now weigh *any* object up to *W* units. *W* has the largest possible value.

> What are Robin's three new weights?

4 Robin wants to get a fourth weight.

> What should it be?
> What about a fifth weight?

5 Robin get a new set of scales. There are two pans on the right. Any weight in pan 2 counts double. So the object in the picture weighs 2 units.

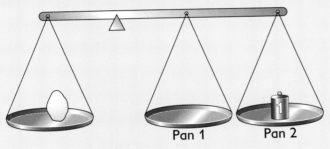

Pan 1   Pan 2

> What weights should Robin get to go with his new scales?

8 JavaScript

JavaScript is a computer programming language.
It is used to add interactivity to web pages.
During this investigation you will look at truth tables and how they are used in JavaScript.
You will edit a template for an interactive web page. The web page allows users to input answers to a question and uses JavaScript to check those answers.

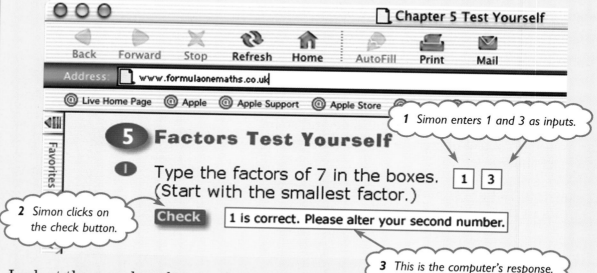

Look at the sample web page above.
Computer programs often use a 1 to stand for 'true' and a 0 to stand for 'false'.
The table, called a **truth table**, shows the different combinations of true and false answers.

Input A	Input B	Feedback
1	1	Both answers are correct. Well done!
0	0	Both answers are incorrect. Please try again.
1	0	1 is correct. Please alter your second number.
0	1	7 is correct. Please alter your first number.

This truth table has four rows.

1 Another web page has the question 'Type the factors of 9. (Start with the smallest factor.)'
  This question requires three input boxes.
  Make a truth table to show the different combinations of true and false answers.

2 A web page has the question 'Type the factors of 6. (Start with the smallest factor.)'
  How many input boxes are required?
  Make a truth table to show the different combinations of true and false answers.

3 Write down a number that has five factors.
  How many rows are there in a truth table for five input boxes?
  Look back at your results so far. Can you spot a pattern?

4 A question has n input boxes. How many rows are there in the truth table?

5 Now you are going to edit the web page shown at the beginning of this investigation.

- Ask your teacher for the JavaScript file required for this investigation.

- Open it by typing **investigation1.html** .

  Use Notepad or SimpleText.

- Using the work you have just done, edit the code for this web page and complete the program.

  Look out for the comment tags.
  ```
  <!-- They look like this and give you
       instructions on what to do. -->
  ```

- Save your work.

- You can view it in a web browser such as Internet Explorer or Netscape.

❾ Polygon rings

1 Diagram 1 shows a tessellation of equilateral triangles. An equilateral triangle is a regular three-sided polygon.

> *Prove* that there are exactly two other regular polygons that tessellate.

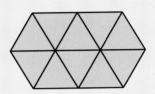

Diagram 1

2 Diagram 2 shows a semi-regular tessellation. It is a ring of four regular octagons. The shape in the middle is a square and this is a regular four-sided polygon.

> Find two other ways of forming a ring of one type of regular polygon with another, different polygon in the middle.

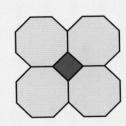

Diagram 2

3 In diagram 3, there is another ring of regular octagons but this time the shape in the middle is a star. All the sides of the star are equal but there are two different sizes of interior angle (in this case 90° and 225°).

> How many other ways can you find to form a polygon ring with a star in the middle?

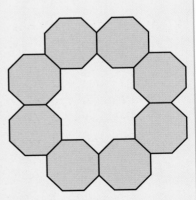

Diagram 3

Answers

1 Percentages (pages 10–11)

1. (a) £1.32   (b) £7.48
2. (a) £141.47   (b) £278.71   (c) £116.09
3. (a) 20%   (b) 6%   (c) $13\frac{1}{3}$%
4. (a) £3.12   (b) No. £2.08 each so loss $13\frac{1}{3}$%
5. (a) (i) 0.1 cm   (ii) 2.2%
   (b) (i) 0.1 cm   (ii) 2.17%
   (c) (i) 10 g   (ii) 2.9%
   (d) (i) 10 g   (ii) 3.6%
   (e) (i) 60 ml   (ii) 9.4%
6. (a) £64.00   (b) £45.00
7. (a) £18.80   (b) £86   (c) £7.60   (d) £36
8. £31 561.92 ≈ £31 600
9. £6885
10. 358 people
11. 10%
12. (a) 9%   (b) 5 years   (c) £2400
13. Time = 7 years   **14** 9%

Investigation

1. (a) £113.10   (b) £528   (c) £28 800
2. (a) (i) £690.79   (ii) £110.79
   (b) (i) £2203.52   (ii) £553.52
   (c) (i) £68 146.10   (ii) £44 146.10
3. The better investments are: 1(a), 2(b) and 2(c).

2 Algebraic expressions (pages 20–21)

1. (a) $6e + 2$ (b) $3f + 7g$ (c) $h + 4j$ (d) $k - m$
   (e) $2m^2 - n^2$ (f) $3p^2 - 4p$ (g) $g^2h - 5gh$ (h) $5rs - 4r^2$
2. (a) $15d$ (b) $10e$ (c) $3f^2$ (d) $5g^2$
   (e) $3hj$ (f) $18gh$ (g) $3pr^2$ (h) $4m^2n$
3. (a) $5a - 10$ (b) $14b - 6$ (c) $6c^2 + 8c$
   (d) $d^2 + d - 12$ (e) $e^2 - 49$ (f) $f^2 - 8f + 16$
4. (a) $3(4 - 2a)$ (b) $3(1 + 2b)$ (c) $c(c - 2)$
   (d) $d(4d^2 + 3d + 1)$ (e) $6e(3 + 4e + e^2)$ (f) $2f^2(5f - 6)$
   (g) $5g(h + 2)$ (h) $11c(3d - 2)$ (i) $12jk(3j - 5)$
5. (a) (i) $a^2 + 2a + 1$ (ii) $a^2 - 2a + 1$
   (b) (i) 40 401   (ii) 9801   (iii) 39 601
6. (a) a^9 (b) b^9 (c) c^9 (d) d^{51}
   (e) e^2 (f) f^4 (g) $g^0 = 1$ (h) h
   (i) i^6 (j) j^6 (k) k^{40} (l) l^{200}
7. (a) $10a^{12}$ (b) $6b^5$ (c) $12c^{13}$ (d) $10d^4$
   (e) $3f$ (f) $4g$ (g) 2   (h) $2h^6$

Activity

$2a^2 \times 3a^4$	$\dfrac{2a^4}{a^3}$	$2a$	$\dfrac{a^3}{a^3}$	a^0	$(2a^2)^3$
$6(a^3)^2$					$8a^6$
$4a^6$	$(2a^3)^2$	$\dfrac{3a^2}{a^2}$	3	$\dfrac{a^3 \times a^2}{a^5}$	1

Investigation

(a) Yes
(b) (i) 2.25   (ii) 6.25   (iii) 30.25   (iv) 110.25
(c) $(n + 0.5)^2 = n(n + 1) + 0.25$

Investigation

1. (a) $(x + 4)(x + 6) = x^2 + 10x + 24$
   (b) $(x + 2)(x + 5) = x^2 + 7x + 10$
   (c) $(x + 3)(x + 7) = x^2 + 10x + 21$
2. (a) $(x + 4)(x + 5) = x^2 + 9x + 20$
   (b) $(x + 2)(x + 3) = x^2 + 5x + 6$
   (c) $(x + 2)(x + 6) = x^2 + 8x + 12$
   (d) $(x + 5)(x + 8) = x^2 + 13x + 40$
   (e) $(x + 10)(x + 1) = x^2 + 11x + 10$
   (f) $(x + 1)(x + 1) = x^2 + 2x + 1$

3 Doing a survey (pages 32–33)

1. (a) 0.4°
   (b) Pie chart with angles as follows:

Education services	232°
Social services	80°
Environmental services	44°
Other services	4°

2. (a) 15–29
   (b) 60–74 and 74+
   This is because women generally live longer than men.
3. (a) Stephen

Time	Tally	Frequency
$0 \leqslant t < 15$		0
$15 \leqslant t < 30$	||	2
$30 \leqslant t < 45$	$\cancel{||||}$	5
$45 \leqslant t < 60$	$\cancel{||||}$ $\cancel{||||}$		11
$60 \leqslant t < 75$	$\cancel{||||}$ $\cancel{||||}$	10
$75 \leqslant t < 90$	||	2
$90 \leqslant t < 105$			1
	Total	31

Anna

Time	Tally	Frequency
$0 \leqslant t < 15$	$\cancel{||||}$ |||	8
$15 \leqslant t < 30$	||||	4
$30 \leqslant t < 45$	||	2
$45 \leqslant t < 60$	|||	3
$60 \leqslant t < 75$	||	2
$75 \leqslant t < 90$	$\cancel{||||}$ ||	7
$90 \leqslant t < 105$	||||	4
$105 \leqslant t < 120$			1
	Total	31

(b) Two frequency charts to show above data.
(c) Two frequency polygons on the same axes.
(d) Stephen has used the computer every day, Anna hasn't. However, when Anna does use the computer she often spends a long time on it.
4. (a) Ask your teacher to check your scatter graph.
   (b) In general, the shorter the time taken to run 100 m, the longer the distance jumped.
   (c) Ask your teacher to check your line of best fit.
   (d) About 1.8 metres.

4 Equations (pages 42–43)

1. (a) $x = 4$ (b) $x = 14$ (c) $x = 4$
   (d) $x = 5$ (e) $x = \frac{1}{2}$ (f) $x = -2$
   (g) $x = 3$ (h) $x = -1\frac{1}{2}$ (i) $x = 1$
   (j) $x = 3$ (k) $x = 0$ (l) $x = \frac{5}{5}$
   (m) $x = 0.2$ (n) $x = -\frac{1}{2}$ (o) $x = \frac{3}{7}$
   (p) $x = 2$ (q) $x = 11$ (r) $x = 1$
2. (a) $10 - 2x = 4$ (b) $x = 3$ (c) $13 - 3x = 1$ (d) $x = 4$
3. (a)

x	1	2	3	4	5
x^2	1	4	9	16	25
$\frac{1}{x}$	1	0.5	$0.\dot{3}$	0.25	0.2
$x^2 + \frac{1}{x}$	2	4.5	$9.\dot{3}$	16.25	25.2

(b) $x = 3.3$ (to 1 d.p.)

4 (a) Total = $14x + 10$
  (b) (i) 35.2 m (ii) 1.07 (to 2 d.p.) (iii) 1.43 (to 2 d.p.)

Investigation 1
(a) $x = 2$ → S (d) $x = 7$ → E
(b) $x = -23$ → U (e) $x = \frac{1}{2}$ → R
(c) $x = 6$ → P

Investigation 2
(a)

2	7	6
9	5	1
4	3	8

(b) All total 15.

(c)

5	10	9
12	8	4
7	6	11

(d) All total 24.

(e) Total = $3x$
(f) All rows, columns and diagonals algebraically sum to $3x$.
(g)

$x-4$	$x+1$	$x+3$
$x+9$	$x-1$	$x-8$
$x-5$	x	$x+5$

5 Working with polygons (pages 54–55)
1 A = 41°, B = 44°, C = 60°, D = 31°, E = 40°, F = 23°, G = 67°
2 (a) (i) 6° (ii) 174° (b) 10 440°
3 13
4 The hexagon is regular.
  Sides must be same length (rhombus).
  Centre angles are equal, therefore 120°.
  Therefore interior angles of rhombi are 120° and 60°.
  Therefore interior angles of hexagon are all 120°.
5 (a) 111° (b) Corresponding angles (c) 900° (d) 99.5°
6 $a = 14.42$ yards $b = 146$ cm $c = 0.604$ m.
7 (a) 150° (b) 30° (c) 30°
8 (a) $x = 10, y = 8$ (b) $p = 7, q = 25$ (c) $r = 36, s = 45$

6 Sequences and functions (pages 64–65)
1 (a) 3, 5, 7, 9 (b) 2, 5, 8, 11
  (c) 1, 4, 9, 16 (d) −1, 8, 23, 44
  (a) and (b) are linear.
2 (a) $a = 4$ and $d = 4$ (b) $a = 3$ and $d = 3$
  (c) $a = 100$ and $d = -5$ (d) $a = -20$ and $d = 2$
3 (a) 57, 54 (b) $63 - 3n$ (c) $63 - 300 = -237$ (d) −240
4 (a) $2n + 1$ (b) $3n + 1$ (c) $2n - 1$
  (d) $5n - 2$ (e) $64 - 4n$ (f) $20.2 - 0.2n$
5 (c) is linear. (a) and (b) are quadratic. (d) is neither.

Investigation 1
(a)

Number of vertices	Number of lines
1	0
2	1
3	3
4	6
5	10
6	15
10	45

(b) In a mystic rose with n vertices there are $n - 1$ lines from each vertex. So there are $\frac{1}{2}n(n - 1)$ lines altogether.

Investigation 2
1 (a)

Jigsaw size n by n	Number of corner pieces, c	Number of edge pieces, e	Number of middle pieces, m	Total number of pieces, t
2 by 2	4	0	0	4
3 by 3	4	4	1	9
4 by 4	4	8	4	16
5 by 5	4	12	9	25
10 by 10	4	32	64	100

  (b) $c = 4, e = 4(n - 2), m = (n - 2)^2, t = n^2$
2 (a) (i) $c = 4, e = 2(n - 2), m = 0, t = 2n$
    (ii) $c = 4, e = 2(n - 2) + 2, m = n - 2, t = 3n$
    (iii) $c = 4, e = 2(n - 2) + 4, m = 2(n - 2), t = 4n$
  (b) $c = 4, e = 2(n - 2) + 2(l - 2), m = (l - 2)(n - 2), t = ln$

7 Circles (pages 72–73)
1 (a) (i) 44 cm (ii) 154 cm²
  (b) $6\frac{2}{7}$ inches (ii) $3\frac{1}{7}$ sq inches
  (c) (i) 35.2 m (ii) 98.56 m²
  (d) (i) 8 m (ii) $5\frac{1}{11}$ sq inches
2 (a) (i) 2.2 m (ii) 11 m
  (b) (i) 4.55 (ii) 45.45 (iii) 4545.45
3 (a) (i) 100.48 inches (ii) 803.84 sq inches
  (b) (i) 81.64 inches (ii) 530.66 sq inches
  (c) (i) 62.8 inches (ii) 314 sq inches
4 18.84 cm, 37.68 cm **5** 36.28 sq feet
6 19.464 m
7 (a) 22.47 m² (b) 9.18 m²

Investigation
1 (b) 741.62 m (c) 88.99 m²
2 Donkey (1413 m²) has larger grazing area than goat (970 m²)

8 Ratio (pages 80–81)
1 (a) (i) 3 : 5 (ii) 5 : 4 (iii) 3 : 2 : 8
    (iv) 1 : 3 (v) 25 : 1 (vi) 3 : 10
  (b) (i) 1 : 125 (ii) 1 : 7 (iii) 1 : 2.4
    (iv) 1 : 12.5 (v) 1 : 2 (vi) 1 : 3
2 (a) 45% (b) 11% (c) The skirt.
3 Cupro-nickel.
4 red ; yellow : black = 5 : 5 : 2
5 (a) 30 (b) 63 (c) 1.8
6 Simon 15 Mandy 33
7 (a) Mrs Craig £42 000
    Ms Fulford £24 000
    Mrs McIntosh £30 000
  (b) £240 000
8 (a) $x = 40$ cm $y = 10.25$ cm
  (b) 9 : 2.25 = 4 : 1
  (c) 40 : 10 = 4 : 1
  (d) 41 : 10.25 = 4 : 1
  (e) Yes, corresponding sides are in the same ratio.
  (f) 16 : 1
9 (a) (i) 3 : 1 (ii) 3 : 1 (iii) 3 : 1
  (b) These cuboids are similar.
  (c) (i) 9 : 1 (ii) 27 : 1
10 (a) $V = 8h^3$ (b) $V = 343$ (c) $h = 4$
11 (a) $z = 384$ (b) $x = 6.35$ (to 2 d.p.)
12 (a) (i) 8 : 1 (ii) 2 : 1 (b) 2 cm
13 (a) (i) 55 (ii) 5.5 (b) (i) 20% (ii) 20%

9 Simultaneous equations (pages 90–91)
1 (a)

x	0	1	2	3	4
$4x$	0	4	8	12	16
-10	−10	−10	−10	−10	−10
$y = 4x - 10$	−10	−6	−2	2	6

  (b)

x	0	1	2	3	4
$2x$	0	2	4	6	8
-3	−3	−3	−3	−3	−3
$y = 2x - 3$	−3	−1	1	3	5

(d) $x = 3.5, y = 4$
(e) No, because it is parallel to the line $y = 2x - 3$.
2 (a) $x = 3, y = 3$ (b) $g = 6, h = 3$ (c) $c = 9, d = 3$
   (d) $a = 6, b = 2.5$ (e) $x = 3, y = 14$ (f) $s = 5, r = 10$
3 (a) $f = 3, g = 2$ (b) $j = 4, k = 3$ (c) $x = 1, y = 1$
4 (a) $a = 3, b = 1$ (b) $x = 8, y = 4$ (c) $r = 9, s = 1$
5 (a) $s = 1, t = 1$ (b) $p = 2, r = 1$ (c) $g = 10, h = 8$
   (d) $a = 6, b = 1$ (e) $x = 4, y = 3$ (f) $c = 10, d = 5$
6 (a) $f = 2, g = 3$ (b) $j = 1, k = 1$ (c) $m = 10, n = 3$
   (d) $c = 5, d = 4$ (e) $a = 5, b = 1$ (f) $x = 2, y = 4$
7 (a) $a + c = 7$ (b) $5a + 3c = 27$ (c) 4
8 (a) $4m + 5p = 30, 8m + 2p = 44$
   (b) Mugs are £5 and plates are £2.
9 (a) $a + 5b = 8, 4a - 2b = 10$ (b) $a = 3, b = 1$

Investigation
1 (a) apple = 2, banana = 3, cherry = 1
   (b) apple = 5, banana = 2, cherry = 3
   (c) apple = 4, banana = 2, cherry = 1
2 (a) $x = 2, y = 1, z = 3$ (b) $x = 4, y = 2, z = 3$
3 5 equations

10 Fractions (pages 96–97)
1 (a) $2\frac{1}{4}$ (b) $\frac{31}{40}$ (c) $\frac{2}{5}$ (d) $1\frac{3}{7}$ (e) $2\frac{11}{20}$ (f) $6\frac{1}{8}$
   (g) $\frac{37}{40}$ (h) $2\frac{13}{18}$ (i) $6\frac{3}{32}$ (j) 15 (k) $1\frac{4}{5}$ (l) $3\frac{3}{4}$
2 (a) $\frac{4}{5}$ (b) $\frac{a}{3b}$ (c) $\frac{1}{3}$ (d) $\frac{1}{x}$
3 (a) $\frac{f + 2d}{df}$ (b) $\frac{2a - b}{ab}$ (c) $\frac{3}{2x}$ (d) $\frac{1}{2x}$
   (e) $\frac{6}{ab}$ (f) $\frac{2}{a^2}$ (g) $\frac{b}{a}$ (h) $\frac{a^2}{b^2}$

Investigations
Discuss these with your teacher.

11 Graphs (pages 108–109)
1
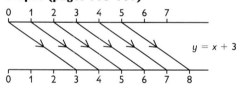

The set of arrowed lines are parallel.

2 (a) $y = \frac{1}{8}x$ (b) $y = \frac{x - 5}{4}$
   (c) $x \to \frac{x - 9}{2}$ (d) $x \to 7 - x$

3 (a)
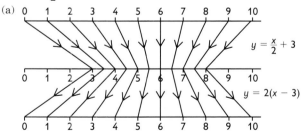

(b) Each mapping is the inverse of the other.

4 (a)
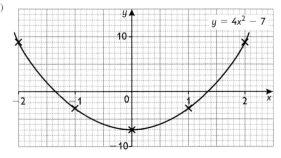

(b) $x = \pm 1.3$

5 (a)(c)
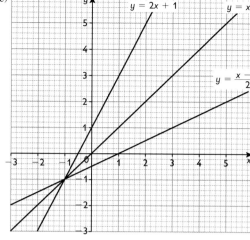

(b) $y = \dfrac{x - 1}{2}$

(d) $y = \dfrac{x - 1}{2}$ is the reflection of $y = 2x + 1$ in the line $y = x$.

6 (a)

x	-3	-2	-1	0	1	2	3
$5x^2$	45	20	5	0	5	20	45
9	9	9	9	9	9	9	9
$y = 5x^2 + 9$	54	29	14	9	14	29	54

(b)
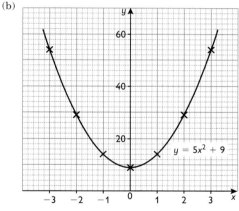

(c) 9   (d) $x = 0$

7 (a)

x	0	1	2	3	4	5	6
$x - 2$	-2	-1	0	1	2	3	4
$x - 4$	-4	-3	-2	-1	0	1	2
$y = (x - 2)(x - 4)$	8	3	0	-1	0	3	8

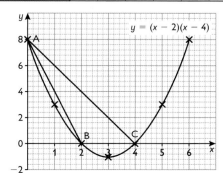

(b) $x = 3$ (c) Area = 8 units^2

8 (a)

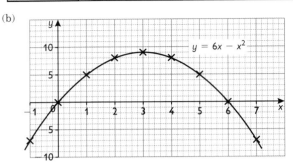

x	−1	0	1	2	3	4	5	6	7
$6x$	−6	0	6	12	18	24	30	36	42
$-x^2$	−1	0	−1	−4	−9	−16	−25	−36	−49
$y = 6x - x^2$	−7	0	5	8	9	8	5	0	−7

(b)

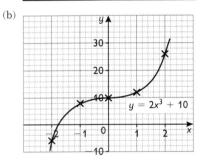

(c) (i) $x = 0$ or 6 (ii) $x = -0.5$ or 6.5

9 (a)

x	−2	−1	0	1	2
$2x^3$	−16	−2	0	2	16
10	10	10	10	10	10
$y = 2x^3 + 10$	−6	8	10	12	26

(b)

(c) $(0, 10)$

Investigation
Victoria's claim is correct.

12 Construction and locus (pages 116–117)
1 (a) 46 cm   (b) 2 cm   (c) 0.7 m² or 7000 cm²
2 (a) 2.5 km   (b) 87.5 hectares
3 59 km
4 (a) Ask your teacher to check your answer.
     (b) The one nearer Crossways.
5 Infinite lines 4 cm from BC and parallel to BC.
6 Ask your teacher to check your drawing.
7 (a)(b) Ask your teacher to check your drawing.
     (c) 16.5 m   (d) 13.8 m

Investigation
1 Parallelogram
2 (a) Rhombus   (b) Rectangle   (c) Parallelogram
     (d) Square   (e) Rectangle

13 Working with data (pages 130–131)
1 (a) 14   (b) 15.5   (c) 11   (d) 15   (e) Girls   (f) Boys
2 1.48
3 (a) 16 | 8 represents 168 m

15*	
15	6 9
16*	4 3 2 2 1 3
16	8 5 9 7 8 6 5 9
17*	2 3 0 2 4 4 3 0 3 4
17	9 5 8 8 5 9 7 6 7 8 6
18*	2 1 4 0 2 4 0
18	5 8 6 5
19*	1 4
19	

(b) 16 | 8 represents 168 m

15*	
15	6 9
16*	1 2 2 3 3 4
16	5 5 6 7 8 8 9 9
17*	0 0 2 2 3 3 3 4 4 4
17	5 5 6 6 7 7 8 8 8 9 9
18*	0 0 1 2 2 4 4
18	5 8 6 8
19*	1 4
19	

(c) Median = 174 cm
(d)

Height (cm)	Frequency
155–159	2
160–164	6
165–169	8
170–174	10
175–179	11
180–184	7
185–189	4
190–194	2

(e) Modal class is 175–179 cm
4 (a) 173.9 cm
(b)

Height up to (cm)	Cumulative frequency
159.5	9
164.5	31
169.5	62
174.5	101
179.5	149
184.5	178
189.5	195
194.5	200

(c) Cumulative frequency graph
(d) 174 cm
(e) Lower quartile 168 cm, upper quartile 180 cm, interquartile range 12 cm.

14 Indices and standard form (pages 138–139)
1 (a) 2^2 (b) 5^{-9} (c) 7^6 (d) 10^{-2}
2 (a) 5^2 (b) 2^{-1} (c) 3^4 (or 9^2)   (d) 3^{-3} (e) 2^{-4} (or 4^{-2})
3 (a) (i) $2^5 \times 3^4$ (ii) 2^3
     (b) (i) $2^9 \times 3^6$ (ii) $5^3 \times 3^2$ (iii) $7^{-2} \times 3^3$
4 (a) 3.67×10^2 (b) 2.5×10^4 (c) 6×10^{-2}
     (d) 3.76×10^{-3} (e) 1.4×10^{-5}
5 (a) 400   (b) 621 000   (c) 0.3   (d) 0.000 000 005 32
6 (a) 3.6×10^3 (b) 1.43×10^6 (c) 8×10^3 (d) 4.5×10^7
     (e) 2.4×10^9 (f) 6×10^5 (g) 2×10^3 (h) 2.5×10^{-4}
7 (a) 1.9×10^8 (b) 3×10^{-4} (c) 1.9×10^{10} (d) 0.000 006 7
8 Ask your teacher to check your answers.
9 (a) 0.000 005 m   (b) 553 m
     (c) 0.000 000 000 000 000 000 000 000 911 kg
10 (a) 2.39×10^5 miles   (b) 2.2×10^{-4} m   (c) 1×10^{-6} m

Investigation
Discuss these with your teacher.

15 Formulae (pages 144–145)
1 (a) $p = \dfrac{a - 6}{3}$ (b) $t = \dfrac{v - u}{a}$

(c) $x = 4(y + 3)$ (d) $w = \dfrac{p - d}{3}$

(e) $t = \dfrac{s - p}{q}$ (f) $y = 2(x - z)$

(g) $s = \dfrac{v^2 - u^2}{2a}$ (h) $u = \sqrt{v^2 - 2as}$

(i) $T = 5(k - 3d)$ (j) $r = \sqrt{\dfrac{4A}{\pi}}$

2 Cost = $15h + 25$
   (a) £55   (b) £77.50
   $h = \dfrac{C - 25}{15}$
   (c) 6 hours   (d) $8\frac{1}{2}$ hours   (e) $6\frac{1}{2}$ hours

3 (a) (i) $w = \dfrac{ml}{50h^2}$ (ii) $l = \dfrac{50wh^2}{m}$ (iii) $h = \sqrt{\dfrac{ml}{50w}}$

   (b) (i) 750   (ii) 450   (iii) 20   (iv) ≈ 15.65

4 (a) $C = 275W + 25N + 150$
   (b) (i) £800   (ii) £1025
   (c) 3 weeks

5 (a) (i) $3^2 + 4^2 = 25$ (ii) Area 1st $\triangle = 6\,\text{cm}^2$
             $5^2 = 25$ Area 2nd $\triangle = 30\,\text{cm}^2$
        $12^2 + 5^2 = 169$
           $13^2 = 169$
      Both the triangles are right-angled.
   (iii) Area 1st $\triangle\ s = 6$ Area 2nd $\triangle\ s = 15$
      $A = \sqrt{6 \times 3 \times 2 \times 1}$ $A = \sqrt{15 \times 10 \times 3 \times 2}$
      Area $= \sqrt{36} = 6\,\text{cm}^2$ Area $= \sqrt{900} = 30\,\text{cm}^2$
   (b) (i) $s = 9$ (ii) $s = 14.45$
      Area $= \sqrt{9 \times 5 \times 3 \times 1}$ Area $= \sqrt{14.45 \times 7.75 \times 5.15 \times 1.55}$
      Area $= \sqrt{135} \approx 11.6\,\text{cm}^2$ Area $= \sqrt{893.9} \approx 30\,\text{cm}^2$

Investigation
Table will contain values depending on the value of l chosen.
A one-second pendulum is approximately 24.8 cm long.

16 Accuracy (pages 152–153)
1 (a) 10   (b) 1.4   (c) 104   (d) 1000
   (e) 0.35   (f) 0.605   (g) 0.002   (h) 0.51
2 (a) (i) 100   (ii) $113.526 = 114$ (3 s.f.)
   (b) (i) 8   (ii) 5.67
   (c) (i) 36   (ii) 32.3
   (d) (i) 1   (ii) 1.21
   (e) (i) 210 000   (ii) $172\,800 = 173\,000$ (3 s.f.)
   (f) (i) 5   (ii) 3.09
   (g) (i) 0.03   (ii) $0.040\,64 = 0.0406$ (3 s.f.)
   (h) (i) 17   (ii) 15.5
   (i) (i) 9   (ii) $11.9025 = 11.9$ (3 s.f.)
   (j) (i) 10 000   (ii) $16\,256.25 = 16\,300$ (3 s.f.)
   (k) (i) 7   (ii) 7.26
   (l) (i) 5   (ii) 5.30
   (m) (i) 0.4   (ii) 0.355
   (n) (i) 32   (ii) 32.8
   (o) (i) 20   (ii) 19.5
   (p) (i) 1   (ii) 0.934
3 $18\,106\,500 \leqslant$ Australia $< 18\,107\,500$
   $5\,228\,500 \leqslant$ Denmark $< 5\,229\,500$
   $58\,285\,500 \leqslant$ France $< 58\,286\,500$
   $125\,155\,500 \leqslant$ Japan $< 125\,156\,500$
   $58\,305\,500 \leqslant$ United Kingdom $< 58\,306\,500$
   $263\,562\,500 \leqslant$ United States $< 263\,563\,500$
4 (a) 0.5 cm   (b) 0.05 cm = 0.5 mm   (c) 0.5 °C   (d) 0.5 g
5 (a) 0.5 m^2 (or 5 m^2, if area has been rounded to the
      nearest ten)
   (b) 0.005 seconds
   (c) 0.05 km per hour
   (d) 5 days (assuming the age is accurate to the nearest 10)

Activity
Compare your answer with the rest of the class.

Investigation 1
1 $3.65\,\text{cm} \leqslant 3.7\,\text{cm} < 3.75\,\text{cm}$
2 Largest value 11.781 cm   Smallest value 11.467 cm
3 Smallest 11.5 cm   Freda's 11.6 cm   Largest 11.8 cm
   These do not agree to 3 significant figures.
4 Discuss this with your teacher but your answer can never
   be more accurate than the measurements given in the
   question.

Investigation 2
(a) To the nearest millimetre (0.1 cm)   (b) 0.5 mm = 0.05 cm
(c) Perimeters   (i) 2 mm = 0.02 cm   (ii) 2 mm = 0.2 cm
   Areas   (i) 0.5675 cm^2 (ii) 1.35 cm^2

17 Three dimensions (pages 160–161)
1 **Prisms**

Shape of cross-section of prism	Number of planes of symmetry
Equilateral triangle	4
Square	5
Regular pentagon	6
Regular hexagon	7
Regular heptagon	8
Regular octagon	9

Pyramids

Shape of base of prism	Number of planes of symmetry
Equilateral triangle	3
Square	4
Regular pentagon	5
Regular hexagon	6
Regular heptagon	7
Regular octagon	8

2 The solid is an octahedron.

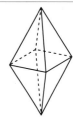

3 Depth of acid in cylinder is 7.07 cm.
4 Volume $= \pi \times 10^2 \times 4 - \pi \times 5^2 \times 4$
             $= 400\pi - 100\pi$
             $= 300\pi\,\text{mm}^3$
   Surface area $= 2(\pi \times 10^2 - \pi \times 5^2) + 2 \times \pi \times 10 \times 4 + 2 \times$
             $\pi \times 5 \times 4$
             $= 2(100\pi - 25\pi) + 80\pi + 40\pi$
             $= 150\pi + 120\pi$
             $= 270\pi\,\text{mm}^2$
5 Depth of water in measuring cylinder is 10 cm.
6 (a) Volume of wood is $12\,974\,\text{cm}^3 \approx 0.013\,\text{m}^3$.
   (b) Area covered with white paint is $10\,317.2\,\text{cm}^2$.
7 (a) VAH, VBI, VCJ, VDF and VEG.
   (b) Not symmetric in any horizontal plane as one end has
      a vertex but the other end is flat.

Activity
(a) Tetrahedron   (b) Tetrahedron   (c) Octahedron

18 Real life graphs (pages 166–167)
1 (a) (i) Object starts moving towards O at constant speed.
         After 2 seconds it begins moving away from O at
         steady speed.
      (ii) In first 2 seconds object moves 2 cm. The speed is
         1 cm per second. In next 3 seconds object moves
         3 cm. The speed is 1 cm per second.
   (b) (i) Object begins moving towards O. After 1 hour
         object is stationary. After 5 hours object moves
         away from O.
      (ii) Object travels 3 km in first hour. The speed is then
         3 km hr^{-1}. Between 1st and 5th hours object is
         stationary. After 5 hours object moves 3 km in
         1 hour. The speed is then 3 km hr^{-1}.
   (c) (i) Object moves away from O in first minute. Object
         is stationary in second minute. Object moves away
         from O in next 3 minutes.
      (ii) In first minute object moves 25 m. The speed is
         25 metres per minute. After 2 minutes, object
         travels 5 metres in next 3 minutes at a speed of $1\frac{2}{3}$
         metres per minute.

2 (a) 60 pence (b) 1–2 days, 4–6 days, 8–10 days
(c) End of day 4 (d) End of day 6 (e) True
3 (a)

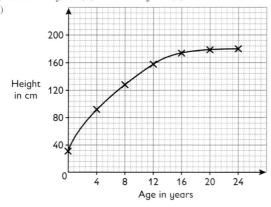

(b) 0–4 years (c) ≈ 146 cm

4 (a)

t	0	5	10	15	20	25	30	35	40
50	50	50	50	50	50	50	–	–	–
60t	0	300	600	900	1200	1500	–	–	–
$-t^2$	0	−25	−100	−225	−400	−625	–	–	–
$v = 50 + 60t - t^2$	50	325	550	725	850	925	950	950	950

(b)

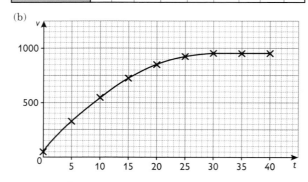

(c) 50 m s^{-1}
(d) 950 m s^{-1}
(e) ≈ 9 seconds
(f) Thrust and weight are both zero or else balance each other.

5 (a)

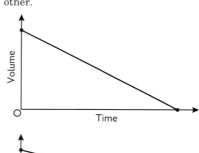

(b)

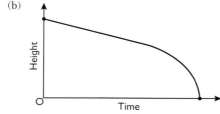

Activity
(a) (b)

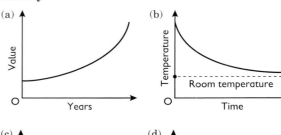

(c) (d)

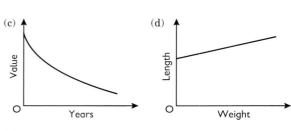

(e)

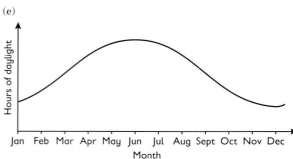

19 Transformations (pages 174–175)

1 (a) Rotation, through 90°, anticlockwise about 0
(b) Reflection in $y = x$
(c) Translation $\begin{pmatrix} -4 \\ 5 \end{pmatrix}$
(d) Rotation through 180° about (5, −3.5)
(e) Reflection in $y = 0.5$
(f) Rotation through 180° about (3, −1)
(g) Reflection in $y = -x$
(h) Reflection in $y = x + 2$

2 (a) One possibility is a translation $\begin{pmatrix} -6 \\ 3 \end{pmatrix}$ followed by a reflection in $y = x$
(b) One possibility is a reflection in the x axis followed by a translation $\begin{pmatrix} -4 \\ 2 \end{pmatrix}$

3 (a) Isosceles triangle (b) Kite
4 (a)–(c) Ask your teacher to check your diagrams.
(d) Rotation through 180° about (2, 2)
(e) Ask your teacher to check your answer.
5 (a)–(c) Ask your teacher to check your diagram.
(d) Ask your teacher to check your answer.
(e) (3, 13)
(f) $\frac{1}{2}$
(g) (i) No change
(ii) Changes by scale factor $\frac{1}{2}$
(iii) Changes by scale factor $(\frac{1}{2})^2 = \frac{1}{4}$

Activity
For A4 $297 \div 210 = 1.414...$ and so on.

20 Inequalities (pages 182–183)

1 (a) $63 \leqslant s \leqslant 175$ (b) $13 \leqslant f \leqslant 37$
(c) $11 \leqslant g \leqslant 39$ (d) $12 \leqslant a < 21$
2 (a) < (b) > (c) < (d) >
(e) > (f) > (g) < (h) >
3 Any four from the following
(a) 7, 8, 9, 10, 11, 12, 13, 14, 15 (b) 1, 2, 3, 4
(c) −2, −1, 0, 1, 2 (d) −7, −6, −5, −4, −3, −2
(e) −5, −4, −3, −2, −1, 0 (f) 18, 19, 20, 21, 22, 23
Fractional answers are also possible.

4 (a) $-2 \leq x < 3$ (b) $-3 < x < 0$
    (c) $-1 \leq x \leq 4$ (d) $0 < x \leq 5$
    (e) $-4 < x \leq 1$ (f) $-3 \leq x \leq 3$
    (g) $x < 1$ or $x \geq 3$ (h) $x < -1$ or $x \geq 3$

5 (a) [number line -5 to 3, open circles]
    (b) [number line 0 to 5, closed circles]
    (c) [number line -3 to 0]
    (d) [number line -4 to 4]
    (e) [number line $2\frac{1}{2}$ to 5]
    (f) [number line -2 to $3\frac{1}{2}$]
    (g) [number line -6 to -4]
    (h) [number line 0 to 5]
    (i) [number line -1 to $1\frac{1}{2}$]

6 (a) $x < 4\frac{1}{2}$ (b) $x \leq 6$ (c) $x \geq 2\frac{1}{3}$
    (d) $x < -3$ (e) $x < 3$ (f) $x \leq 5$
    (g) $x > 2$ (h) $x > -10$ (i) $x \geq -4$

7 (a) (i) $<$ (ii) $<$
    (b) (i) $<$ (ii) $<$
    (c) (i) $=$ (ii) $=$

8 (a) $-4 < x < 3$ (b) $0 < x < 5$
    (c) $-1 < x < 0$ (d) $0 < x \leq 4$

Activity
Region 1 $y \leq 14, y \geq 9, x \leq 0, y \geq x^2$
Region 2 $y \leq 14, y \geq 9, x \geq 0, y \geq x^2$
Region 3 $y \leq 9, y \geq x^2, x \leq 0$
Region 4 $y \leq 9, y \geq x^2, x \geq 0, y \geq 3x$
Region 5 $y \leq 3x, y \geq x^2$

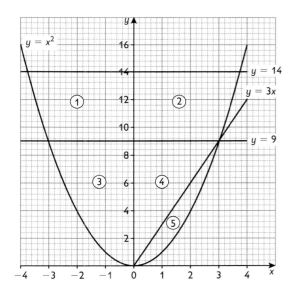

21 Probability (pages 190–191)

1 (a) 0.1   (b) 40   (c) 6
2 (a)

HH	DH	CH	SH
HD	DD	CD	SD
HC	DC	CC	SC
HS	DS	CS	SS

    (b) (i) $\frac{1}{4}$ (ii) $\frac{1}{4}$ (iii) $\frac{1}{2}$ (iv) $\frac{1}{8}$
3 (a) 0.15   (b) (i) 60   (ii) 20   (iii) 30
4 (a) (i) 0.36   (ii) 0.1   (iii) 0.3
    (b) Red 6, yellow 5, green 2, blue 7
5 (a) 4
    (b) 1
    (c)

Red die

		1	2	3	4	5	6
	1	1	3	5	7	9	11
	2	0	2	4	6	8	10
Blue die	**3**	-1	1	3	5	7	9
	4	-2	0	2	4	6	8
	5	-3	-1	1	3	5	7
	6	-4	-2	0	2	4	6

    (d) (i) $\frac{1}{12}$ (ii) $\frac{1}{6}$ (iii) $\frac{1}{12}$ (iv) $\frac{1}{18}$ (v) 0

22 Trigonometry (pages 200–201)

1 (a) $x = 9.03$ m, $y = 11.98$ m
    (b) $x = 2.60$ m, $y = 8.41$ m
    (c) $x = 8.39$ m, $y = 12.31$ m
2 (a) 72.8°   (b) 28.6°   (c) 47.8°   (d) 83.2°
3 (a) 36.87°   (b) 200 m
4 (a) 14.24 cm   (b) 53.13 cm
5 (c) 63.43°
6 (a) $x = 5$ cm, $y = 5.55$ cm
    (b) $x = 25.98$ m, $y = 30.96$ m
    (c) $x = 4.00$ mm, $y = 6.93$ mm
7 (a) 4.59 cm   (b) 6.55 cm   (c) 15.04 cm^2
8 (a) 24.81°   (b) 54.80°   (c) 59.58°

Activity 2
(a) (i) OB $= \sqrt{2}$ cm   (ii) OC $= \sqrt{3}$ cm   (iii) OD $= \sqrt{4} = 2$ cm
(b) (i) 6   (ii) 17

24 Reasoning (pages 216–217)

1–2 Check your proofs with your teacher.
3 (a) 57   (b) 57   (e) Proof by exhaustion.
4–5 Check your proofs with your teacher.
6 (b) $a^2 + 2ab + b^2$
    (c) (i) $(a + b)^2$ (ii) $2ab + c^2$
    (d) $a^2 + b^2 = c^2$
    (e) Pythagoras' theorem
7 (i) False
    (ii) True
    (iii) False
    (iv) False